Three Masquerades

Three Masquerades

Essays on
Equality, Work and Hu(man) Rights

Marilyn Waring

UNIVERSITY OF TORONTO PRESS
TORONTO BUFFALO

For Gaye

First published in New Zealand in 1996
by Auckland University Press with Bridget Williams Books.
First published in Australia in 1996 by Allen & Unwin.
First published in Canada
and the United States in 1997
by University of Toronto Press Incorporated.

ISBN 0-8020-4230-9 (cloth)   ISBN 0-8020-8076-6 (paper)

Canadian Cataloguing in Publication Data

Waring, Marilyn, 1952–
Three masquerades : essays on equality, work and
hu(man) rights

Includes bibliographical references and index.
ISBN 0-8020-4230-9 (bound)   ISBN 0-8020-8076-6 (pbk.)

1. Women's rights.   2. Sex discrimination against women.
3. Equality.   4. Women in politics.   5. Women – Employment.
I. Title.
HQ1236.W374 1997   305.42   C96-932407-3

Contents

Acknowledgements

I am grateful to all those whom I have met who have taught me. I have not always agreed with them, but where they have prompted a question or a comment, where I have pondered the event or behaviour, where I have sought clarification or further evidence, I have been taught.

I am grateful to those who have trusted me, who have confided matters previously unspoken, or who have admitted me to observe where I otherwise had no place to stand.

I am grateful to all those who have listened as ideas evolved – friends, family, students, and feminist sisters – and have supported, fed back, added evidence, questioned, sending me on further research adventures.

Specifically I want to thank Gaye Greenwood, Amanda Greenwood, Prue Hyman, Antony Shaw, Sandy Stephens, Bridget Williams, and Elizabeth Vaneveld for their comments on different parts of the manuscript at various stages. Annette Carne, Liz Winthrop, and Deirdre Shaw answered crisis deadline calls to assist with typing and referencing.

The book could not have been written if my farm animals had not been cared for. The responsibility for this fell chiefly on the shoulders of the late Dave Weston. In the copy editing period, the work was shared by Cheryl Worthington, Gary and Wendy Inger, and Gaye and Sam Greenwood.

I am not easy to be around during my writing binges, and I am so grateful to those who take me away from it all for play. Here special thanks are due to Lee Beston, Anita McNaught and Tainui Stephens, and to Abby for the jamming sessions.

To my parents, who don't get to see me enough when I set off on another writing project, thank you again for your love and support.

Finally to my friend and publisher Bridget Williams, my special gratitude for providing such a supportive environment and a constructive outlet for my politics and my passion.

While all those above add to my life and work in their various ways, I take sole responsibility for the politics and passions on the pages of *Three Masquerades*.

List of Abbreviations

ACC	Accident Compensation Corporation
ADB	Asian Development Bank
APP	Agricultural Perspective Plan
CEDAW	Convention on the Elimination of All Forms of Discrimination Against Women
EEO	equal employment opportunities
FAO	Food and Agriculture Organisation
GATT	General Agreement on Tariffs and Trade
GDP	gross domestic product
GEP	gross economic product
GHP	gross household product
GMP	gross market product
ICCPR	International Covenant on Civil and Political Rights
ICESCR	International Covenant on Economic, Social and Cultural Rights
ICSE	International Classification of Status in Employment
ILO	International Labour Organisation
IMF	International Monetary Fund
IPU	Inter Parliamentary Union
IRRI	International Rice Research Institute
ISCO	International Standard Classification of Occupations
LEAF	Legal Education and Action Fund
NGO	non-governmental organisation
NHSCP	National Household Survey Capability Programme
NPC	National Planning Commission
OECD	Organisation for Economic Co-operation and Development
UN	United Nations
UNDHR	United Nations Declaration on Human Rights
UNDP	United Nations Development Plan
UNESCO	United Nations Educational, Scientific and Cultural Organisation
UNFPA	United Nations Family Planning Agency
UNHRC	United Nations Human Rights Committee
UNICEF	United Nations Children's Fund
UNSNA	United Nations System of National Accounts
WHO	World Health Organisation

Preface

When equal does not mean half, when workers are informed they are at leisure, when the lives of the 'leisured half' of people on the planet are clearly not the intended subjects of international human rights guarantees, lies masquerade as truths.

The concepts of equality, work, and human rights hold centre stage in philosophical debates at the most esoteric academic conferences, and at the dinner tables of the folks down the road. We use the words with such frequency and in such clichéd contexts, that the impacts of their disguises are seldom revealed. Institutionally reinforced, and buoyed by male power, the pretences are everywhere endorsed and supported.

These essays represent my outrage at the perpetuation of these lies. They reflect on the privileges I have had as a parliamentarian, a development consultant, a farmer, an academic, and an activist to be privy to the voices, actions, passions of those most abused and brutalised by the masquerades, the women of the world. Their experiences are filtered through the lens of my particular experiences, but I am always struck by the similarities between us, the echoes of phrases and feelings, in spite of our outward and visible differences.

The completion of this book is one of life's synchronicities. I needed the catharsis of the opportunity to write about my years in parliament, an experience of counterfeit equality. My experience in the development field and my own passion for farming meant that I was daily confronted with the travesty of excluding women's unpaid work from the policy-making process. My activist work for women imprisoned, or denied refugee status because of feminist political issues beyond the restricted definitions and practices of international human rights, demonstrated that for most women, these guarantees were a false outward show. It dawned on me that there was a coherent framework within which to weave them all together.

Three Masquerades expresses considerable anger, but I refuse to seek refuge in depression. Women's sense of humour, and their remarkable resilience in the face of the very real obstacles to their rights to equality, visible work, and female human rights, keeps me strategising and scheming and writing.

Equality 1

Imagine yourself a woman member of Parliament, or congresswoman, or deputy. You are in the major opposition party. A woman in the governing party is appointed to the Cabinet. The woman's former husband then visits the Leader of the Opposition to advise him, man to man, that his wife, the new minister, has had silicone breast implants and also alleges that, when the separated couple were students, they had participated in key-swapping parties.

The Leader of the Opposition does not send the former husband swiftly from the room and discard the information. He has much delight in passing the story on to his opposition colleagues at his party's next weekly caucus. You are present as one of three women in the room. On receiving the information, most of the men hoot and guffaw, and ribald, smutty comments continue for some minutes.

In Parliament in the years that follow, the woman minister endures taunts about whether or not she feels pumped up, and frequent irrelevant interjections ask whether or not she wishes to swap her keys.

The woman telling me this story was disclosing it for the first time some years after it had occurred. By being present when the allegations were related to her caucus and by not commenting at that time, she felt co-opted as a guilty party to the situation. What was she supposed to do? She did not feel able to tell the woman minister what had happened. She could not rise to take offence at the comments made in Parliament, for to do so would place them on the parliamentary record and would require an explanation of the insult in the innuendoes. So she sat in silence, and every woman in the House suffered the indignity and harassment of the result of this disgusting male collaboration.

Imagine that this is not an isolated incident. Imagine that you are subjected to such experiences every day. Imagine what you might do in such a situation.

Hannah Arendt has observed that 'Truthfulness has never been counted among the political virtues, and lies have always been regarded as justifiable tools in political dealings.'[1] But, for the political woman in office, where lies silence? I agree with Adrienne Rich that 'lying is done with words, and also with silence',[2] but silence is also the tool of the political prisoner, an element of informed passive resistance. Silence is often survival. The silence of a battered woman is a wall of resistance. It is often effective protection, but it also keeps other women removed from truth.

I served in the New Zealand Parliament for three terms, from 1975 to 1984. The past twelve years for me has been a period of another life, and of continuing silence. I have not been possessed of a desire to return to Parliament. I have not sat again in the gallery, I do not listen to broadcasts of the House. I have not dwelt on the past. Therapists may say I have 'blocked' the experience, and this could be true. Events surrounding the 1993 suffrage centenary commemorations in New Zealand, and the invitation to participate in the South Australian centenary of suffrage in 1994, have forced some contemplation and it is time to lift the lid on our silences.

While few who serve are left with the courage to speak truly about the experience, as a reality check I have been reading the words of many other women who have won elected political office, to establish for myself that my reflections are not selective or bitter or unrepresentative. There is also the responsibility that an essay such as this could not only give succour to those who do not wish to see women serve in equal numbers in Parliament, but also dissuade women of integrity and principle from ever offering themselves as parliamentary candidates.

But I have known and talked with too many of us since 1975 to see my experiences as exceptional. At conferences and congresses and assemblies, on trade missions and good-will visits, at demonstrations, or because we've heard about each other and asked to see the other, we have sought each other out. From whatever point on the party political spectrum, whether elected or appointed, regardless of religion or culture or age or marital status or sexuality, wherever we come from, because there are still so few of us and we are hungry for company that understands, we share the secrets of abuse and survival.

Joan Kirner was a member of the Victoria State Parliament in Australia for ten years and state premier from 1990 to 1992. Her response to my first breaking this silence, to my deciding not to protect the abusers any more, was, 'I haven't allowed myself to feel yet.'

Many of us stay silent for a long period, and some of us are silent for life. There is the self-contempt of co-option, of knowing when we played the game, became 'like'. There is the knowledge that we enjoyed the privileges of power and, consciously or otherwise, abused them. There is, for many, a desire to return to that place because they enjoyed more power and prestige than will ever come their way again, or because, frankly, they were outstanding at that job and every other option is boring beside it. There is the silence of those who were so abused they may never speak of it, or who think to do so displays a certain weakness. There is the silence of those who think that abuse is relative, that we were, after all, never violently physically beaten, never went hungry, and had a home to go to even if we rarely saw it, so who are we to complain? There is the silence of those who care more for seeing increased numbers of women in Parliament than they do for breaking the silence, and see telling such truth as implicitly putting women off standing for office.

I felt a combination of all of these for twelve years. Then I reflected on the politics of breaking silences, on emotional battery, and the coalitions of press, political parties and parliamentarians who are desperate for the silence to remain. The silence protects the co-options, the dualities of personality, the attempts to isolate, the punishments for not playing the game.

Speaking as a feminist in the struggle for the liberation of Palestine, Hanan Ashrawi said, 'Each of our experiences of pain is unique, but there is commonality. We have to emphasise the common denominators. We cannot afford to become captors of our own pain. Victimisation has to be shared – and transcended together.'[3]

Other women's words provide an awakening, an echo, a reminder, a companion, as I work now. They are not a replacement for my own experience. But this essay is more than mere self-disclosure. In it I hope to trouble the prescribed and accepted vocabulary of the experience of surviving as a woman politician.

I had at no time in my life contemplated being a member of Parliament as an ambition, nor had I set out to attain such a position. I was not aware of any family history or activism in local or central government and politics, although after becoming the National Party candidate for Raglan I discovered that my great-grandfather had stood in a by-election for what was presumed to be a safe seat, and had lost it.

I had no party history, no public profile, no savings or real income, and no delegations approached me to stand for office. My activism in Wellington, where I attended university, was for 'unpopular' issues – anti-apartheid, abortion and homosexual law reform. I didn't campaign properly for pre-selection, and more than 70 per cent of the voting delegates for the primary were men, and those overwhelmingly farmers. In the context of 1975, my selection was unusual. I did have an obsessive interest in international politics, which was a major part of my degree in political science, and I had worked part-time as a researcher in Parliament.

Elizabeth McCombs, Catherine Stewart, Mary Dreaver, Mary Grigg, Mabel Howard, Hilda Ross, Iriaka Ratana, Ethel McMillan, Esme Tombleson, Rona Stevenson, Whetu Tirikatene-Sullivan, Dorothy Jelicich and Mary Batchelor were the thirteen women who preceded Colleen Dewe and me when we were elected as members of the New Zealand Parliament in 1975.

I had studied New Zealand politics in my university degree, but despite this I could not have given you the names of all of those women. I knew that in 1933 Elizabeth McCombs had taken her seat as the first woman member of Parliament in New Zealand. When the business of the House began, she gave notice of two questions she wished to ask. When she rose to speak, six leading members of the Arawa tribe of the indigenous Maori people stood and left the House, later explaining their belief that it was not a woman's place to be involved in politics and public speaking. The first Maori woman member of the same Parliament, Iriaka Ratana, met similar opposition from the Arawa and other tribes who shared this view. From the beginning, women were to be silenced.[4]

I knew Hilda Ross's name only because I came from the Waikato region, which she had represented, and Mabel Howard's name only because of the sensationalised parliamentary episode when, during a speech on consumer interests and manufacturing standards, Mabel produced a pair of bloomers to illustrate her point. Rona Stevenson's name was known to me because, like so many women before and after her in New Zealand, Australia, the United Kingdom and many other places, she held by a handful of votes a seat that should have been lost on the swing in a general election, and most assuredly held it because she was a women. Whetu Tirikatene-Sullivan, whom I honour as the longest-serving woman member of the New Zealand Parliament (and another who entered the House with a degree in political science), was the member for Southern Maori, having succeeded her father in 1967, when I was of an age to take an interest in the women who were breaking barriers.

As an undergraduate student in politics, I do remember stories that appeared in the newspapers. There were few facilities for women MPs. In the 1940s Mabel Howard did manage to secure the provision of bath facilities, but only by offering to break through the window of the only bathrooms to avoid passing the sign which read 'Gentlemen'. Hilda Ross was appointed as Minister for the Welfare of Women and Children in the first National Government in 1949, but it was a position without a department and was less well paid than those of her Cabinet colleagues.[5] Women members were turned away at the Members and Guests dining-room of Bellamy's (the parliamentary dining-rooms), because women were not entitled to bring women guests to dine with them. Until the 1970s, no woman was allowed to take a seat at the back of the debating chamber on the floor of the House to observe the proceedings.

After the 1969 election, Esme Tombleson was offered a Cabinet position as Associate Minister of Social Welfare, a department that did not then exist. She turned it down, commenting that 'I would have been Associate Minister of Nothing'. She regretted this lost opportunity. The message was that women who refused such offers did not get a second chance, while refusals from men had no after-effects. In 1967 she described the dilemma of a woman in the House. 'She [owes] it to the nation as a whole to delve into certain aspects of life to help womankind, but at the same time she must realize she must not go too far along these lines or no man will vote for her.

'But if she becomes too male in her outlook, too interested in indus- trial and scientific matters, she will find she has every woman complain- ing she is not looking after women's affairs. . . . She must remember she is a woman and not try to be a man or outdo a man in anything she does. It is not an easy task. But there is *tremendous satisfaction in being accepted* [my emphasis].'[6]

I remember Mary Batchelor and Dorothy Jelicich and their efforts to gain admission to the billiard room. Now the billiard room had no atmosphere, and I'm not even sure that many women members before 1970 were particularly enamoured of playing pool. It was, however, an enormous room with very large comfortable chairs. It contained the sole publicly available television set for members of Parliament and it was the only place in the whole building where you could sit undisturbed by a messenger, the telephone or other visitors. Until 1972 no woman member was entitled to enter the room.

In 1984, on her retirement after fifteen years, Mary Batchelor commented: '[Parliament] was absolutely geared to males. We had to walk miles even to find a ladies "loo" . . . at cocktail parties I was often asked: "Whose wife or secretary are you?" It was so annoying. Why did I have to belong to someone else?'[7]

Beyond New Zealand, the two key names in the press that drew my attention in the mid-70s were those of Bella Abzug, in the United States Congress, and Bernadette Devlin, in the House of Commons.

Bella Abzug was a visual memory at once, from the pages of *Time* magazine or the international pages of the newspapers, with her amazing hats. But under the hat was a 100 per cent voting record in the US Congress on human rights. Here was the first person in Congress to call for the US to get out of Vietnam, the first person in Congress to call for the impeachment of President Nixon. I noticed this person was a woman.

Because Bernadette Devlin had entered the British House of Commons at such a young age, and as a 'fiery Irishwoman', New Zealanders read of her too on the international pages. When I was selected as a candidate, her name was mentioned with mine – and so was that of Margaret Thatcher, then leader of the opposition Conservative Party in Britain. Thatcher had been committed from 1953 to becoming a member of Parliament, and had been consistently turned down by selection committees saying she should stay home and look after her twin children.

There were other books for me to read, by and about the widows and daughters – Bandaranaike, Gandhi, Bhutto – and I read everything I could lay my hands on. In those days, the mid-70s, there wasn't much. Sirimavo Bandaranaike, Prime Minister of Sri Lanka from 1960 to 1965, and 1970 to 1977, is supposed to have said, 'A woman's place is everywhere and anywhere duty requires her to be, and also in her kitchen.'

Indira Gandhi, Prime Minister of India from 1966 to 1977, and 1980 to 1984, had made her first appearance before the Lok Sabha on 1 March 1966, at a time of economic crisis, unparalleled drought, the renewed Indo-Pakistan war and the cessation of US aid. Not surprisingly, she was strained and jittery, and did not speak confidently.

Opposition members of Parliament interrupted her and nicknamed her the 'Dumb Doll', a name which remained with her as a long-time taunt.[8]

Few of these role models knew 'the tremendous satisfaction of being accepted' as a woman in the male political world. Whoever we are, we woman come from and belong to a different political culture. Unlike men, who do not believe there is anything outside or beyond patriarchy (of course, there are other 'cultures' in the sense of indigenous peoples, or race, or class, but they are, all of them, defined by male so-called leaders), women's lives are spent moving between patriarchy and what Jessie Bernard calls 'the female world'.[9]

So what did I find of this culture when I arrived in the capital, Wellington, as a parliamentarian in 1975?

We were four women out of 87 MPs, with an all-male Cabinet of nineteen and five male parliamentary under-secretaries. All heads of government departments were men and, while there were nine women private secretaries to ministers, all 43 principal private secretaries were men. Thirty-one men and eight women members of the parliamentary press gallery fed their views from central government to 37 major metropolitan and provincial daily newspapers, all edited by men. The law courts were presided over by 23 male judges, and only three out of 26 major city councils by women mayors. Legislatively there was no Juries Amendment Act, no changes in matrimonial property legislation, no domestic violence legislation, no Evidence Amendment Act for rape trials. There was no Human Rights Commission; there were no rape crisis centres, no women-run refuges, no women pilots, fire-fighters or jockeys. We still had nuclear ship visits, played apartheid sport, had no Official Information Act, and much much more.

An early and continually brutal lesson for the woman politician is the attention now given to your life, and the images of you that are portrayed. I should not have been surprised by this. The editor of my regional newspaper, the *Waikato Times*, had advised me on my first visit to him as a candidate in 1975, 'I am a salesman. I have a daily product. I am not here to educate, I am here to sell.'

Women have a particular difficulty with self-marketing when seeking political office, and this is a reflection of their motives for doing so. Socialised as selfless rather than selfish, we face a shortage of role models; we are often insecure about image-making and feel discomfort at being seen as or feeling like a product. The intimidations built into the system will feel alien. The printed *curriculum vitae* forms of political parties, for instance, were established for men, not women. Mine requested information on such things as local authority positions held and war and military service. Years of volunteerism and community service were forced into a small paragraph marked 'Other – please specify' at the bottom of the second page.

Helen Clark, a member of the New Zealand Parliament since 1981 and in 1996 Leader of the Opposition, recognises the image-making as a political statement. 'Commentators have an image in mind and they trot it all out again. "But the media say she has an image problem" is a male media construction. There are no appropriate standards available by which to assess women in leadership. To be strong or to be assertive, characteristics appropriate for male leaders, are seen as unwomanly.'[10]

An interview with Gro Harlem Brundtland, while she was Prime Minister of Norway without the comfort of a parliamentary majority, illustrates this point. *The New York Times* in 1987 reported revisionist critics speaking of Brundtland as having 'matured' and of behaving less 'emotionally' and 'confrontationally' than in her first term as Prime Minister in 1982.

She responded: 'Because you're a woman they try to say she should be "more feminine", which means she should have less deliberate and well thought through meanings and she shouldn't express them as well . . . But what they're really saying, when you come to the bottom line, is: "A woman should not lead because she shouldn't be like a leader in what she says or does."' The report continued: 'Norwegians have accepted and now even enjoy the flush of anger their leader can show. . . . "Showing feeling is part of communications", said the Prime Minister, who concedes she works more at controlling herself in her second incarnation.'[11]

Brundtland's ascension as Prime Minister on each occasion came at a time of economic crisis. She has observed wryly that she and her seven other women ministers had often been described in male media as having been brought in 'to do the dishes after the party', but noted that 'the fact that there are eight women around the [Cabinet] table will influence the weight put on different aspects of human life'.[12]

Joan Kirner describes the hardest lesson in public life as being the lesson of image. 'The image makers who constantly and often viciously depicted me as the overweight harassed housewife in a spotted shift and moccasins did not simply denigrate me personally, they were out to destroy me politically. Once I realized they were making a political statement rather than a personal one, I was able to deal with it. I was able to react politically rather than personally.

'I could then ask the questions: who is this attack serving; what is the intent behind focussing on my appearance; who profits as I respond in kind; how can I turn the attacks around?'[13]

When Edith Cresson was Prime Minister of France in 1991-92, a daily television puppet-show, *Babette*, satirised her as the sexy slavish creature of the President. Cresson denounced it as 'grotesque, brainless, a synthesis of all stereotypes of women'. Michele Barzach, a former Health Minister, commented that the programme had never been so horrible to anyone before. 'This attitude, that women who succeed at the top level of politics must have done so through seduction, is so pervasive among men that they now dismiss the reaction of many women to the show as hysterical and paranoid.'[14]

When Mitsui Mariko won an election to fill a vacancy in the Tokyo Metropolitan Assembly in 1987, the mass media described her as 'a Madonna' who magnificently transformed herself from a mere high school teacher to an assemblywoman.[15]

While there is no doubt that some women seek to portray themselves as the best 'man' in the squad, in the unfortunately correct assumption that this will assist any hierarchical ambitions they might have for power and promotion, one or all of these experiences are universal for the woman politician.

Most of us know only too well the experience described by Greek parliamentarian Virginia Tsouderos. 'This reporter calls me a chatterbox. Does he know me? If there is a characteristic one cannot attribute to Tsouderos, this is it . . . Still, it is the first thing that came to his mind – she is a woman so she must be a chatterbox . . . they brand me as meddlesome, a busybody, they accuse me of sticking my nose in everywhere, of being superficial. If a man were to be meddling in so many sectors they would call him 'dynamic' . . . When a woman is not meddlesome and nothing is heard about her, then they say: "What did she enter Parliament for? To be cute?" Whereas we know of men MPs who without talking and by keeping quiet, are re-elected without difficulty, and don't become anyone's target.

'The fact is that they attribute to women certain characteristics that are considered "female characteristics" until the moment you can persuade them of your worth. Then, when they start considering you dangerous, their attitude towards you becomes much more antagonistic than it would have been towards a male opponent . . . From a woman they expect basically goodness, understanding, meekness, and not competition . . . and not abilities. Whereas male competition is part of the game.'[16]

Writing of her move to the South African Parliament from a prison cell, ANC representative Thenjiwe Mtintso writes that there is a real problem with the women who 'enter the sphere of parliament with an acceptance of its male orientation and thus play the game according to the rules dictated by male domination instead of trying to change the whole game and its rules. To the extent that this leads to the creation of domineering, strong, competitive, unemotional people, it does not help in the restructuring of society and the changing power relations.'[17]

Her colleague Lydia Kompe echoes these observations. 'Some women have adopted the same style as men – push, jostle, and some assert themselves in whatever way possible. Some are men in skirts.'[18]

There are senses in which the game is inevitable and the dual consciousness begins, although it became increasingly unclear to me where I was drawing the line between life and the game. At first it can be light-hearted. I used to say to myself on waking, 'What costume will I need to wear today? What image do I need to project for them to see me, hear me? What will convey credibility?'

Some feminist commentators believe that conformity of dress is a sign that women in such positions of authority are co-operating in the divisions of class and sex which reinforce stereotypes and enable white men to stay secured to the top. Others who play the game ('what costume shall I wear today?') do know that the guises are disguises and in that sense deceptions. But there is a point at which the disguises are so effectively part of the male expectation of femaleness that they render the woman invisible.

Both Dr Carmen Lawrence, Australia's first woman state premier, and New Zealand MP Ruth Richardson, one of the first women Ministers of Finance in the world, undertook major image transitions as they gained more political power. They were deliberate in seeking that power. But even those who do not seek higher office can submit (or choose) to follow fashions.

Former Irish Cabinet minister Gemma Hussey has written: 'Women in politics have all sorts of extra criteria to cope with, extra dimensions of comment: it did one no good, politically, to be found on the worst dressed list, as I once was. [I was chosen as the worst-dressed person in New Zealand one year: I was outraged.] If one looked tired or less than immaculate on television or in press photos, it was widely commented upon and seen as a sign of weakness.'[19]

In office I wore designer clothes, preferably Italian, and my favourite suit was pinstriped. I think I did it to please myself, within what I knew was a restricted dress code. But I also knew that, if I was to break so many other rules, this was a place for obvious compromise. I've never worn those clothes, or that style of clothing, since I left Parliament.

But I entered Parliament with shoulder-length 'honey-blonde' hair (as the press described it.) At one stage I had it permed and had a red rinse through it. At another time it was cut very short with blonde highlights 'frosted' in it. When I left office I grew a thin plait from the nape of my neck and had the strands dyed purple, green and white before plaiting them. In this, as in many things, I pleased myself, though it would be true to say that I would not have attempted the tri-colour plait while in office.

Upon my selection as a candidate, I learnt quickly that when I was recognised few people around me behaved normally. Men tried to monopolise my public time. Even 'private' conversations with new people who knew who I was turned to the one subject I was desperate to escape. A male friend with whom I shared a house in Wellington found that it affected his social life too, until he printed a badge to wear which read 'I don't know, ask her'.

I was elected to my first term in November 1975. From my work in Parliament Buildings as a Legislative Department researcher I knew a little about what to expect of the public arenas of political performance. And a sixth sense was already at work about what might be in store behind the closed doors.

On my wall I wrote the words from Katherine Mansfield's Journal: 'Risk – risk anything. Care no more for the opinions of others, for those voices. Do the thing hardest on earth for you to do. Act for yourself. Face the truth.' It joined T. S. Eliot's

> And right action is freedom
> From past and future also.
> For most of us, this is the aim
> Never here to be realised;
> Who are only undefeated
> Because we have gone on trying . . .[20]

Nothing short of being metaphorically clubbed over the head could have prepared me for the Neanderthal sensibilities about women that confronted me when I entered Parliament. And the cavemen were quite happy about revealing themselves. It's not dissimilar wherever you look. Some particularly stooped and hairy specimens are found in the House of Commons, for example John Carlisle (Conservative, Luton North): 'Women are natural bitches. They mistrust other women and have a general sense of insecurity about their representing their interests. The day's work here at the Commons, is more naturally tackled by a man. Once you start giving women special privileges and pushing them forward – and it is the same with ethnic minorities – you give them a false sense that they are equal to the task.'[21]

Diane Abbott, a black woman Labour backbencher in the Commons, is forced to work with such 'representatives', and in an institution obsessed with male traditions. Typical of these is the story she tells of the cloakroom where members of Parliament hang their coats. 'Every member has a peg with his or her name on it. From every peg hangs a loop of red ribbon. At first I was baffled as to what the red ribbon was for. Later I found out that it is to hang your sword on. Now, no one has worn a sword in the British parliament for over a hundred years. That is about how long it takes for the place to adjust to change.'

Further, she says, 'the atmosphere of the place exudes masculinity. It is full of wood panelling and leather armchairs. All around there are messengers and flunkies to wait on MPs. It all conspires to massage a specifically masculine sense of self-importance.'[22]

Lydia Kompe views the architecture of the South African Parliament as ominous, unfriendly and male. 'The building itself', she says, 'gives you the creeps. The place is cold, unfriendly, and unwelcoming. As I walk in these passages I feel lost. It was meant to make people feel the power in the buildings themselves.'[23]

Angela Rumbold describes the chamber of the House of Commons as 'a cockpit designed for men to attack each other with words. That is why the two sides are seated face to face. The whole structure of competitive debate is alien to a women's nature. When they are given the verbal equivalent of a punch on the nose their instinct is to retreat shocked by the aggressiveness of the unsolicited attack.'[24]

I don't know of any woman MP who enjoys the House, particularly because the level of debate is an insult to our intelligence. My colleague Colleen Dewe spoke frequently of the futility of the debate. 'It's banal on most occasions and it's repetitive point-scoring to no avail. The tone of it generally does no credit to anyone. I get so frustrated, so infuriated.'[25]

The House is also a breeding-ground for rank hypocrisy. Labour member of the House of Commons, Jo Richardson, says: 'Yes, I hate the chamber, I am not the best chamber attender. It is partly because I have other things to do but partly because I find it so macho. It's all so formalized and you get sucked into it. I just find it irritating and the trouble is I am irritated with myself for doing it. I can get up like anybody else and say "will the Honourable gentleman give way", or "I do thank the Honourable gentleman", but I don't thank him at all.'[26]

This hypocrisy is public and audible. But there is a constant underside to sitting in the chamber. The boys persist in their *sotto voce*, snide, cutting commentaries, seldom picked up by radio or television microphones. They think these are very funny. Women don't. These commentaries are overwhelmingly sexist, jeering and demeaning of women – those on the other side of the House, or visitors in the gallery. Every one of these tests something inside you. There is no room to turn and confront. You are expected to laugh along, to 'be one of the boys'.

Imagine the reaction if you were to raise a point of order, against a member of your party, for the frequent, dirty, snarling, insidious male rumblings that you are surrounded by whenever a woman on the other side of the House is speaking.

So often, when we complain, we are greeted with raised eyebrows and a kind of 'what planet are you from?' reaction, because, as far as the boys' club is concerned, nothing unusual is going on. In the New Zealand Parliament in 1980, Mary Batchelor was asking why so few women were represented at inter-government negotiations. A senior colleague of mine interjected and asked who she slept with, and, though she called for him to be publicly identified, she was forced to accept the Speaker's ruling that this could not be done.

New Zealand Alliance Party deputy leader Sandra Lee describes the sexual obsession with a story about question time when her colleague, Jim Anderton, was absent. 'Rather than say "on behalf of my colleague the Member for Sydenham", I said "on behalf of my member". That set the dogs barking.'[27]

Marcia Freedman, recalling the abortion hearings in the Israeli parliament, writes: 'I came to the abortion hearings more expert than most of the expert witnesses, but the facts were hardly central to the committee's deliberations. Sex was on everyone's mind throughout the months and years of committee hearings on abortion. The committee room often filled with jokes and lurid remarks, guffaws and snickers, these meetings always loud and excited, so dismissive of women and punctuated with suggestive jokes. These meetings enraged me.'[28] I can recall four abortion debates in my time in Parliament. Fortunately, I never had to sit on a select committee on the issue.

These instances were in public, on the floor of the House. In 'private', I experienced the omnipresent boys' brand of humour delivered over the tables in Bellamy's, in the members-only dining-room, drawn together in one long line so that they could still pretend they were all prefects at a boys' boarding-school and act in much the same way. Lunch could be a gross experience. MP number one: 'How can you legislate against rape in marriage? It couldn't be implemented.' MP number two: 'That's not the point, why should you be able to rape your wife in the bedroom but not beat her up in the kitchen?' MP number three: 'Then beat her in the bedroom and rape her in the kitchen.' Honourable members: 'Ha ha ha.'

In another 'private' situation, Jennifer Cashmore tells the story of voting in the lobbies at 3 a.m. in the South Australian state Parliament. The lobbies were full of men, and one drunk MP pinched her on the bottom. She was shocked and bewildered, and cried at him, 'How dare you do that?' Five minutes later he returned and did it again. 'I hurled my drink in his face', she said, 'and all the men who thought of me as a quiet conservative woman just looked on in stunned amazement, as if it was I who had committed the offence.'

Late-night and all-night sittings of Parliament are inhuman without qualification. But there was an element of them that was also physically frightening. The voting lobbies of the New Zealand Parliament were long narrow corridors. On one side, from floor to ceiling in steel cabinets and shelves, were bound copies of statutes and of previous parliamentary debates. On the other side were large old leather couches alternating with large heavy cylinders serving as ash receptacles and rubbish bins for the smokers. It was difficult for two moderately built men to pass shoulder to shoulder in the space between couches and bookshelves.

It was in this space that around 40 adult men, and one or two women, would queue to vote in lines like infant schoolchildren, quite literally locked in this area until the result of the division was reported to the

House. When sufficient numbers of your bored male colleagues had had too much to drink, they behaved like infant schoolchildren in the queue, pushing, shoving and tackling each other. It was not unusual for my 57 kg frame to be thrown against bookshelves or old leather couches as I ricocheted from being hit by some 100 kg hooligan 'playing' with his friends as we ran the country.

I also learnt early of other procedures in Parliament which were unbelievably infantile. We were engaged early in my first term in repealing a large piece of legislation, and this required a vote on every one of 300 plus clauses. The House adopted the procedure known as 'urgency' on a Wednesday afternoon: that is, the parliamentary sitting would be continuous, with no adjournments at all. Since there was no break in the proceedings, and while the rest of the country knew that it was nearing midnight on Saturday, it was still Wednesday in Parliament and the calendar on the floor of the House still recorded that fallacy.

The Standing Orders, the rules by which Parliament runs itself, stated that Parliament could not be in session on a Sunday, and must adjourn at midnight on Saturday. So at midnight on Saturday, when there was a motion to adjourn the House, there ensued a debate on whether it was now Sunday or still Wednesday. Common sense did finally prevail, but not before I was seriously questioning whether I had entered the right institution at the beginning of the week.

Another rule, perhaps peculiar to the New Zealand Parliament then, was the need for the Government at all times to maintain a quorum of 20 MPs in the House during debates. Given the exhaustive and differing calls on my time, which required making phone calls, or researching in the library, or meeting with lobbyists and delegations, this was an especially galling requirement and one imposed overwhelmingly on junior backbenchers.

I felt as though I was wasting vast amounts of time sitting in the House helping to keep the ridiculous quorum rule. I thought, 'If I have to sit here, I'm going to do something creative.' So I began knitting. It helped curb a major frustration of not being able to use my hands enough, of getting to the end of another long, long day without a sense of achievement and not seeing anything concrete in my wake, because it had all been just words. And it gave me time to observe just how much more time is spent on intrigue as opposed to innovation, and how many beliefs are sacrificed on the altar of promotion.

More than 100 years ago, Susan B. Anthony was right when she wrote: 'At every political convention all matters of right, of justice, of the eternal verities themselves, are swallowed up in the one all-important question, "Will it bring party success?" '[29]

And I began to realise just how exhaustive the insidious pressures on non-conformists were. The first black woman member of the US Congress, Shirley Chisholm, had warned of this, when she reflected, 'There is little place in the political scheme of things for an independent, creative personality, for a fighter. Anyone who takes that role must pay a price.'[30] The attacks came for being different – for being a woman. Anything I brought to the institution was because I was a woman. And this was a politics which had been left out of that world, an element which did not exist. It was distinctly unwelcome. Therefore, differentiate it, ghettoise it, separate it.

The way that women could work together, and across party lines, was also distinctly unwelcome. It could be seen, for example, in the debate in the House of Commons for 24 April 1990 on the Human Fertilization and Embryology Bill.[31] There is a contextually stunning speech by the Conservative Teresa Gorman, with strong interventions from Clare Short, Harriet Harman and Mrs Mahon. Such collaboration is frightening for male MPs, especially when the central issue is debated in terms of women's right to power.

The presence of women in more than single figures also shifts the tenor of debate when our experiences are reflected. Men are no longer the experts on everything, and there are too many of us to bully. In the 103rd US Congress elected in 1992, when a record number of women were elected,[32] Lynn Woolsey (Democrat, California), a former welfare mother, helped lead a fight for welfare reform. Carrie Meek (Democrat, Florida) recounted her own experiences as a domestic worker to argue for changes in social security that would help increase benefits to such workers. When the Family and Medical Leave Bill was discussed in the Senate, Dianne Feinstein (Democrat, California) spoke of the struggles of working with a young child.[33]

On the day all the new congresswomen were sworn in, one of Congresswoman Patricia Schroeder's male colleagues pulled her aside. 'Well, you finally got your dream – this place is starting to look like a shopping mall,' he said. Schroeder responded: 'Where is it that *you* shop where only 10 percent of the customers are women?'[34]

Patricia Schroeder also observes: 'It's really funny when two women

stand on the House floor. There are at least two men who go by
and say, "What is this, a coup?" '[35] This was my experience also, particularly if I shared a meal table in the members' dining-room with a
woman member from another party. We would be subjected to
constant interruption, with great concern expressed about what we
might be 'plotting'. The paranoia is not entirely misplaced. We are
usually having conversations we would not have with male colleagues,
using a different tone and style, and generally on a subject on which,
experientially, they would have little to offer. Frequently the subject,
conveyed in coded messages, is the last humiliation or put-down made
of a woman colleague or of women in general.

Khunying Supatra Masdit was still in her 20s when she entered the
Thai parliament in the late 1970s. She too experienced the 'ghetto'
treatment. 'If a woman runs for election her opponents would attack
her on her weakest point – being a woman.' (What she did not say, but
what is also true, is that this same behaviour will be displayed by her
party colleagues.) Speaking at the Global Summit Meeting of Women
Parliamentarians in 1991, she said, 'Women parliamentarians who participated have all had similar problems of male bias against them, no
matter what country they come from.' On retirement, she explained,
'Women's priorities are too often side-lined.'[36]

The devices used to sideline women's priorities are various. Doris
Lessing's description of Zimbabwe in 1980 has always seemed appropriate to the situation of women elected to political office. 'There are
always a few mad people screaming, "For God's sake, look, this is what's
going to happen." They got put into concentration camps or ignored or
treated as we were treated, a sort of humourless patronage: "O listen to
them" . . . There are many different ways of dealing with minority
opinion. It's often just as effective to treat people with indulgence as it is
to put them in concentration camps, you know. If the object is to
silence people there are many different ways of doing it.'[37]

But, while we are consistently a minority in representation, we are
not a minority of the population. This was fine while we were not in the
corridors of power, and while men could presume to speak for us and
continue the pretence that they somehow legislated and budgeted for
the good of all, and not for their gender interest. Now, though, our
presence, our reflections of our female culture, our unwillingness to
remain silent, hold up a mirror to reflect both their bias and their
ignorance, as well as their sustained self-interest. We will not be told

what to say or think. We will not be controlled. In general, the men elected to political office do not like this experience.

Women of courage and defiance articulate what women know, and what we learn. Joan Kirner explains: 'For me the politics of learning means women matter as much as men do; women have the right to determine our lives; women's experiences matter; women should be able to freely describe and share these experiences; women's experiences should be part of decision-making.'[38]

Clare Short, a British MP, explains it this way: 'You realize you're feeling differently than most of them in here, you bring your womanness with you. If you didn't have it there all in a package before, you find it once you get in here, you're responding in a different way and you have a different understanding.'[39]

Nowhere was this more apparent than in the weekly meetings of the party's parliamentary caucus. In my first year I watched the games and verbal rituals of caucus with dumbfounded awe, not recognising them, taken in, not realising I would see these moves for years. Caucus was compulsory for all the party MPs, including the Prime Minister and members of Cabinet, every Thursday from 10 a.m. until 1 p.m. The most testing agenda items would be left until 12.45 p.m.; tired issues, such as a national price for milk or national two-channel television coverage, would be raised from the chair and be a safe bet for an inconclusive and wasted hour, when there was major electoral discontent that should be aired. The good old pre-Budget kites – prescription charges, more indirect taxes – would be flown, to let the backbenchers feel they had been consulted. If Cabinet had had a division of opinion at its Monday meeting, and the issue was referred to caucus, none of those Cabinet ministers who disagreed with the Prime Minister would be called to give their opinion. When just enough new members entered every three years, and just enough older members thought they might jeopardise promotion chances by getting involved, and just enough thought it was a pointless waste of energy anyway, old dogs didn't need new tricks.

Helen Clark describes her weekly party caucus meetings as a back-bencher. 'I have drawn back from some outright confrontations because it was just getting too difficult, too emotionally demanding to go into savage fights. It was really upsetting me and I found it profoundly depressing. Politics is conflict ridden anyway with all the conflict from the opposing party, but when you are experiencing even more intense hatred and conflict from people who are supposed to be on your side that's an impossible situation . . . People get out of control in caucus, men in particular lose control entirely. They scream and shout and are personally abusive, it's really quite extraordinary.'[40]

I clearly remember occasions when colleagues would have to be physically restrained from crossing the caucus room to beat up on another MP. And the language and lack of self-control from this mass of boys together is frequently disgusting. Then there are the issues they just don't want to talk about. While you are on the floor of the House, only so much control can be exerted on your exercise of rights to speak on whatever you wish, and, because the efforts to silence you in that forum, while still exerted, are at least subject to public and press scrutiny, a different standard prevails in the privacy of the party caucus room.

Elected to the Israeli Knesset in 1973, Marcia Freedman experienced this conspiracy of silence. 'The walls of denial are especially thick around family concerns. Women's issues always seem to reveal shameful secrets about family life, secrets that the state has a vested interest in protecting.'[41]

I recall in my first term considerable concern being expressed about the number of young women (my colleagues called them 'girls' and they were in 'girls' homes') who would abscond just before the end of their institutional terms when, in accordance with government policy, they were to be returned to their family homes. I was not much older than these young women, and made several trips to these institutions to talk privately with them, to see what explanations they might give if I could gain their trust. It was soon obvious that the reason many of them ran away was because the state was about to return them to places where they were raped, beaten or abused by fathers, uncles, brothers or cousins. I returned to caucus to raise quietly the question of our part as an accessory to incest and other offences. There was a stunned silence. Then one of the caucus members said, 'Normal women don't think like that,' and we moved to the next agenda item.

Philosopher Joan Eveline has reflected: 'Men who are openly hostile towards a woman in authority find ways to define and depict her which leave little doubt of their misogyny. One of the primary ways that this is done is to define the woman who speaks out as deviating from her designated female place. The inference is not only that the woman is manly, but that the presence of manliness in a woman becomes one of the most undesirable – in every sense of the word – things for her to be.'[42]

Walls of denial were not limited to sexual politics. Racist politics, and in 1981 the issue of apartheid and the South African rugby tour of New Zealand, brought forth the evil of political men in the secrecy of a government caucus. I retain many images of that period. I recall them as moments of innocence and brutal savagery. The marches of hope before that team arrived – every sort of New Zealander, including me, represented – trusting that there might still be time to stop this nightmare. There was the cynical political manipulation of other genuinely caring but politically ignorant people, for whom sport was apparently divorced from politics, and to whom the denial of entry visas to the Springbok team was a denial of freedom somehow exceeding the bounds of the struggle to overcome apartheid.

Adrienne Rich has written: 'We assume that politicians are without honour. We read their statements trying to crack the code. The scandal of their politics, not that people in high places lie, only that they do so with such indifference, so endlessly, still expecting to be believed. We are accustomed to the contempt inherent in the political life.'[43]

I know about the lies – I was there. Every Thursday morning I sat with those who protested publicly their opposition to this tour and who, safely ensconced in the National government caucus, dealt with the logistics of ensuring it would proceed and succeed. There was an election to be fought and to be won in the provinces, bastions of that right-wing, lower-class, sexist, racist, male-supremacist mentality. For their love of the game of legitimised violence called rugby, and its vested political conservatism, we were to tear ourselves apart.

You cannot be too cynical about such politics. The Prime Minister, Robert Muldoon, claimed that he had asked the rugby union to stop the tour. Publicly, the best he had managed, in a grotesque television performance, was to invite us to believe that because New Zealand and South African soldiers (of English descent) were buried alongside each other in the cemeteries of war dead, we were somehow brothers. For this reason he asked the New Zealand Rugby Football Union to 'think again'. He claimed he privately asked Ces Blazey, the president of the union, to stop the tour. Blazey said he did not. One of them was lying, and I have no doubt at all that it was the Prime Minister.

I watched in caucus meetings as a game in an opposition-held marginal provincial seat was cancelled on the basis that the ground could not be sealed from demonstrators. Since many Labour voters supported the tour, this was designed to have them change their vote. The game in a government-held seat would have to go on, and so would be protected by the army, barbed-wire fences and teams of police. I watched a Minister of the Crown (coincidentally the Minister of Police, an executive member of the New Zealand Rugby Football Union, an elder of the Latter-Day Saints Church and a Maori) say publicly that he supported the tour and apartheid. In the practice of the Westminster system of ministerial responsibility, he should have resigned. He was retained, and his honesty was praised as a virtue.

I protested – on the streets, on television, at public meetings. I leaked whatever I knew to leaders of the demonstration movement. I was the only member of Parliament of any party to participate in the protests on the days of the matches. All others were instructed by their various party leaders not to be seen near the stadiums. For my efforts I was assaulted by a male constituent and thrown down a bank. All this was recorded on photographs immediately made available to the police. While demonstrators were arrested on the basis of photographic evidence for trespass and property damage, no effort was made to speak to my assailant.

In caucus, I was advised to shut up and fall into line for the good of the Government. But it was more than that. There were explicit descriptions of 'what my wife is going to think of you, and what my children are going to think of you'. And comments such as, 'What do you want to be backing this group of people for?' Did they mean demonstrators? victims of apartheid? 'They are not important to you.' The real intent was to wear me down – to break my spirit, or what remained of it.

The tour was a horror time. I was just one young woman, and the only woman in government, getting chewed up if I spoke up and said Muldoon was telling lies – and he was – and chewed up by the protesters if I was not in the front line every Saturday. The battery was effective. Within weeks I was hospitalised from exhaustion.

The stress of the South African tour and the lies played their part in this, but so did the craziness of the life. My only woman party colleague from 1975 to 1978, Colleen Dewe, believed that being a member of Parliament 'is a two person job which the tax payer is too niggardly to pay for. I believe there has to be a lot of change to the system to allow single people, particularly single women, to enter the system.

'Men usually have some tame lady, be it a sister, a girlfriend, or even an electorate woman, who can do your laundry and make sure you have a meal in your deep-freeze, or even have you around for a meal. That didn't happen to me. Perhaps being a woman you don't confess your need for this sort of help . . . you have to be seen as superwoman.'[44]

When she was defeated after a three-year term, Colleen most remembered the intolerable tiredness. She was approached to stand again, but 'when I sat back and said "What was my life like?" I knew I could not go back . . . I had a sense of overwhelming relief that I could be a free person and a real person all over again'.[45]

Gemma Hussey has echoed her concerns about support. 'The organization of politics . . . is presently based on the increasingly unrealistic concept of the "serviced male": a man who has a full-time spouse looking after his physical needs, caring for children and home, to the exclusion of all other activities. The answer is not to ask women in politics to become mirror-images of the stereotyped male politician: rather it is to change perception and practice of how roles can be shared between two partners. I am talking child-care, education, parental leave for both parents.'[46]

Adequate childcare facilities in houses of parliament would be a good start. At the Women, Power and Politics Conference in Adelaide in 1994, Amanda Muir, former national director of the 300 Club in the UK, told the story of the most recent attempt to establish crèche facilities in the House of Commons. The Palace of Westminster has a shooting gallery, and it was suggested that this space be used for crèche facilities. As both men and women MPs suffer from not being able to see their children, and 85 per cent of all staff are women, this seemed a sensible suggestion. It was rejected. The chairman of the Commons Shooting Club, Michael Colvin (Conservative, Romsey and Waterside), admitted that space within the Commons was at a premium. He also admitted that there had been an attempt to raise the membership of the Shooting Club to counteract the crèche proposal.

The stories that women have to tell of what their male colleagues say in private always show up their extraordinary hypocrisy around these issues. Diane Abbott has written of her experience that she has 'had to fight to have a semblance of a normal domestic life. My marriage broke up because of the pressures of my political career . . . I have no live-in help. I take [her three-year-old son] to nursery every morning. Since he was born I have had to cut back on my activities . . . But I have no regrets. A political career that didn't give me time for my child would not be worth having. Many older male MPs have taken me aside and told me to spend as much time with my son as possible. They say, sadly, that when their children were growing up they didn't see them and they regret it now.'[47]

In the New Zealand Parliament a crèche has finally been provided for all workers. But the large billiard room remains even while there is no provision for MPs' school-age children other than the so-called members' wives room.

Given the manipulative games to ensure that logistical support is not available to prospective women MPs, and the priorities typified by the battles to retain shooting galleries and rooms for shooting pool, it seems that only the lonely, the naive, the chronically ambitious or the truly anarchic woman would seek to set foot in the place. I would not have considered myself to be over-endowed with any of these characteristics when I became the candidate in 1975, but at various times and in various survival modes over the following nine years I probably experienced them all.

First comes the campaign. The people close to you, and you yourself, must understand that this will be an enormous change. They must privately and publicly advocate your candidacy. They must accept a lower standard of household servicing, take over household chores, and be prepared to pay for a housekeeper. They must not be threatened by the power you have, or seek to demean you or put you down. They must be able to accept the outcome if you disagree on policy. They should be prepared to give advice if asked, but should not expect to make decisions. They should not expect to change you. They probably do not expect the change that will come to you, but then neither do you.

If you are in a relationship, fellow workers and 'mates' can make it hard for your partner; if you have children, teachers and pupils can make it tough for them. There will be swings between pride and envy at the attention you get. There will be resentment at how frequently you are absent, and demands for even more attention when you are present, usually when you are at your most vulnerable and needing the comfort and support yourself. Any male partner will receive more attention from other women than he has received in a long time, and you will receive a similarly increased amount of attention from other men. The innuendoes will be sexual, and you should both be prepared to deal with this.

Not many women who write about their 'parliamentary life' describe what happened at home. Early into her first year in the Irish Cabinet, Gemma Hussey noted in her diary: 'I've been working very hard to keep up a presence at home as much as possible so that the stress there won't become too great; despite all our knowledge before I took the job, we didn't know how bad it would be.'[48] In this, as in too many aspects of the lives of the women who serve, the silence is most revealing.

Any woman who has stood for office, and many who have been interviewed for employment in male bastions, have known the indignity of 'What if you get married?', 'Do you want to have children?', 'What about your husband? How does he feel?', and the rest of this sexist line of questioning. I am reliably informed by women in both the Labour and National parties that, after 1975, a regular question asked was 'Are you a feminist?' – and if you said yes – the follow-up was, 'Not like Marilyn Waring?' So that too many women answered no.

But not all of them. In the New Zealand parliamentary context, only a feminist would speak of 'the unequal power relationships between men and women', as Margaret Shields did.[49] Only a feminist parliamentarian would remember history the way Katherine O'Regan does: 'I believe strongly in choice. I will do all I can to retain that option for girls and women. I recall at 16 my outrage when it really dawned on me that women's suffrage had had to be fought for, that women couldn't vote because they were born women. Every cell in my body asked why, and it wasn't until much later that I found the answers. We weren't taught that at school. I had never heard of Mrs Kate Sheppard or Mrs Elizabeth McCombs, the first woman Member of Parliament, or any other of the women who had helped build this country. They were invisible in our history books.'[50]

When Judy Keall was selected as candidate for the Glenfield seat, she said her major qualifications were that she was a women and a mother.[51] The only time I recall such terms being used by men running for political office was in the contest for the selection of a candidate for the new Waipa seat in 1978. In 1976 a tabloid newspaper had run a series of articles on my sexuality. In 1977 the Electoral Boundaries Commission, in redrawing constituencies, had managed to eliminate my seat of Raglan completely, splitting it three ways. In 1978, having indicated that I would stand for the new seat of Waipa, I was challenged by three white, middle-aged, middle-class men, two of whom vigorously insisted that their key qualifications were that they were 'strong family men with Christian moral values'. I won the Waipa nomination on the first ballot, and within months one of those two men was declared bankrupt and the other was left by his wife.

And, in this first term in Parliament, I am learning even more about my naivety. I learn that a woman in government might be said to change attitudes on minor issues, but I doubt whether she changes ethics. If women are seen as an important voter population, and if the government has a small majority, then policies might change – but expediently, not ethically. I find I am presented with a dual mission: to do what needs to be done yesterday, and to transform that rigid, walled, prison-like institution into a fluid, flexible creation quite without boundaries. This is extremely threatening to the male power structure, and to the souls of the women who find themselves inside.

What I had to say from day to day and from issue to issue did not make the men there happy. The words I chose as a feminist politician had a resonance, or a decibel level, that exacted a different realm of responsibility for their use. I was constantly alert. Am I translating correctly? Am I conveying the complexities, the subtleties? Am I inside this phrase? Will this come back to haunt me? If this cynicism is mis-reported, how will it sound on the page? To what extent does the perceived need to speak reasonably obscure the truth, the outrage, the injustice?

I would look at their faces, their body language. I would see discomfort, aggression, masked as a patronising 'Oh, just let her talk, let her blow off steam. Let's get this part over with. Then we can just ignore her and get on with the real work.'

I would get angry. This was not about me. It was about the misuse of power and the consequences for the lives of people who for me had names and faces – and they were not always all female people. The guilt that I was letting them down would crowd in. Some of the inner truth of the utter loneliness of these moments would take over my self-control. Sometimes I would break down.

In an outstanding autobiography, former Governor of Vermont Madeleine Kunin has observed: 'Women cannot risk revealing public emotion; they are asked to take the toughness test each time they appear in public. A silent assessment is made by the audience as a woman approaches the podium: Can this woman be as strong as a man?'[52]

Women who weep in Parliament are reported, and labelled as emotional or lacking self-control. Men who weep, and it happens not infrequently, are labelled 'moving'. The male media moved by male tears also determines that male anger is not 'emotional', nor does it demonstrate a lack of self-control. But this is not our experience.

Male reporters are obsessed with women's emotions and pleased to portray them as a form of weakness, rather than as those scarce political characteristics of honesty and vulnerability (to me, vulnerability is the characteristic that is most required to truly demonstrate political courage). Take, for example, a recent major feature in a New Zealand monthly magazine, profiling Alliance Party deputy leader Sandra Lee. The male journalist reports: 'She speaks softly. So much so she sounds like she's on the verge of tears . . . Women are heard in the House but only if they bark like a man.'

Later in the article we read: 'Finally she greets three Maori women, two of them from the South Island, who have come simply to offer their support. "We know it's been hard on you, Sandra," says one softly in a kindly, motherly way. "But we just want you to know that we and all of Maoridom are behind you and that if there is anything that we can do." Sandra Lee, touched by these words, has her head in her hands. She is crying.'[53] In context, the impression the writer is keen to convey is that this leader is not strong enough for the job.

What a contrast this is with the reporting on men. Male parliamentarians are not unfeeling. I have seen them weep during debates on abortion and adoption, and with horror in recognition of the reality and depth of domestic violence. They weep in greater numbers, however, in saying farewell to Parliament. Unless these scenes have been televised, the public are unlikely to know about this, since it implies weakness on the part of the patriarchs and must not be revealed.

My electorate executive did not like it if I was reported to have wept, or to have acted on my conscience in the reproductive freedom debates, or to have carried out party policy to oppose the racist Springbok tour, or to have asked for constructive implementation of our policies on nuclear arms. They then had to suffer the tedious and arrogant letters of other National party electorate executives 'disapproving or condemning' the member of Parliament for Raglan, or subsequently Waipa. I used to wonder aloud how many letters had been sent to the electorate executives of alcoholics or adulterers? But, in the male world, that was so-called normal behaviour, which apparently did not cost votes. I began to believe that it was just thinking and feeling and researching and honesty which caused so much trouble.

But breaking down pleased the boys in the caucus band. They looked reassured. I was stereotypically unstable, too emotional, probably pre-menstrual, couldn't take it. They had a victory.

There is a scene in the movie *Broadcast News* when the character played by Holly Hunter excuses herself briefly from her companions, and goes to her hotel room. She throws herself on the bed, and in the space of a few moments runs the gauntlet of massive self-contempt, extreme fatigue, a minor emotional breakdown, and an hysterical weep. Then she gets up, takes some good deep breaths, checks herself in the mirror, and rejoins her co-workers as if nothing had happened. For me that was not a character in a film. That was me, every day.

My tears did not come just on the issues. They came with immense fatigue. They came because the constant compromise of language was a lack of truth to myself, and a cost to my emotional health. Even victories were hollow with this lack of truth, not to the principle of the argument, but in the tactics and the culture that I had to adopt and work within to achieve those results. And the effect of this denigrating of one woman's passion was to silence others also, including men, who might have been there to offer public support.

So the isolation increased. They were trying to humiliate me, they were trying to put me down, they were trying to isolate me. This was real and deliberate. I was not making this up. This felt dreadful.

Meanwhile, back with the inner me it was getting tough. Helen Clark explains how it gets to be: '[I'm] . . . tired all the time, [I'm] . . . exhausted for most of the year. [I'm] . . . giving up so much personal space in time and privacy. I don't read as much as I'd like to. I don't get to plays or films or music . . . I've lost a lot of friends simply because I don't have time for friendships anymore. The friends I've kept are those who tend to give more to me than I do to them, who are prepared to be supportive. Social occasions become very demanding. I have come to positively dislike going to parties unless I know exactly who's there and whether I can tolerate them.'[54]

But that's too bad. It's nice that you still remember how it used to be, but too bad. The 'real world' waits at work.

There is no doubt that women in parliaments have a compromising influence on the maleness of the House, but they are frequently sucked into the deceit. There is the temptation to think that the parliamentary institution is the be-all and end-all of politics in the country. It should not be surprising that the people who work there think so. The media report them avidly every day; they are institutionalised for more than half the week in one building, and there for long hours. When answering a telephone call from out of town, I not infrequently had to walk to the window to discover the answer to a question about the current weather in the capital.

Some women seek power as an achievement in itself; some do not want or need it; some boast that they have more by manipulating behind the scenes, (and fool only themselves). Some women seek it because it shuts out another patriarch. Some infiltrate, passing on the secrets, confusing the male world from bounding on on its hitherto-unquestioned male course. Some use the position to mobilise others. All of these routes are more valid than remaining contentedly power-less, you tell yourself as you rationalise staying for more emotional battery.

And, like the classic battered woman, you try another approach. You try the tactics of the batterer. I rationalised this too. For those people who trusted in me, for their words to be articulated, I would become whatever I had to be. I would taste the seductive nature of power. I would adopt the tactics, the culture. In my mimicry I would reinforce the historical male models. I could change my behaviour, and sense the commanding presence of the new me. I could feel the adrenalin rush of the competition. I could change my language and use the battle metaphors.

Women generally do not like fighting, and we are unused to fighting for ourselves. We can go to battle for others, but we do not consider it a mark of self-respect when we discover that we are good at it. A major problem arises. If the woman politician is generally loved for her expressions of passionate anger, her fortress defences against male attack, and her refusal to concede ground to male political compromise, and she is invited to behave like this for sixteen hours a day, then who is she with the intimates in her life, her partner, and especially her women friends, who do not find these traits acceptable in a personal relationship?

Madeleine Kunin recalled: 'I was astonished . . . by what I discovered in myself. I had a fierce drive . . . I wondered, Have I always had that capacity for combat, and is it only now exposed? What happened to the feminine side of me, the lady who smiled pleasantly and was nice?'[55]

This combative style requires no courage. Being co-opted to reinforce the male order may lead to a debilitating self-contempt, but only if you constantly examine how it feels to play this game. Many women transit to this role and never again engage their emotions. It is easier to play the head games. Since there is nothing elevated or cerebral about these, you soon discover that you are good at them.

They discover this too. This is very threatening. You are better than them at their own game. And, what is more, if you are a feminist your competition breaks the rules. This is not because we compete, but because we do so for reasons other than self-promotion – for principles, for ideals. (It should be clear that this is the point where the women who decide to be 'one of the boys' and the rest of us part company. But it should not be overlooked that the price paid by every woman in parliamentary life, captured in Bernadette Devlin's foreboding title *The Price of My Soul*,[56] is paid also by these women.)

But your success on their terms is not part of their game-plan either. The new tactics begin. You find yourself being constantly set up by the men against all other women. You are responsible, they say, for the Wonaac (Women's National Abortion Action Campaign) activists in the gallery during the abortion debate, who arrived as pregnant women and then released message-strewn helium balloons to float around the ceiling during the debate. I wish I had thought of that, but after a few years in that institution such theatrical tactics were beyond my imagination.

Alternatively, I was being set up against the women in the religious right on a variety of issues, and ordered by Whips to follow the women in the opposition in debates. The price of refusing this little proposal was removal from the speaking lists when I really wanted to participate. The attitude seemed to be that, since the male battleground has always pitched men against men, if we sought to invade, how dare we try to change the rules?

But that wasn't their point. Pitch one woman against another: they cancel each other out. They lose their credibility. We don't have to listen to anything that makes us uncomfortable. One women alone could be controlled, could be contained. But women together, especially from 'opposing sides', was disorder, a real threat, a revolution. Their perception that we intend to act with the same abusive exclusivity and hierarchical control, to 'keep men in their place' with the same brutality with which women have been kept in theirs, could not be more wrong.

And every day the constant invention needed to transform the system, to break the rules, to create precedents, requires exposure to vulnerability. And every day is fatiguing beyond the ability to dream, beyond the capacity to picture ideals.

In the midst of this very serious game I hoped I was still surviving deep down inside, but I had no time to check 'her' out. I had to hope that one day, when I went to retrieve 'her', 'she' might still be there. I introduce the third person here to recall a process that I became conscious of only years after my retirement.

I had begun my first term with the already edited use of the first person. I moved to the passive 'one' when I meant 'I'. Next I used 'you', and I notice as I listen to today's women leaders how frequently they respond to personal questions or inquiries in the second person. Helen Clark reported recently: 'A woman politician's life is often a rather lonely one. We all go into political life with our network of friends and acquaintances supporting us. But once we are there we don't have the time to nurture our networks. Politics has a tendency to become all absorbing. What one soon learns is that the best friends are one's old friends and family who believe in you and will stick with you through thick and thin. Politicians attract many fair weather friends. None of them will ring you after you or your party's defeat. They are off to cultivate acquaintanceships with the newly successful.'

In the final years I spoke of myself in public, and to myself (although a different self) in private, in the third person. Yet in all this time I did know, as Madeleine Kunin has noted, that 'the political audience is always searching for the genuine person who they suspect is hidden under the political facade'.[57] And there is always the other constant pressure on public performance, beautifully captured by Gemma Hussey in two diary entries: 'The final function was . . . utterly exhausting, moving around chatting with a million different people with their own strong points of view, but I kept my smiling, greeting, listening, interested air to the end';[58] and, 'Now I must wash and dress and put on the capable bright, ministerial front again, charming and chatting . . .'[59]

For my second term in Parliament, as the only woman in government, the most overwhelming characteristic was an acute loneliness. To my surprise, 20 years later Glenda Jackson, first-term Labour MP in the House of Commons, expressed the same sentiment. It was particularly difficult, she explained, because coming from professional theatre she had always, literally, worked with a company. But the woman member of Parliament is seldom with company she can rely on, or in company she can trust.

Just being there for another woman – on select committees, in board rooms, receiving delegations – the non-verbal support of other women is food for the soul. I was always so grateful to see women enter the parliamentary gallery or a select committee room or be present at official events. I was delighted to learn, years later, that my lonely presence had had a similar effect on the visitors. A poet, Rachel McAlpine, spoke of visiting with male colleagues to give a reading one evening during the dinner adjournment, and of feeling quite desperate and alien until I walked into the room.

When I review the interviews I gave in this period, or the pieces I wrote, the loneliness shows. In 1979 the tone is suspicious and angry: 'I cannot but feel more and more cynically resigned to a hopelessness that sees necessary social decisions deferred, that sees bigoted and anachronistic laws upheld and that sees difficult decisions postponed.'

In 1980 I wrote:

> How creatively as a politician do I avoid being distracted from wider political questions by a plethora of issues which act in some cases to pit us against each other? How do I cope with the contradictions implicit in a feminist belonging to a political party? How do I explain that the policies of leadership, the concepts of power, what is said in programmes, what is done, how things are done, are all offensive to me? How do I explain to women that it's not important to delineate a way of getting 'there', that we needn't limit ourselves, that we don't truly know our resources, our own collective strength. By remaining how much am I part of the problem?
>
>   How do I control and redirect the anger I feel when a woman in a leadership position criticizes those who describe 'man as the enemy', not because she has heard many other women do that, but because it will produce, predictably, a charged emotional response from her audience? To what extent does my being here perpetuate oppression? How much credibility do I give this patriarchal institution by being part of it and having to comply with its rules?[60]

And there was yet another obvious predicament, described so succinctly by Marcia Freedman, the sole feminist in the Israeli Knesset between 1973 and 1976: 'My role in politics was to place feminist issues on the agenda and try to keep them there. It was a mission that in political terms was doomed. Unless I turned my back on the cause that had put me in office I was bound to fail as a politician. To succeed I would have to fail as a feminist.'[61]

It was not a healthy time to be a public, proud and active feminist. It was not just a personal problem. In 1981 Helen Clark remembers: 'It was a difficult campaign. As a single women I was really hammered, I was accused of being a lesbian, of living in a commune, having friends who were Trotskyites and gays, of being unstable and unable to settle to anything. "If you elect her," my political opponent said, "she's for abortion on demand and your whole society will change overnight." I was fighting on all fronts. On top of all that I could do without the living in sin label. That's the only reason I married the man I'd been living with for five years, I was really tired of being extended on the personal front as well as on political issues. Personal accusations do hurt me but over time I've got to cope with them better. When I married a lot of the personal criticism stopped but I felt really compromised, I think legal marriage is unnecessary and I would not have formalized the relationship except for going into Parliament. I have always railed against it privately.'[62]

Living with compromise and hypocrisy becomes as common as cups of tea. Lots more becomes commonplace: the chronic exhaustion . . . the schedule eight months in advance . . . the recognition . . . how organised you have to be . . . how frantic that is . . . how impatient you are when you have to change pace, when the driver isn't good enough. . . . Having to hide some illnesses – menstrual cramps, depression, vomiting, bleeding fissures.

Of this period I wrote: 'sometimes I'm not sure I am surviving, and if I do, I owe it to women's energy, women's words, pain, strength, love . . . I am still afraid of getting too tired, of giving up. I am still afraid of staying in the job, and afraid of leaving it. . . . I am recognised in every corner of the country; and I don't hear normal conversations any more, as people posture and play within my hearing or sight.'[63]

I became afraid to ask what good I had done, what had changed for the better. I was part of a process that appeared more intent on harm than good, and all for the sake of electoral victory. There was the constant battle on all fronts not to lose ground.

I would resort to women's words on the page to convince myself that my feelings were justified, that I wasn't extreme. That in terms of the truth of women's lives I wasn't even radical. It was hard not to think I'd blown it for those who remained silent, that I'd let them down. But I

refused to intellectualise the debate so that the men might take refuge
in avoiding the real issues. I had to trust what I called my 'gut instincts',
those remnants of the woman somewhere still inside.

By 1983 I had made my decision not to contest another election. I
hadn't told anyone, but reports of interviews from the time show the
distancing that had begun. I said: 'I really have the confidence to work
alone now. Frankly I'm not collaborating with anyone, I'm not consulting. I know what I think, I know what I'm trying to do and I'm very
happy to get on with it and not have other people try to compromise
me . . . or score petty political points. If I work on my own, I can just
stick with the issue. I don't have to play games.'

I was on my own inside the institution, but never on my own outside.
That is what keeps so many of us going. It continues as it begins. After
her Cabinet selection, Gemma Hussey was 'astonished at the flood
of messages, letters, telegrams, flowers – so many women all round
Ireland have written to wish me luck; God, it's a responsibility. I'm
delighted for all the sisters who have slogged and worked and encouraged, but I have a sinking feeling that I'm hardly ever going to see them
for as long as this lasts, or anyone else either.'[64] You don't get to see
them as much, but your sisters read of you daily, and identify the
battering times, and respond.

Clare Short explains: 'After I arrived at the Commons I became
perceived as a strong feminist, probably before I used that same label
about myself. It was both their reaction to me and other women's
reaction to me that strengthened the very joyous sense in me of being a
woman, of being different, of being there connected with lots of other
women who aren't in and who ought to be here in the Commons. For
me that was a lovely experience . . .

'I got hundreds of letters and cards from women saying I was just
doing the ironing and I had to stop and I'm quivering with anger and
are you okay and don't worry we care about you. Not just trying to say
we agree, but also there is an enormous sense of worry and concern for
me to look after me which was just lovely.'[65]

Women like these would also invite me to be with them. Often I had
to make some kind of presentation or speech, and it was always an
emotional time for me, like a homecoming when you know you have to
leave again immediately. I was so hungry for those spaces and opportunities. Madeleine Kunin knew this too. 'What a new sensation it was to
be in a room filled with political women; here I was effortlessly being

understood . . . The emotional energy I expended functioning in the men's world could only be calibrated when I turned off the switch and relaxed in this comfortable space.'[66]

It was experiences like these that gave me the strength to act from that core of being a woman, however alone I felt. These moments of 'going home' gave me courage to engage issues, whatever the consequences. I recognise this in other women too.

Nikki Coseteng, on first winning a seat in the Philippines Parliament standing for Kaiba, the women's political party, was appointed to chair the Human Rights Committee in the first post-Marcos Parliament. She describes the move as a clever male tactic. It was an unsafe chair to have. No male politician wanted to risk the wrath of the military, or to be antagonising the rebels. 'That's her coming. Get her into trouble. Kill her off as a candidate. That will stifle her.' How wrong they were. Coseteng worked assiduously, and often underground. She asked too many difficult questions. They had to remove her for doing too good a job.

Vigdis Finnbogadottir became President of Iceland in 1980. In 1985 on International Women's Day the women of Iceland staged a strike. The President intended to strike too. On 8 March, the Althing (parliament) passed a bill forbidding the female flight attendants on Icelandic Air to join the protest. When Vigdis refused to sign the bill, the Prime Minister put great pressure on her, arguing that if air traffic was disrupted Iceland would suffer economically. Vigdis signed, then quickly went home, and silently applauded when the flight attendants joined the strike anyway.[67]

During her first campaign in 1990, Irish President Mary Robinson was never afraid to criticise 'the patriarchal male-directed presence of the Roman Catholic Church' for holding back women's rights. She was portrayed by Fianna Fail as an agent of abortion, homosexuality and promiscuity, and as a mother who had only passing interest in her children. She replied: 'My views are known. What I would represent is more space and more pluralism and more tolerance.'[68]

Often a sister's story has resonance for me, and I recognise a similar experience. Gemma Hussey recalls that, when she was Minister of Health, 'a row was blowing up about my refusal to go to the Surgeons Charter Day dinner because of the male-only guest list. Victor Lane of the College of Surgeons rang me at home, very upset and quite angry about a *Sunday Independent* piece on it, wanting me to withdraw it or correct it, but how could I since it was true.'[69] I refused those sorts of invitations too.

On one occasion, when I had been invited to some literary awards during the tea adjournment, I rang the minister's office to find out whether the award had been won by a woman. I had another engagement, but intended to make an effort to be present for a time to provide a woman's presence if I thought that was necessary. A man was the winner, so I made my apologies and went to my other function. The male private secretary informed the press that I had refused to attend because a woman hadn't won the award, and a tedious and patronising editorial followed.

For so many women politicians, if Parliament was hell, the constituency was the space to recover, the opportunity to heal, to replenish in order to go back one more time. Here I could help, I could be an agent to change lives, to deliver what was due, to be constructive. And I would be taught – by example or through experience. The privilege of trust invested in me by constituents and by women throughout the country was a salutary and humbling experience, and however much I felt myself drowning and fighting (metaphorically) for my own life, the cases of courage and survival challenged me to battle on for the many.

Audre Lorde, commenting on the events surrounding her writing the poem 'Power', mirrored the voice inside me, the torment it was all becoming: 'How do you deal with the things you believe, live them not as theory, not even as emotion, but right on the line of action and effect and change . . . to put myself on the line to do what had to be done at any place and time was so difficult, and not to do so was the most awful death. And putting yourself on the line is like killing a piece of yourself, in that you have to kill, end, destroy, something familiar and dependable, so that something new can come in ourselves, in our world. And that sense of [political activity] at the edge, out of urgency, not because you choose it but because you have to, that sense of survival – once you live any piece of your vision it opens you to constant onslaught. Of necessities, of horrors, but of wonders too, of possibilities . . . like meteor showers all the time, bombardment, constant connections.'[70]

But only for so long. By the end there was nothing left to work with, however much I tried.

On Friday evenings, after the flight from Wellington, I picked up my car at the airport, and if I was especially lucky, perhaps once a month, I could drive straight home. I'd pull into the drive of a modest wooden house close by the town boundary, collect the mail, and deposit my briefcase and suitcase inside the back door.

Then, even on balmy evenings, I liked to collect the dried pine cones, the kindling, the driftwood collected last summer on a constituency beach of black sand, and light a fire in the old stove and then in the open fireplace in the sitting-room. Once they were established, I took a torch, the secateurs and a bucket of water, and walked the garden, picking flowers, noticing the seasonal changes reflected in the fledgling buds and blossoms.

When the house was full of vases of flowers, I assembled the yeast, flour, cracked wheat and molasses and began the process of making bread. I'd open a bottle of claret, and during the periods while the dough was rising I'd lie in front of the fire and listen to some recordings from the old life, when I had been a trained classical musician.

By 1 a.m. the house smelt of the freshly baked loaves and the flowers, the damp of four days of a home being uninhabited was disappearing, and so was the red wine. I thought these hours were a peaceful happy time, and imagined that this was what 'normal' people might get to do when they had the opportunity.

I could not afford to examine the implications of the favourite piece of music on such occasions. Dame Janet Baker was singing a Bach cantata. The recitative began 'Ich habe genug'. I spoke German – it meant 'I've had enough'. The aria followed: 'Schlummert ein, ihr matten Augen' (Go to sleep, you weary eyes). But it was not an aria about wanting to sleep. It was about wanting to die.

Despair – and the failure of imagination. The poets know this. Adrienne Rich has written: 'We see despair in the political activist who doggedly goes on and on, turning in the ashes of the same burnt-out rhetoric, the same gestures, all imagination spent. Despair, when not the response to absolute physical and moral defeat, is like war, the failure of imagination.'[71]

In 1980 I had written: 'Those male politicians who fought the suffrage less than a century ago on the grounds that it would masculinize women were describing their own political lives, lives of oppression, competition, conflict. Their mistaken assumption was that women would assume or acquire the same characteristics in the same environment . . . The task is to find a way to get there and survive without becoming in any way like'.[72] I was wrong. It requires a woman of super-human qualities (and an extraordinary lack of personal ambition) not 'to assume or acquire the same characteristics in the same environment'.

Helena Kennedy, describing colleagues in the English legal profession, writes: 'Some women say they never experienced discrimination, and they may be the lucky few. However, there are women who sail through the process having made a conscious decision to identify with their male colleagues and become 'one of the chaps', albeit a feminine version.'[73]

In politics, the same pressures operate for women to become 'one of the chaps'. But I consider something quite tragic has happened if they do. Listen to these voices.

'There isn't a separation between me as a person and my job. I am that same person. If you're asking "does one never get hurt" the answer is "of course I get hurt". Yes of course one gets hurt.'[74] This from Edwina Currie, former Secretary of State for Health in Thatcher's Conservative Government.

Or 'I have tended to become the political and public persona I present myself as. I've become the mask as it were . . . I deliberately suppress a lot of my feelings in public life, I have become so controlled that I don't have many personal reactions, I wasn't like that before.'[75] This is Helen Clark, leader of the New Zealand Labour Party.

Listen to Teresa Gorman, Conservative member of the House of Commons: 'My advice to new-comers to this game is to always be on your guard with the press and never never be your natural self . . . The system is merciless so you have to be calculating in order that the public doesn't get the impression that women are superficial and light weight.'[76]

While in office, few women can speak of the brutalising impact of political life. Surviving takes all your emotional energy. Some only speak of it later. Madeleine Kunin expresses the predicament so honestly in her autobiography, and at a depth few have so extensively braved on the page. 'I had become familiar with my political demons: fear, self-doubt, and paranoia. Through practice, I had gained the capacity to keep them under control. Each time I got the upper hand, I felt a sense of accomplishment; I had triumphed over myself again . . . I would feel a rush of adrenaline, as my stronger self flaunted its prowess over my weaker twin, forcing it to beat a retreat . . .'

'Politics imposed an artificial order, a ritual, that allowed me to delude myself into thinking that my life was under control . . . I could

close the door behind me and move to another house . . . Compart-
mentalized, I felt better. This is who I was for the moment. But
who had I left behind? . . . Was politics another form of constriction,
rather than a liberation? . . . [Was I] moulding myself to an outwardly
defined model? In Sylvia Plath's poetry she had turned over rocks
and uncovered the less manageable and more conflicted emotions that
swarmed there. Her life could not contain the passions she had
released; one look and I knew that neither could mine. I rolled the
rock back. . . .'

'This sense of wholeness was coming apart. The person I appeared in
public and the person I was in private were no longer the same . . . I
did not want to become a political figure whose sense of self-worth
depended on looking in the mirror each morning and saying, "You are
the Governor". Having felt the seductive nature of power, I wanted to
free myself of it and prove that I could live without it once again.'[77]

I mentioned at the beginning of this essay that the circumstances surrounding the centenaries of women's suffrage in New Zealand and
South Australia had provoked reflection and writing of my own on my
parliamentary experience. It also provoked others who had shared that
position, often whether we liked it or not, because we became the
subjects of a plethora of books, and newspaper and magazine articles,
and all received many invitations to speak at commemorative functions.
In New Zealand, it meant reading that I was not alone in any of the
desperation I had felt at the end.

Ann Hercus had described why she had retired: 'Working 100-plus
hours a week, the continual flying on planes to get home, the lack of
privacy, the crank phone calls in the early hours of the morning, the
obscene letters and so on . . . I also recognized the inevitability of doing
the sane and sensible thing for my family and myself.'[78]

The New Zealand Suffrage Centenary also offered me the opportunity to accept the invitation to present the annual Hocken Lecture at
the University of Otago, where I ventured, but very carefully and in a
highly edited form, my first public reflections on the emotional battery
of women politicians.

In 1994, the invitation to address the South Australia centenary conference gave me a stage outside New Zealand, where I could be braver
in my disclosures. During and after my speech, many women who have
held, and who hold, political office wept openly. Breaking the silence
was like lancing a festering boil. They approached me, and told me

more stories. I am grateful for all that they shared, and the courage it takes to share it. The only words that I could find at the time, about why I had to retire, were that I could feel proud of what I had accomplished at the end of each day, but that I was utterly self-contemptuous about the methods I'd been forced to use to achieve that result. In the end, I think, this is why we go.

After my Adelaide address, Jennifer Cashmore, who had served twelve years in the South Australian Parliament, offered me a piece of paper 'on which [she] had scribbled in despair and frustration' near the end of her final term. It read: 'Oh, if only I could be out of it! Every time any energy or feeling or conviction bubbles up inside me it gets suppressed, one way or another. If only the next few weeks would pass quickly, so it will all be over and the sham of being a front-bencher will cease.

'There is something dehumanizing about being required, or rather being willing, for whatever reason, to submit to this fraudulent existence of allegedly representing people while knowing you are not really representing them at all . . . The great dilemma is to see where loyalty lies. With the party, by conforming to the lowest common denominator? With myself, by speaking out against all the things I think are wrong? . . . Jill Ker Conway was right when she said Australia is not "psychologically energizing" for women. Twelve years in the Party Room have certainly sapped my psychological and intellectual energy.'

At the airport, when she saw me off after the conference, Jennifer told me of her decision not to stand again: 'I was discussing whether to stay or go after twelve years with my adult daughter, and she said to me, "If you stay one more term, something essential to your identity will be destroyed." '

I returned home from the conference and was soon engaged in a telephone conversation with Margaret Shields. We had been in the New Zealand Parliament together for three years, although on opposing sides of the House. Margaret had been an active feminist before her election, and experienced that enormous dislocation from and loneliness for our old friends and support structures. She told me: 'Especially in campaigns I felt as if I was clinging to my identity with my fingernails. Everyone wanted to see you better than you are, bigger than you are, worse than you are. I couldn't go back to the well. There was no time for reflection, for reading. I felt as if I was getting closer and closer to my bones and there was no flesh there . . . You'd be fighting like hell for the people you represent, often at great pain, and then have to follow the party line, and never be able to tell the truth either way . . . No one has the right to encourage women in unless they're prepared to stay there for them, to know how to support them and not put them down.'

Former senator and leader of the Australian Democrats, Janine Haines, explains: 'The fact is that women often have to be tougher if not smarter than men to survive in politics and it goes without saying that they have to be tougher as well as smarter in order to succeed.'[79]

What are we saying here? That it is vital to play their game? According to their rules? That it is vital to suppress emotion? That it is imperative never to be ourselves, and never be true to ourselves?

What truths should we tell?

Madeleine Kunin explains: 'The inner life . . . gives the public person that most critical ingredient – courage . . . It temporarily blinded me to what everyone else could see clearly: that the political life is brutal . . . I began to fear that the private stockpile had run low. I wanted the opportunity to be alone, to write, to observe, and to create ties with a few individuals one at a time . . . The luxury of an unscheduled day, of a meandering conversation with no agenda, of a walk that had no destination, these are the things I yearned for.'[80]

In her essay 'Three Guineas', Virginia Woolf writes: 'if people are highly successful in their professions they lose their senses. Sight goes. They have no time to look at pictures. Sound goes. They have no time to listen to music. Speech goes. They have no time for conversation. They lose their sense of proportion – the relations between one thing and another. Humanity goes.'[81]

Humanity goes. And when humanity goes you have become the mask. And it is painful for all who find themselves battered into this hiding-place, even for men.

Jim Anderton made the following comments at a press conference when announcing his resignation as leader of the Alliance Party in the New Zealand Parliament, and his intention to resign as a member of Parliament at the next election. 'Politics is also a bruising and demanding arena within which normal sensitivities are a luxury which one quickly learns to hide. As a result politicians themselves can become desensitised. I do not criticise them for that because the pressures are very great, but becoming desensitised allows them to deal with their opponents and even those on their own side in ways which, if they studied objectively, they would surely be horrified . . . Parliamentary politics has become a brutalising arena to which I can no longer subject myself.'[82]

All this brutality masking itself as power, and in situations where it is simply not necessary. Maria de Lourdes Pintasilgo was appointed Prime Minister of Portugal in 1979. She has observed: 'Women who are very competent in their fields feel that political life is less pure, that they're going to have to make compromises on an intellectual or moral level.

'The whole realm of life, which I would call the poetic side of life, is very dear to me. Politics by itself is a highly dry thing . . . In the Greek universe you need politicians and you need poets, and you put the two things together.'[83]

In case the reader is tempted to stereotypes here, this woman Prime Minister was trained as an engineer. But Vaclav Havel, President of the Czech Republic, and a man brutalised as a political prisoner, is a writer and a poet. He has outlined what he believes are the characteristics necessary for those who seek a career in politics. 'If your heart is in the right place and if you have good taste, not only will you pass muster in politics, you are destined for it. If you are modest and do not lust after power, not only are you not unsuitable for politics, you belong there. The sine qua non of the politician is not the ability to lie; he [*sic*] need only be sensitive and know when, to whom, what and how to say what he has to say. It is not true that a person of principle does not belong in politics; it is enough for his principles to be leavened with patience, deliberation, a sense of proportion, and an understanding of others. It is not true that only the unfeeling cynic, the vain, the brash, and the vulgar can succeed in politics; all such people, it is true, are drawn to politics, but in the end decorum and good taste account for more.'[84]

It is always tempting for a writer, and particularly one who also has been a lecturer, to try to leave their reader with a sense of hope at the end. I have noticed, in the dozen years since I retired from Parliament, that women and men comment to me that it must have improved since I was there – and women add quizzically, 'hasn't it?'

In the time of writing this essay, I looked out for indications of the current situation, to see what I might offer in response to this query. A year after the triumph of democracy in South Africa, ANC backbencher Thenjiwe Mtintso wrote: 'There seems to be no holistic understanding from the cabinet to the National Assembly on the notion of gender. Individual ministers throw in paragraphs in their long speeches meant to be addressing "women's problems and affirmative action" without any clear understanding of the relationship between national liberation and women's emancipation. Though the constitution specifies this equality, neither the cabinet nor parliament has begun to address the main issue of patriarchy and the very patriarchal state, cabinet, civil service and society at large.'[85]

I looked for evidence of change in New Zealand. A speech delivered in 1994 by Jo Fitzpatrick, a member of the Labour Party executive, came my way. I read: 'Men assume power as a natural right. They are used to having it . . . They give us bits of it when it suits them or when they think we are becoming uncomfortably restless.

'Our most recent leadership change in the Labour Party was the same as any other but for the fact that it put a woman into power. It is a caucus where women are still the minority and it is unlikely that gender was a reliable predictor of support for either contender. Despite that it became a women's conspiracy in the media. Women were labelled and attacked – lesbian (therefore manhaters) or husbandless (therefore dangerous and out of male control) and women got an unfair share of all the vitriol. I staffed the phones at the Labour Party throughout and much of the male response was blatantly sexist. I was horrified and enlightened by the degree and depth of it. The women office staff reeled under the attack and eventually got angry. They blanch at being called feminists but they know how to stick up for themselves. It was sobering and shocking listening to the seedy sexist slurs and vicious misogyny.

'In the Selwyn by-election, after we had finished decorating the hall for the campaign opening, with posters of Helen Clark and the candidate Marian Hobbs, some of the men suggested that the presence of so many women's images made it a difficult space for them.'[86]

In the magazine story on Sandra Lee, she commented on the behaviour in Parliament. I read: 'I sometimes look up to the public gallery at the faces of kids coming in school groups and almost without exception you can see how unimpressed they are with what they see going on in the floor of the House . . . One day for a split second the House was quiet and a child turned to her father and said, "They think they're very clever, don't they, dad?" Everybody heard it and everyone looked up stunned.'[87]

In a recent weekly magazine, in a feature story on New Zealand

MP Christine Fletcher, I read: 'We are supposed to be entering a new era, but Parliament is still run along strict whipping lines, the working hours are programmed to break up the togetherest family, and there's a constant undertow of sexism aimed at women MPs.' The report continued: 'It has taken her longer than most MPs, but she gives the impression of finally having grown the extra layer of skin necessary for survival in politics. "You grow it at the expense of a certain sensitivity, but if you show you're vulnerable around the House", she says, "you're dogmeat". She has imposed what she calls emotional discipline on herself, has learned to work the system and has not only won a couple of battles but, to her surprise, rather enjoyed winning . . . The game goes on and, in order to compete, Chris Fletcher has had to become a player. "It's amazing what you can do when you flex your muscles", she says. "There's quite a competitive side to me which often surprises me. The tragedy is that I've probably learnt to be a better strategist now."'[88]

Imagine yourself a woman member of Parliament, or congresswoman, or deputy. Imagine yourself tormented, harassed, silenced and emotionally battered for six or more years. Imagine this relationship with these men you live with in this institution as a marriage. Imagine you have hoped it would change, that you have worked for change. Imagine that you have stayed because of the insecurity of leaving, knowing at the same time that staying provided no security. Imagine you have stayed for the sake of the children (constituents, women, minorities, causes, issues). Imagine all imagination spent.

Imagine what you might do in such a situation.

After her retirement, Madeleine Kunin describes walking on the beach in the late afternoon, alone, singing to herself, swinging her arms, stretching. She writes: 'I felt a sort of exorcism, the stirring of a physical relief from emotional pain . . . *Schmerzen*. All that accumulated pain covered up by layers of self-control began to reveal itself here, by the sea. I don't understand it, and I am afraid to confront it, but as I began to breathe deeply, I felt a weight begin to lift from my chest.'[89]

Ich habe genug.
Schmerzen.
Ich habe Schmerzen genug.
There has been enough pain.

Work 2

I do my shitwork with shovels, wheelbarrows and motor vehicles, and transport it on sealed roads. Let me explain.

I bought my farm in a dry, hot New Zealand summer. City friends who vicariously enjoyed the pioneer experience of rural life would come to stay; how long they stayed depended largely on the facility with which they acquired useful skills and how hard they worked. But the time of year, and their habituated need for an urban social life (plus our desire to wash in something a little bigger than a bucket of boiled water taken from the stock trough, and to eat other than from the barbecue), saw us making the trip back to town for Christmas/New Year parties.

The tradition of these events is that you 'take something' – generally food or drink to be consumed on the occasion, sometimes a frivolous or impractical little item which has already come your way in the season of good cheer, and which, having ascertained that that particular benefactor will not be present, you are able to move onwards.

This year no such items had come my way. I had no cash to spare for seasonal gifts, no garden yet established and productive, no hens laying healthy free-range eggs. But everywhere I was invited that summer was a city home with a garden ravaged and cracking from the combination of heat, wind, and water restrictions. So, to the horror of the transient pioneers who were with me, I would take myself, a shovel and some stout rubbish bags down to the wintering barn that came with the property, and fill them with stinking rotting worm-infested cow dung. And then, slinging them on the back of the old utility, we'd head off for town.

My companions would tell me that I couldn't take cow dung to the party. They would threaten not to come with me, and would insist on stopping *en route* to buy their version of the socially acceptable gift.

On arriving they would leave the utility very quickly to distance themselves from the shimmering exotic-smelling goodies on the back of the
truck.

The hosts, however, were beside themselves with joy. Steaming
towards their compost bins, or into buckets to make liquid manure, or
directly onto their desperate plants, came the gift likely to rescue their
beloved gardens. Much to the chagrin of my companions, they then
told everyone else how superb my present was – superior indeed to the
customary offerings that had also arrived that day.

Nine years later, there are eggs and fruit trees and the year-round
production of vegetables, but the first choice of my visitors remains
fertiliser – now principally of the goat kind, even more sought-after
than cow dung. Recycled containers carry away the droppings from
under the ribbed floors of the goat sheds, seasonally supplemented with
mushrooms, watercress, blackberries, pinecones and fallen tree boughs
split into logs.

This cleans my shed environs, gets rid of contributors to foot scald,
helps in general hygiene, clears the paddocks of wood which inhibits
growth and can get caught in machinery during haymaking. The
bargain struck is that I get half the bucket gathered, and that some is
always left for the next visitor. The only losers are the goats, who adore
blackberries and watercress, and are not averse to the single bite out of
fresh field mushrooms.

This production is immensely satisfying. We all enjoy the exercise, it
seems ecologically sound, it makes for tidy farming. It enhances further
production, especially in nutrition and food security. It saves the use of
fossil fuels in home heating. And, while it is undoubtedly enjoyable the
way it is done on my farm, there is no doubt that it is hard work.

But I have watched women in many parts of the world following
herds of animals to scoop up steaming dung in their bare hands, placing
it in woven baskets which they then hoist onto their heads and carry.
The loads they bend for, lift and carry are very heavy, and the work is
very tiring. In the context of the lives of these women, dung is not a
summer city-garden rescue; access to it is a matter of daily survival. In
addition to providing fertiliser, it is a primary source of cooking fuel
and is also used as a building material and plaster.

When used as organic manure, the dung must be dried for several
months and then carried to the households' farming plots. These are
seldom contiguous, and may be several kilometres from the household.

I recall images of women walking bare-footed along rough narrow paths on the side of steep hills, for example, in Indonesia or Nepal. Entire days are spent carrying on their heads baskets full of fertiliser for the small family plots before ploughing.

In many places in the developing world, livestock are held in a small enclosure immediately next to the home, since the pressure on land use means that, with a few seasonal and agro-ecological exceptions, fewer livestock are allowed to wander freely or are herded. Gathering fodder for the animals and then bringing them water become more arduous tasks for women and children, with longer and longer walks. At least the dung is closer to the household.

In parts of Africa and Asia, dung is also used as a basic material for building construction, maintenance and decoration. Adobe houses are covered with a mixture of mud, dung and straw and replastered several times a year. The mixture is spread by hand, and only women do this work. In some villages, the plaster is mixed with coloured pigments, and spectacular decorative patterns often adorn the outside of the houses.

As a result of forest depletion, women increasingly need dung to burn as an alternative to wood fuel. After collection, they mix it with straw and water and make it into flat cakes. Then it is dried, usually in the sun, and the women need to turn each cake several times in this process before it is dry enough for storing. Making dung cakes can take up to two hours a day and, when the cakes are stacked, there is the further process of thatching and sealing the pile to keep out the rain.

Making dung cakes to be used as fuel appears to me to be an entire manufacturing process, with clear inputs and outputs of an economic nature. In mining or gas extraction, for example, paid workers harvest the primary resource. Machines transport it to processing plants. The raw material is refined, the product manufactured. It is sold, then consumed. The traditional economic model is followed: workers process raw materials for the market. This counts. But when dung, the 'non-product', is carried as a 'service' by 'housewives', to sustain land, dwellings and households, then, according to the economic model, nothing happens. There is no economic activity. But dungwork is only women's work, so it is a safe assumption that in the official definitions of productive work it will be invisible.

All over the planet, and for centuries, organic manure has been recycled and frequently returned to the soil to increase productivity. But environmental degradation has increased the value of dung as an alternative fuel, and the lack of available manure has translated directly into declining soil fertility and declining crop yields.

And let's get something else quite clear before we go any further. Dung is not a primary product, whatever we might have assumed in the past. Dung itself appears to be taken for granted as a 'free gift of nature'. Nowhere have I found it recorded with milk, skins, meat, or animal by-products in a nation's livestock production accounts, or recorded in energy production accounts. In addition, we will not find the hours women spend in gathering, transporting, cooking with, processing, manufacturing from, or decorating with it recorded as work.

The area of human activity generally excluded from economic measurement is household activities, the products of which are seldom or never marketed, i.e. the unpaid services of housewives and other family members, household maintenance, subsistence agriculture performed by children or 'housewives', voluntary work, and reproductive work: most of the work that most of the people do most of the time.

'Growth' figures register 'market' activities, i.e. cash-generating activities, whatever the nature of that activity and regardless of its legal status. The figures will include, for example, agricultural production, but they will also include munitions and armaments production, prostitution, the sale of children, deforestation – provided cash is exchanged. Female sexual slavery, wars, ecological devastation, the huge trade in illicit substances, graft and corruption all contribute to growth.

In New Zealand, companies dry dung products and sell them in pelletised form for the home gardener. The process is called manufacturing. The results are marketed. The workers are paid. When the rural women of the developing world recycle dung, nothing in the process, the production or the labour has an economic value.

The value of this most primary of all forms of production, and its links with women's unpaid work, raise crucial policy questions which have seldom, if ever, been contemplated by the arbiters of what does and does not count. As a consequence, much of the rhetoric intended to ensure continuing exclusion of these activities, and large amounts of women's other work, from measurement is made on the basis that all this has little or no effect on most micro and all macro economic activity.

Yet the consequences for micro and macro policy planning are immense. While dung can be a replacement fuel for scarce wood, and therefore ease the rate of deforestation, this use is a major loss in terms of soil conservation and fertility. For example, it is estimated that in Nepal eight million tonnes of dung are now burnt each year, equivalent to one million tonnes of forgone grain production.[1] At the same time, the use of dung as a fuel is a major instance of import substitution, and is a national saving in terms of the debts that would be incurred through the importation of fuel if resourceful women had not processed the alternative.

According to the economic experts, this import substitution of considerable proportions (in the millions of dollars saved in overseas debt) is of no account. But the land is deprived of its needed organic fertiliser. Then, when plans to import and subsidise chemical fertiliser are announced, development consultants are puzzled by the significant differences between their forecasts and the low actual usage of the expensive alternative. But, if the marginal cost of a farmer's invisible labour to collect, process and transport this free gift of nature is considered to be zero, why should he/she put him/herself to any expense to replace it? Why should he/she assist in increasing the burden of debt from imports? Do the 'experts' designing a nation's economic development plan even begin to address such questions? The answer is no, and the reasons lie in the half-baked data bases they use for such planning, and in women's invisibility.

THE RULES ON WORK

Readers familiar with my earlier work on the United Nations System of National Accounts[2] will understand the need to outline briefly the rules that pervade what is and is not 'economic activity', and who does and does not count as a 'producer' in a nation's economy.

The method for measuring growth and production throughout the world is called the United Nations System of National Accounts (UNSNA). The rules of this system state that there are areas of human activity which lie outside a 'production boundary' (i.e. outside the market) established for the purposes of the national accounts.

Any economic report of the World Bank, the International Monetary Fund (IMF), United Nations (UN) agencies, or national governments, is based on national account statistics. The UN uses these figures to assess annual contributions, and to appraise the success of regional development programmes. Aid donors use the UNSNA to identify deserving cases, 'need' being determined by 'per capita gross domestic product' (GDP). While the most in 'need' would tend to register low growth figures, donors prefer to invest in countries showing high rates of growth, paving the way for their own exports and investment opportunities. In the same way, the World Bank uses these figures to identify nations that most urgently need economic assistance, but prefers those with higher rates of growth, making it easier for multinational corporations to use the same figures to locate new areas for overseas investments. The availability of IMF loans and loan roll-overs comes with contingencies to force changes in government economic policies to increase growth rates based on these figures. Companies in turn use these national accounts projections to project the markets for their goods and to plan their investment, personnel and other internal policies.

Resources are mined, skies are polluted, forests are devastated, watercourses are turned into open sewers and drains, whole populations are relocated as valleys are flooded and dammed, and labour is exploited in chronically inhumane working conditions. The statistics record economic growth.

There are many caveats to be considered in the interpretation of growth figures.[3] In this context we will confine ourselves to those expressed in the best-selling UN publication *The World's Women*.[4] It explains: 'Generally, the lower a sector's share in GDP, the higher the amount of informal activity in that sector and the greater the participation of women . . . Women's average economic situation in most developing regions is certainly worse than GDP figures show, as GDP averages do not take any account of distributional considerations.'

For individual countries, the uses made of national accounts and their supporting statistics are manifold and have far-reaching effects. They are used to create frameworks or models for the integration of economic statistics generally. They are used to analyse past and current developments in the national economy, and to project the possible effects of changes in policy or other economic changes. They are used to quantify all areas of what is considered the national economy so that resource allocation decisions can be made accordingly. Governments project public service investment and revenue requirements for the nation, and plan the new construction, training and other programmes necessary to meet those needs, all by using their national accounts. They are used to forecast short- and medium-term future trends. They are also used internationally to compare one nation's economic performance with another's.

It is claimed that national accounting provides factual information. As I have demonstrated, dung cakes are a manufactured product that requires hours of labour. And that is a fact. But not according to the UNSNA, where facts are carefully selected in a way that predetermines public policy.

The UNSNA measures the value of all goods and services that actually enter the market. It also measures the value of other production that does not enter the market, such as government and non-profit services provided free or at a nominal charge, and accommodation provided by owner-occupied dwellings.

From the UNSNA are derived the figures for the GDP. This is used to monitor rates and patterns of growth, to set priorities in policy-making, to measure the success of policies and to measure 'economic welfare'. Activities that are outside the production boundary – that is, in every nation the great bulk of labour performed by women in an unpaid capacity – are left out of the GDP. It is not a large step from that point to leaving them out of policy considerations altogether.

Cooking, according to the UNSNA, is 'active labour' when cooked food is sold and 'economically inactive labour' when it is not. Housework is 'productive' when performed by a paid domestic servant and 'nonproductive' when no payment is involved. Those who care for children in an orphanage are occupied; mothers who care for their children at home are 'unoccupied'.

The policy implications are stark. The company jet ferrying executives to football or cricket or hockey to host business colleagues in 'hospitality boxes' is a tax-deductible expense. Compare this with the treatment by governments everywhere of the need for tax-deductible quality childcare facilities.

The authors of the UNSNA boast that per capita GDP in any country is a measurement of the well-being of its citizens. A major reason that only cash-generating activities are taken into account is to ensure that countries can determine balance of payments and loan requirements – not as a comparative exercise, but as a controlling exercise. Those to whom money is owed (first world governments, multinational banks and multilateral agencies) are primarily interested in gauging the *cash-generating* capacity of the debtor countries, not their *productive* capacity.

Women have argued against this myopic approach to production for decades. In 1900, Charlotte Perkins Gilman wrote: 'the labour of women in the house, certainly, enables men to produce more wealth than they otherwise could; and in this way women are economic factors in society'.[5]

Following the calls made by women at their successive United Nations world conferences in Mexico City and Copenhagen, the final document of the end of decade conference for the United Nations Decade for Women, held in Nairobi in 1985, included this paragraph: 'The remunerated and in particular the unremunerated contributions of women to all aspects and sectors of development should be recognized, and appropriate efforts should be made to measure and reflect these contributions in the national accounts and economics statistics and in the Gross Domestic Product. Concrete steps should be taken to quantify the unremunerated contributions of women to agriculture, food production, reproduction and household activities.'[6]

This suggests to me that all the work with dung, whether as a fertiliser, cooking fuel or building material, should be quantified. But in 1993 the UN published a revised edition of *A System of National Accounts*, and in the context of the Nairobi document the rules make interesting reading. Of particular importance is paragraph 1.22, describing the UNSNA as a 'multi-purpose system . . . designed to meet a wide range of analytical and policy needs'. It states that 'a balance has to be struck between the desire for the accounts to be as comprehensive as possible' and their being swamped with non-monetary values. The revised system excludes all 'production of services for own final consumption within households . . . The location of the production boundary . . . is a compromise, but a deliberate one that takes account of *most users* [my emphasis – it is difficult to make extensive use of statistics in which you are invisible] . . . If the production boundary were extended to include the production of personal and domestic services by members of households for their own final consumption, all persons engaged in such activities would become self-employed, making unemployment virtually impossible by definition.'[7] Yes, that's the reason they give!

I would have thought that this was a reflection of the inappropriateness of the definition of unemployment, rather than an excuse to leave most of the work done by most women out of the equation. In fact, the more the international male response squirms to find containment definitions in which to straitjacket women's work, the more the system becomes nonsense. We now find that we are 'productive' or 'informal' or 'subsistent' or 'engaged in personal or domestic services', and the rules do not allow for our reality, which is to be all of the above, and often all of them at the same time.

In official statistics, women's contribution to both productive and subsistence[8] agricultural production anywhere has been poorly estimated or ignored. Where women's contribution has been noted, arbitrary demarcations between formal and subsistence production have been imposed, never reflecting the blurring of such distinctions in the working day of the hundreds of millions of women concerned.

The most widely used definition of unpaid productive activity or work was expressed in a 1971 Canadian study by Oli Hawrylyshyn[9] as 'the value of those economic goods and services produced in the household and outside the market, but which could be produced by a third person hired on the market without changing their utility to the members of the household'. This definition would include all aspects of dung work, but only hypothetically, since it is most unlikely that any man or woman could be hired to do the work.

A more recent definition, which I find both more useful and more political, is that of Australian economist Duncan Ironmonger: 'The household economy can be defined as the system that produces and allocates tradeable goods and services by using the unpaid labour and capital of households. The household economy transforms inter-mediate commodities provided by the market economy into final items of consumption through the use of its own unpaid labour and its own capital goods.'[10] This too would include dung work.

But neither Hawrylyshyn nor Ironmonger is responsible for the international rules on what does and does not count as work. A plethora of international agencies and rule books occupies that territory.

In 1982, the International Labour Organisation (ILO) defined the 'economically active' population as including all persons of either sex who provide labour for the production of economic goods and services.[11] All work for pay or in anticipation of profit is included. In addition, the ILO standard specifies that the production of economic goods and services includes all production and processing of primary products, whether for the market, for barter or for home consumption. Where it is for home consumption, though, such production must be 'an important contribution' to the total consumption of the household. Now this certainly includes dung work, because we know, even if economists do not notice, that there is no product more primary than dung. And the provision of fuel is unquestionably an 'important contribution' to the household. It would be difficult for the household members to survive without this fuel.

In a 1993 resolution concerning the international classification of status in employment, the International Conference of Labour Statisticians defined subsistence workers as those 'who hold a self-employment' job and in this capacity 'produce goods and services which are predominantly consumed by their own household and constitute an important basis for its livelihood'.[12] Surely, I think to myself, this includes all unpaid women's shitwork. The idea of 'an important basis for livelihood' suggests work of many kinds, the nature of which falls beyond the definition of subsistence agricultural and fishery workers in the International Standard Classification of Occupations (ISCO-88). This definition is:

> Subsistence agricultural and fishery workers grow and harvest field or tree and shrub crops, grow vegetables and fruit, gather wild fruits, medicinal and other plants, tend or hunt animals, catch fish and gather various forms of aquatic life in order to provide food, shelter and a minimum of cash incomes for themselves and their households.
>
> Tasks include –
> (a) preparing the soil, sowing, planting, tending and harvesting field crops;
> (b) growing vegetables, fruit and other tree and shrub crops;
> (c) gathering wild fruits, medicinal and other plants;
> (d) tending, feeding or hunting animals mainly to obtain meat, milk, hair, skin or other products;
> (e) fetching water and gathering firewood;
> (f) catching fish and gathering other forms of aquatic life;
> (g) storing or carrying out some basic processing of their produce;
> (h) building shelters and making simple tools, clothes and utensils for use by the household;
> (i) selling some products at local markets;
> (j) performing related tasks.[13]

While it might appear that the intention of the words 'an important basis for . . . livelihood' in the ICSE, or the words 'performing related tasks' in ISCO-88, is to admit the multitude of women's tasks which sustain the life of the members of the household but are not specified in the list, this is not the case.

Compare the concept of 'an important basis for livelihood' with the specific exclusions from production in the 1993 *System of National Accounts*.[14] (Here we have to remember that all these definitions have a hierarchy of importance, and that the UNSNA is the biggest daddy of them all.) Paragraph 1.25 establishes the 'consumption boundary', describing the domestic and personal services which do not count when they are produced and consumed within the same household. These services are the cleaning, decoration and maintenance of the dwelling occupied by the household; the cleaning, servicing and repair of household goods; the preparation and serving of meals; the care, training and instruction of children; the care of the sick, infirm or old people; and the transportation of members of the household or their goods.

These services do count when supplied by government or voluntary agencies, and when they are paid for. Women all over the planet perform the vast bulk of this work. But the authors of the *System of National Accounts* call these tasks indicators of welfare and, out of a breathtaking conceptual ignorance and undoubted Western bias, fail to grasp that there is no demarcation for the women in a subsistence household between the tasks outlined in the ISCO and the UNSNA omissions. All tasks of survival in such circumstances are 'related'.

RHETORIC AND REALITY

Now, in case you think I am being crude for the sake of it, let's get out of the shit for a moment and clean up the argument with a little water. If a woman spends an hour or more a day fetching water (which in some circumstances, according to the 1993 revised *System of National Accounts*,[15] may be a subsistence economic activity), she will use it critically and sparingly. She may use it in the care of livestock and poultry, she may use it to assist in food storage or the preparation of food which is marketed or bartered, she may water the vegetables in her garden – all of which may be classified as subsistence activities. She will also use it in food preparation, cooking, cleaning dishes and utensils. She may wash children or other dependants, or clothes. It will also be the household's drinking water. However critical these activities are as an 'important basis to livelihood', they are 'services' and do not count as subsistence production.

The organisation of rural household production does not recognise such arbitrary demarcations. Outputs from crop production are used as inputs in livestock production, and vice versa. Outputs from both contribute to household resources. All these influence one another. Deprived of female input, most rural households would cease to function productively.

By now we are thoroughly confused about the status of the time-consuming, basic livelihood tasks dealing with dung and water. The situation gets even more confusing when we look at further definitions.

Because definitions used in national surveys and censuses have relentlessly excluded the great bulk of work performed by women, women's productivity has been assumed to be pitifully low. This is especially so in agriculture and in work in rural areas, where the majority of women on the planet are to be found. The direction of census questions to the male head of the household, the expectation that most heads of households will respond that the primary occupation of the adult women of the household is 'housewife', the instructions in the enumerator's handbook to the same effect, and the use of male enumerators, have all accentuated this invisibility.

Using the concepts of 'holding' and 'holder' have also played a part. The UN Statistical Division has noted that 'a dividing line between what is and is not an informal sector agricultural unit is difficult to establish'.[16] The UN Food and Agriculture Organisation (FAO), which sets the international guidelines for the agricultural census, defines a holding as a unit of agricultural production comprising all the land used completely or partly for agricultural purposes and all livestock operated under the management of an individual or group without regard to legal ownership.

In some countries, the minimum size for holdings to be included is set on the basis of cash crop production, or limited to those above a certain area. This overlooks a significant number of holdings engaged in food production. Women are more likely to be involved in such work. On this basis, the most vulnerable section of the agricultural population is not investigated at all. This omission, the FAO itself concedes, 'results in a loss of information that is of great importance for policy formulation and planning in areas such as improvement of living conditions of rural population and food security'.[17]

For collecting data on agriculture and in survey programmes, identification of agricultural households is described as follows: 'A household is considered to be an agricultural household when at least one member of the household is operating a holding (farming household) or when the household head, reference person, or main income earner is economically active mainly in agriculture.'[18] The 'holder' is the person who controls the operations of the 'holding' and is responsible for the utilisation of available resources. These definitions further increase the proportion of households connected with agriculture which will not be covered, including those households that do not operate a holding or those where the head, reference person or main income-earner (interpreted as the senior male in the household) is not 'economically active mainly in agriculture'. This further isolates large numbers of women from visibility in the processes of policy formation and delivery.

A discernible trend in available data shows a growing proportion of the agricultural workforce throughout the world to be female. Male migration, seasonal and permanent, leaves more women as the 'farmers', with heavier work burdens and little access to credit and other critical planning inputs. But the absent men, for census purposes, remain the 'heads', 'reference persons', or 'main income earners'.

Much of my confusion with the constant exclusions resulting from rules determined by one group of UN agencies is because I find continued calls by other UN agencies for inclusion. Whole forests have been devastated to produce the miles of rhetoric that fill libraries on the subject. Wherever I look I find this.

For instance, the FAO declares that 'women should participate and contribute on an equal basis with men in the social, economic and political processes of rural development and share fully in improved conditions of life in rural areas'.[19]

The UN Convention on the Elimination of All Forms of Discrimination Against Women (1979) (CEDAW) (see Appendix 3) states that 'discrimination against women violates the principles of equality of rights and respect for human dignity, is an obstacle to the participation of women, on equal terms with men, in the political, social, economic and cultural life of their countries, hampers the growth of the prosperity of society and the family and makes more difficult the full development of the potentialities of women in the service of their countries and of humanity'.[20]

The Nairobi Forward Looking Strategies for the Advancement of Women state: 'Development strategies and programmes, as well as incentive programmes and projects in the field of food and agriculture, need to be designed in a manner that fully integrates women at all levels of planning, implementation, monitoring and evaluation in all stages of the development process ... so as to facilitate and enhance this key role of women and to ensure that women receive proper benefits and remuneration commensurate with their important contribution in this field.'[21]

Men join the call. 'Development plans generally by-pass women. The major cause for this omission is the lack of adequate statistics', declared Muhammed Hafiz Sheikh, Director-General of the Federal Bureau of Statistics, Pakistan.[22]

The Vienna Declaration of the UN World Conference on Human Rights in 1993 argues that 'the human rights of women and of the girl child are an inalienable, integral and indivisible part of universal human rights. The full and equal participation of women in the political, civil, economic, social and cultural life, at the national, regional and international levels, and the eradication of all forms of discrimination on grounds of sex are priority objectives of the international community.'

After years of reading from the harvest of forsaken forests, I find the UN reports have a vacuity exceeded only by their hypocrisy.

While decades of comprehensive, detailed, well-researched documentation from a plethora of agencies and researchers, both national and international, have now been published on the issues, few male economists or policy planners demonstrate a familiarity with or a working knowledge of this material. It depends on the circumstances of the women in their immediate family. It depends on their limited observational powers. It depends on their own strength of character, or their weakness, which sees gender equity as a threat to their personal and collective political power as men. The inefficiency and insufficiency of this approach have reached a critical level.

Among key staff in ministries of economic planning throughout the world, there are several clear categories of consciousness. The economic imperative is seldom addressed operationally, although some lip-service references can be found in speeches and papers from a variety of individuals. They express the political will, but have no idea of the planning vehicles for delivery or institutionalisation. Where awareness does exist, based usually on project or personal experience, it does not permeate the system because of general male resistance to the empowerment of women, and because the systems of measurement render so much productive work invisible.

The pervasive approach to the policy of integrating women into the mainstream of development displays a total conceptual misunderstanding of the principle. It is the 'ghetto' approach of women-only projects, or separate training modules. Women are not regarded as mainstream producers. They are burdens, special cases, welfare. The welfare approach is not the point of view from which to address the policy crisis caused by the neglect of half the world's population. Yet too often it is the point of view which participants in gender sensitivity training take away with them from a course.

Staging a multilateral workshop on statistics and indicators on women in development seldom sees the attendance of highly ranked male economic ministry personnel. Women are not perceived as economic actors in the mainstream. This attitude is reflected by producers of statistics. Many still do not see women's advocates as an identifiable group of users. They often misunderstand what is sought and specify the need as the production of statistics on women only, and for a user group consisting only of women. This, of course, reflects the point of view of the authors of the 1993 *System of National Accounts*, who, you will recall, thought that 'most users' were not interested in household production. And even if they see that women are important contributors to the economy, it is, they say, just too hard and too expensive to collect data on their lives.

THE INCONVENIENCE OF ACCURATE DATA

Now, I am the first to accept that there are major logistical difficulties in data collection. A 1993 report of the Statistical Commission noted that problems encountered by countries in implementing their survey programmes included a lack of strong commitment to statistics by governments, inadequate donor support, failure to present results of surveys attractively, lack of co-ordination between different producers of survey data, lack of timeliness, poor-quality results, delays due to processing bottlenecks, and unsatisfactory distribution of survey findings.[23]

Frequently, the difficult terrain, vast areas to cover and communication difficulties reduce the effectiveness of supervision and control of the field elements of the surveys. Quality of data may suffer because of the temporary nature of field staff, or the heavy workload of enumerators in multi-purpose surveys. Surveys often impose heavy burdens on interviewers and respondents, giving rise to fatigue. Survey data is often under-utilised, owing to a lack of analytical capabilities, especially in national statistical offices. Many statistics offices have serious shortcomings in report-writing and analytical skills. There remains a large amount of data collected on women which is simply never analysed.[24]

Where various units within an agency are responsible for different components of the survey – such as sampling, fieldwork and data processing – lack of co-ordination among those units poses problems for the design and implementation of the survey. Delays in data processing are often caused by the absence or late design of a processing system. The data-processing system for any application has three important components: personnel, machines, and methods. Monitoring progress and effective quality control are also vital. If one ingredient is missing, the whole programme is in jeopardy. Frequently, surveys are promoted when no software package has been specifically developed for processing the data collected.[25]

The influence of donors often plays a part in the difficulties encountered. In one developing country under the regime of *ad hoc* surveys, for Survey 1, Donor A provided a data-processing expert with the necessary computer equipment. For Survey 2, funded by Donor B, the country wanted to keep the same data-processing expert so that the systems and programmes he had designed could be further developed. It also wanted additional micro-computers compatible with those used for the first survey. The expert could not be retained because Donor B fielded its own adviser, and the equipment brought in was incompatible with the previous set.[26] Even in the poorest countries, in competitive 'aid' schemes, Toshiba competes with IBM.

The situation generally is complicated by the status of statistics. One expert, noting that by the end of 1992 only seven countries from Asia and the Pacific were participating in the World Bank National Household Survey Capability Programme (NHSCP), commented that governments' commitment to statistics was 'suspect in many countries in the developing regions'. This is attributed to three main factors: 1. governments tend to give priority to projects whose outputs can be clearly identified, such as bore holes or bridges; 2. users in the government sector are generally not so statistically sophisticated that the lack of data causes them any significant uneasiness; 3. the statistical offices have not yet found an effective way to promote their products. The lack of commitment by governments mainly explains the inadequate resources given to statistical offices and to survey work.[27]

Further logistical difficulties can be located in the operational demarcations of UN agencies. For example, the FAO's mandate is to work with ministries related to food and agriculture and rural development. Its work is almost always with agriculture, livestock, forests, fisheries, food and rural development, and occasionally with ministries of local government or the interior (community development), health (nutrition), commerce (food processing, exports, food standards), but extremely rarely with women's affairs or statistics. This means that the ministries most likely to seek assistance for better indicators on women and rural development are not targeted for FAO assistance.

And I would be dishonest to overlook the corruption and manipulation I have observed surrounding data collection in much of the world. Data is manipulated by governments for electoral purposes. It is manipulated to control different ethnicities. Economic data is invented to please the World Bank or the IMF. Literacy rates are manipulated to get UN Educational, Scientific and Cultural Organisation (UNESCO) funding, and fertility rates are manipulated to get UN Family Planning Agency (UNFPA) funding.

The need for data collection provides great wish-list opportunities for corrupt government officials seeking aid donors. High on the agenda are lots of vehicles, especially of the four-wheel-drive variety, along with many motorcycles. Mainline computers, and portables or notebooks, are on the list, along with vast amounts of software. In the field, there's even more fun and games, where census responses are invented by the interviewer seated under a shady tree on the outskirts of the village, if they bother to get that close to the intended respondents. Study tours to foreign countries are also fun.

RUBBISH IN, RUBBISH OUT – DATA AND POLICY PLANNING

Given the exclusive definitions, and the practical problems outlined above, it proves extremely difficult to gauge the full extent of women's production, subsistence or otherwise, in agriculture, and in unpaid production and reproduction. So I play with the numbers, not for what they can tell me, but to gasp and guffaw at the preposterous pictures they paint in their fictional portrayal of women's lives. Let me demonstrate.

Imagine I am a development adviser in economics and agriculture, committed to targeting the productive, as opposed to income-generating, labour force in Bangladesh. When I arrive there, I ask for the census and survey data on rural women's work to assist in the development of the next five-year plan. I am told that, in the 1984 census of population in Bangladesh, 90 percent of the active-age rural female labour force were classified as housewives. But in 1983–84, I find the Bangladesh Bureau of Statistics manpower survey question-naire reported 90 percent of all those listed as housewives as having extra main activities, including food processing (91.5 percent), livestock or poultry care (37 percent) and fuel and water collection (32.3 percent).

I compare the census of population statistics with the labour force survey of 1989, in which 18.2 million men and 18.7 million women listed agriculture, forestry and fisheries as their major occupation, and 16.7 million of these women were unpaid family helpers. This was when the total population of women in rural areas was estimated at 50 million.

I then discover that, while the Bangladesh labour force survey of 1992 continued to exclude housework from its revised definition of economic activity, it did include unpaid agricultural work. The result was that female labour force participation for this sector jumped from 25 percent in 1985–86 to 89 percent in 1989, while the total labour-force participation rose from 9 percent to 62 percent.[28]

It is not clear that being counted in 1992 guarantees the rural women of Bangladesh access to credit facilities, agriculture extension classes and the range of inputs available in agriculture development projects, whatever I write in the five-year plan. What is clear is that, when women were not counted, there would have been no recognition at all. Now, at least, there are no excuses.

In the 1990–91 census round the Government of India made special efforts to see that all of those intended to be captured by the ILO definition of economic activity were visible. In recognition that it is not enough to adopt a new definition and expect decades of past practice to disappear in the field, considerable effort was made to put the change into effect. Given the numbers in the Indian population, this was a significant attempt. Gender ratios of interviewers were changed so that for the first time the number of women in the field exceeded the number of men. Special intensive-training workshops focusing on the new definition were held for the census interviewers, and a new handbook of census guidelines was issued. Television advertisements and radio jingles publicised the change.

The handbook for census interviewers demonstrated attempts to capture women's invisible work.

> Before making an entry make sure whether he or she is engaged, even if
> only for a few days a year, in the following activities: Work on the family
> farm; sale of home made dairy products; rearing of poultry and sale of
> the products; sale of fruits, vegetables etc; sale of fish; making of
> cowdung cakes or collecting wood for fuel, fodder, grass and other
> forest produce and selling some of it; engaged in household industry
> such as weaving, spinning, bee-keeping, sericulture, tanning and
> making of leather products, leaf plate making, block printing, making
> cane bamboo products, rope-making, etc; providing services on
> payment for others such as laundry, domestic work, hair cutting,
> tailoring, etc. or working on piece rate for making agarbathies, match
> boxes, bidi-rolling, assembly of various parts, making and selling of
> garments, pickles, papad, masala, jam, snacks and other food products.

Yet all this effort provides an example of the substantial amount of
work that remains invisible. The handbook makes the exclusion
explicit.

> Question 14A seeks to find out if a person had done any work at all
> (including unpaid work on a farm or in a family enterprise) during the
> last year or whether he or she did not work at all and if it is the latter
> how the person spent his other time as a non-worker [*sic*] . . . However,
> any person who is engaged only in household duties but doing no
> other productive work to augment the family's resources should not be
> considered as working . . . A man or woman may be producing or
> making something only for the domestic consumption of the household
> and not for sale. Such a person is not a worker, even though from his or
> her point of view the activity is productive . . . *Those who produce goods*
> *for the self-consumption of the members of the household like persons collecting*
> *wood, preparing dung cakes, etc for domestic consumption . . . are not workers*
> [my emphasis] . . . The term 'unpaid worker' may not be confused with
> these persons . . . NOTE: Please note that persons who cultivate land
> to produce for domestic consumption only will be treated as workers.

The continued exclusion of this subsistence work showed in census
results. In the 1991 Indian census, the percentage of women to the total
number of workers in the primary sector rose from 19.5 percent in
1981 to 27.2 percent. There was a rise of only 3.9 percent in the
cultivation category and 2.4 percent in the livestock, forestry, fishing,
plantations and orchards activity.

Total rural population figures from the 1991 census show another
picture. The total rural population was 622,812,376, of whom
301,532,971 were females: 26.67 percent of these women were classified as workers (8.04 percent of whom were in the marginal worker

category), 32.3 percent of the total rural workforce; *73.21 percent of the total female rural population were classified as non-workers.*[29]

Other studies demonstrated the extent of invisible work. For example, a survey by the Indian Ministry of Planning in 1987–88 showed that, of all the females engaged in household duties, 60 percent of all rural and 15 percent of all urban women collected firewood or fodder or food-stuffs, maintained kitchen gardens or fruit trees, or worked with poultry or cattle within the household area. Fifty-two percent of rural women and 9 percent of urban women prepared cowdung cakes for use as fuel, and 63 percent of all rural and 32 percent of all urban women carried water for household use from outside the premises.[30]

In a 1988 study in rural India, Richard Ankar, M.E. Khan and R.B. Gupta[31] asked the following sequence of questions and obtained increasing estimates of women's economic production activity (the percentage figure is the total number of women recognised as econom-ically active according to the question asked):

What was your main activity?	15.7%
[*most would reply housework*]	
What was your next most important activity?	41.2%
[*they may reply getting wood or water*]	
Did you work for earnings in the last 12 months?	47.6%
[*perhaps seasonal agricultural work*]	
Did you do something else for which the family earned income?	55.3%
[*sold home preserves, for example*]	
Subsistence-type and other activity in terms of time?	93.0%
[*tending a home garden, making dung cakes*]	

The census said that 73 percent of rural women did not work. This study found that 93 percent of rural women did work productively. In a country with more than 620 million rural residents, where basic food security, water, fuel and shelter are daily policy imperatives, the gap in credible data is critical.

The most recent data available from neighbouring Pakistan, given to me on a visit there in May 1994, claimed preposterously that 91.55 percent of women over ten years old were 'inactive'. The tables claimed that only 0.5 percent of all women in Pakistan were active in agricul-ture. (Muhammed Hafiz Sheikh had obviously retired.) The data was prepared from a pilot study conducted by the World Bank and the

Statistics Bureau of Pakistan, and the processing of the figures was supported by Canada's aid assistance. I don't believe this data series has been published yet, and for good reason.

In Pakistan, rural women are major contributors in four sub-sectors of the rural economy: crop production; livestock production; cottage industry; and household and family maintenance activities, which include transporting water, fuel and fodder, food preparation and preservation, and caring for children, the elderly and the disabled. Yet the measurement of women's participation varies chaotically.

For example, in 1981 the population census reported a participation rate of 3 percent, and the labour force survey the same year a rate of 12 percent. A World Bank report estimated that as many as 12 million economically active rural women were disregarded in this data, and the 1980 census of agriculture estimated that 9.5 million (or 42 percent) of the 22.8 million economically productive people in agricultural households were women. This placed the female participation rate in rural areas at 73 percent for women, compared with 93 percent for men.

The rate would be even higher if the agricultural census did not exclude non-agricultural households, which typically have higher participation rates than agricultural households and comprise 31 percent of all rural households. In addition, 62 percent of economically active rural women were classified as part-time workers by the agricultural census, compared with only 14.5 percent of all males. Women thus made up 76 percent of all part-time workers, and only 25 percent of those recognised as full-time workers. But full-time workers are defined as those who do only agricultural work on the holdings. Since most women also do other household work, they fall outside the definition of full-time agricultural workers.[32]

In Sri Lanka, the labour force survey results in 1990 for all people aged 10 and over recorded a female labour-force participation rate of 34.7 percent overall, with a rural sector rate of 36.2 percent. Twenty-six percent of the total number of females 'employed' worked as unpaid family members, with 96 percent of those being in the agricultural sector. Half of all females not then in the labour force were 'engaged in household work'.

In Nepal's 1991 census, 54.5 percent of the female population was described as economically inactive.

It is beyond belief that half the women of Sri Lanka and Nepal are engaged 'only' in housework. When the figures are further extrapolated and given substance by micro studies, it can be concluded that the majority of the women of the Asia-Pacific region live in rural areas, work longer days than men, and, in all age groups, perform most of all work classified as subsistence agriculture, as well as most of the 'housework'.

The non-recognition of this work is not only an issue of equity. It has resulted in inappropriate and misdirected policy planning and targeting. The consequences are significant, particularly for women in agriculture. Food, fuel and water are the main items of subsistence production. Women participate as unpaid family workers in the family holding, gather fodder as well as fuel and water, and keep a small garden for family consumption, providing food security for basic survival.

Subsistence households are often landless, but not always. Nor should it be assumed that a subsistence household is comparatively poor, though the composition of income may vary. In Nepal, the key difference between poor and non-poor subsistence households lies in the contribution cash crops make to the household income.[33]

Further, while the internationally recognised definition of subsistence work is confined to agriculture and fishing, it should not be assumed that subsistence production is found only in rural or coastal areas. Millions in urban areas survive on subsistence livelihoods, particularly those who have migrated from rural areas. Access to the fundamentals for survival is frequently limited in the urban environment.

In the time–use studies of subsistence households in Asia, females are found to work comparatively longer hours than males in all age groups.[34] In addition to preparing and cooking food, cleaning dishes, washing clothes, cleaning the house, and looking after children – with little assistance from men in the household – women will also spend long hours collecting fuel, fodder or water, and will frequently spend more hours in paid farm labour, because, of course, women are paid a lower hourly rate and it is cheaper to hire them.[35] Studies in the region reflect the observation in the ISCO that 'the necessary skills [for subsistence agriculture] – an understanding of the natural environment and the crops and animals worked with, as well as manual [sic] strength and dexterity – are usually acquired by working from childhood with other members of the household to produce the necessities for subsisting'.[36]

The pattern for the inter-generational cycle of subsistence for the overwhelming number of girls in such households is established early.

They will be unlikely to inherit any assets or land and will have little or no capacity to raise collateral to enable access to tools, animals, seeds or other such inputs. Since many of them are seen as a liability, for whom a dowry payment will one day be necessary, they are regarded as a poor investment in terms of education.[37] As early as age five, girls have charge of younger siblings to free their mothers for other work. If they do enrol at school, they remain the additional hands during harvesting periods and other times of peak labour need, and will be withdrawn so frequently that they will soon cease to attend. Regardless of the legal requirements on the age of marriage, they will be married off as early in their teens as their parents can arrange. And here the subsistence cycle of rural women's lives will start again.[38]

The contributions of the agricultural sector to a nation's economy are recorded as a percentage contribution to GDP. These figures substantially understate agriculture's contribution to all production, because vast amounts of agricultural production are done by unpaid labour, overwhelmingly that of women and children, and because a large proportion of production occurs in non-marketed areas.

The problem with numbers is not confined to the developing world. In Australia, the official number of women directly employed in agriculture has doubled in the past 30 years to one-third of the rural workforce.[39] What this really means, of course, is that women are now being paid, or at least acknowledged as book entries. At the same time as the rural population has declined, the proportion of women involved in farming is said to have increased. These figures more than likely reflect a category transition, for half the farming women in Australia still describe the work they do as 'home duties'.

Those of us urging them to change this label are not concerned with converting them to a ready feminism, as some of them seem to think is the effect of our efforts. Nor are we making any judgement on the value of the work they do. We are suggesting that their farms and family livelihoods, their access to basic services and the ability of their communities to survive depend more and more on the political consequences of the nomenclature they adopt.

Whether done deliberately or simply out of ignorance, the effect of describing vast numbers of agricultural workers as housewives has major policy consequences for future productivity, and particularly for food security.

For example, while there are no reliable 'access to' figures for agriculture extension training, accurate comments can be made about general patterns. Throughout Asia, 15 percent is a high figure, for either women participants in extension courses for farmers, or the percentage of women farmers reached by mainline agriculture extension.[40] Regardless of farming system or culture, the reasons are the same and can be briefly stated as follows.

- Most agriculture planners, district chiefs, extension workers and contact farmers are men.
- Extension targets the head of the household, assumed to be a man.
- Extension concentrates on commercial crops, not the food (security) crops usually grown by women.
- Extension is more easily delivered to those who have some functional literacy, overwhelmingly men.
- Extension policies fail to address the gender division of labour within households.
- It is assumed that information conveyed to the head of the household is then conveyed accurately (if conveyed at all) to other family members.
- It is assumed that women's time is flexible and that women are available for extension activities at the same places and times as men.
- It assumes women's interests are concentrated on home economics.

Even where there are women agriculture extension agents, they are more likely to be trained in home economics than agriculture and reinforce the stereotypes of women farmers as mainly housewives and farm helpers. Studies in Thailand found that, for new crops, fertilisers, pesticides and planting techniques, more than 60 percent of principal male farmers and less than 30 percent of principal female farmers named the agriculture extension officer as their source of information.[41]

Where there are dedicated, determined women extension workers, they are subject to discrimination in employment, lack of promotion opportunities, sexual harassment and often physical danger. Near Jessore in Bangladesh, for example, I have watched men who were so threatened by the sight of a women alone in such a job that she was daily pelted with mud and stones as she manoeuvred her pushbike – no motorised vehicle for her – around her district.

Even where a country's data base is sophisticated enough to illustrate a significant female presence, the future investment policies can be significantly misdirected. In South Korea, where the 1991 census showed that 55.9 percent of rural women were full-time farmers, and 8.9 percent combined farming with secondary income-raising activities, women were explicitly excluded from training programmes in agricultural machinery until 1988. While women's contribution to farm sector labour increased from 38.7 percent in 1965 to 44.3 percent in 1986, this was not reflected in planning and policies. In South Korea's sixth five-year plan (1985–91), 36,716 women were targeted to enrol in courses out of a total number of places of 1,434,000. During the same years, the government training for young farmers in agricultural management skills selected 1509 women as 'future farmers', 3.1 percent of all those selected.[42]

Studies in Canada further illustrate the economic and policy consequences of the failure to account for women's economic contribution to agriculture. Echoing calls with which we are all familiar, the *Ontario Women's Farm Network Newsletter* has noted discrimination in the treatment of women's off-farm income, the inability of many farm women to make significant contributions to the Canada pension plan, the urgent need of farm women for access to appropriate training, the absence of adequate, appropriate, affordable childcare, the lack of access to shelters for victims of domestic violence and to appropriate health and counselling services for rural families, and the lack of representation and participation in policy development at all levels, including parliamentary, producer and farmer lobby groups.

Women contribute substantially to agricultural production and related processing, trade and industry. Undervaluing this economic contribution has resulted in policies that are ineffective and inefficient in achieving the distributive as well as the output goals of agricultural development. Overall progress is less than optimal because of the failure to observe the part women play in the dynamics of agricultural development, and the consequent failure to utilise their potential.

The key tool needed to mainstream women in the economic process is information – well-based, reliable, timely and relevant information. Most government machineries, established with line ministry responsibilities, present planning problems for the macro policies needed for major issues such as the integration of women into agriculture and rural development, or the preservation or sustenance of the environment. These planning problems go well beyond the inadequacy of dominant economic indicators, such as GDP, as tools. The continued predominance of old colonial planning techniques, with departments and ministries proliferating laterally, and with poor mechanisms for horizontal relationships between departments in the planning process, accentuates the challenge. For example, there are very close linkages between the status of women, subsistence food production, literacy, poverty, the rate of population growth and policies of structural adjustment. No government appears to have found a satisfactory mechanism for making the connections.

Fragmentation of knowledge accompanies technical development. Specialists have a limited capacity to discern what knowledge is relevant, where to find it, how to use it. Doctrine and economic dogma do not cultivate a sense of responsibility. And there is a paucity of examples in policy planning which demonstrate an understanding of the interrelationship of phenomena.

We all have these stories to tell at a micro economic level, but how, and why, does this continue to happen? And what is the scenario when the whole future of a nation's most important productive sector is at stake?

GENDERED PERSPECTIVE – A CASE STUDY

I had the opportunity to observe at close quarters how women are left out when I spent some months working in Nepal in 1993. So this will serve as a case study to examine the practice of exclusion.

The Agriculture Perspective Plan (APP) began in a paper entitled 'Nepal in 25 Years: the Agriculture Perspective Plan – an Optimistic Vision and Guide' by John Mellor. An academic at Cornell University with significant development-project experience, Mellor had been described to me as 'the man behind the green revolution in Asia'. I had thought that the bent bodies of women planting, weeding, harvesting and storing were the human forces behind that particular change, but I suppose that too depends on your perspective.

I had been informed by the Minister of Agriculture, the National Planning Commission head of agriculture and the major donors that they consider this plan the key for the agricultural development of Nepal and the guide for change in the next twenty-five years. It ought to be stating the obvious to expect that such a plan would highlight the specific participation of more than half the human resource component in agriculture – women farmers.

In Nepal, as in much of the rest of the world, women's direct

contribution to agriculture is increasing because of three key factors:
1. female labour input to family farms increases as cropping patterns
shift to commercial food and non-food production; 2. women's own-
account production increases under the pressure of rising costs of
feeding, further family care and less availability of children's labour due
to schooling; 3. women's own-account production necessarily increases
with the increasing number of households headed by women, through
divorce, desertion, urban migration and widowhood.

Studies demonstrate that, in most communities throughout Nepal,
much of the agricultural work and in many cases much of the trading
and many of the cottage industries are carried out by women. Rice,
maize, millet, barley and potatoes are major crops in Nepal. All these
crops require intensive care and weeding, and these activities are mostly
the responsibility of women. Statistics on the cost of rice production in
selected places in the Terai show that, for the entire production process
from land preparation to harvesting, from 87 to 93 percent of the
labour involved is spent on planting, weeding and harvesting. Likewise,
the labour required for weeding and harvesting maize and potato
(almost exclusively a female undertaking) constitutes the bulk of the
total labour requirement for these crops. Kitchen gardening, which
supplies the most necessary vitamins to the family, is another female
undertaking.[43]

In addition, the APP was developed at a time when comprehensive
data demonstrated conclusively that women worked longer hours, and
at a greater variety of tasks and with a greater simultaneity of tasks, than
men in the agriculture sector in Nepal. In all age groups, women's total
work burden exceeded that of men.

The APP also appeared in a political context in which His Majesty's
Government of Nepal had guaranteed women the right to equality in
the Constitution of the Kingdom of Nepal.[44] It was conceived at a time
when the government had ratified CEDAW without reservations. It was
drafted in the period of the eighth five-year plan, in which, in the
Women in Development Sector, taking 'necessary measures to amend
laws and acts that hinder women's development' was recognised as
a priority.

Thirty years of official publications repeat a litany of rhetorical
concern. Barber B. Conable, the former president of the World Bank
(the major donor for the APP project), wrote in 1990: 'Improving
opportunities for women is not only a matter of human justice, but also

a sure route to faster and more sustainable development . . . There is a direct relationship between expanded opportunities for women and improved health and learning for children, slower population growth, and the easing of environmental pressures . . . The World Bank identified women in development as a priority and has integrated this concern into its analytical work and lending operations.'

In the country briefing paper, the Asian Development Bank (ADB) wrote: 'the implication of this information [on women in agriculture] for the Bank is that any agricultural project in Nepal should assume from the start that women make a contribution to the activity at least equal to that of men. The project should then determine the gender division of labour in the particular case. Only then can the project be designed to promote development most effectively.'[45] The ADB was also a donor in the APP.

In addition, almost without exception, all donor governments involved had published their own policy guidelines on the full integration of women in development projects. The rhetoric of these statements makes it abundantly clear that, operationally, these policies can be fulfilled not by a few women's income-generating activities, nor by ghetto-ised or token 'women's components' in major projects, but by the consistent technical targeting, in conception, operation, delivery, monitoring, evaluation – and distribution of benefits – of half the human resource component in the country.

But the rhetoric is the easy part. So it was no surprise to find in the APP terms of reference this Paragraph 6, headed 'Poverty Reduction and Gender Analysis':

   (i) Within the framework of a plan designed mainly to generate output and income growth within agriculture, develop mechanisms and approaches which ensure that the poor including poor women participate in the growth process and share in its benefits; and

   (ii) Evaluate the impact of the plan in terms of income increases for the poor and participation of women in national development. This should be done partly as one measure of the plan's objectives, but mainly during the planning process to assist in guiding the selection among alternative courses of action; and

   (iii) Carry out gender analysis as the plan is developed and analyze the impact of agricultural policy choices and recommendations on women.

There are, of course, conceptual problems with grouping 'poverty' and 'women', but for now there are other concerns to deal with.

In mid-March 1994, having been apprised of the importance of the APP, I visited the office of the project consultants. I asked about the progress made in implementing the gender analysis paragraph above. None of its provisions had been met and, I was told, it was too late to commission an expert paper, or to have oversight of all draft chapters to mainstream the development interests of women farmers.

To be fair, this state of affairs did not appear to have been the objective of the plan's principal consultant. In a draft paper dated 28 February 1994, entitled 'A Strategic View of the APP', John Mellor wrote: 'Because of the tendency for women to be left out of the development of modern institutional structures, specific attention is given in each chapter to the means by which women can fully participate in the key activities. Particular note is given to women's participation in institutions such as those for credit that are critical to the development process.'

But he was premature in anticipating that anyone in the consultancy team would pay any attention to Paragraph 6. They never had on any previous project, so why should they start now? Besides, it was highly questionable whether any of them had the knowledge or expertise to fulfil the terms of reference of Paragraph 6. At our meeting, Mellor admitted that he had no idea that Nepali women had no effective access to land ownership. He had not asked. He had not read the Nepal constitution. He was not aware of the ratification of CEDAW. He submitted that to obey the constitutional guarantees given to women, or to insist that the APP was doomed without access to land on behalf of the majority of the country's agricultural producers, would be to 'interfere in Nepal's domestic politics'!

In the four sub-groups of the APP facilitation group, out of twenty-three participants only four were women, and two of these women were assigned to the group on poverty, food security and environment. No woman was on the key sub-group dealing with data, macro policy and, most important, strategy. All the authors of the draft papers were men and, yes, in one, the livestock sub-sector paper, there was a whole paragraph on women, and overall, in more than 20 other papers, there were six references to women, usually grouped with the poor. In my experience there was nothing unusual in all of this. But it was too late in the century to call it oversight, too late to claim forgetfulness, too late for those of us who constantly receive platitudinous and patronising excuses to be polite any more. The APP ignored constitutional guarantees, five-year plan priorities, and multilateral and donor policy guidelines. It was illogical, and defied balanced economic analysis. If the great plan had perspective, it was chronically imperceptive.

Why does this happen? Certain men are threatened by policies which give women any form of access to independence. Data gaps are enormous, but there is a more than substantial literature in Nepal to meet all requirements of the APP.

Isn't it time it was acknowledged that the strategic perspectives of gender analysis require expert skills, comparable with the expertise required to be a doctor or an engineer? Isn't it time it was recognised that such analysis is a disciplined skill requiring years of study, field work, experience and application, and that few men anywhere have this? Isn't it time the gentlemen asked for help?

The singular glaring omission in the APP was the lack of women's right to property. In any business expansion which presupposed access to income, or collateral with which to gain credit, in which 60 percent of those expected to participate had little, if any, access to either, and particularly if those 60 percent were male, the proposals would be recognised as at best elitist, and at worst doomed to failure. This was economic nonsense. While Chapter 2 of the APP mentioned institutional impediments to the success of the proposal, no mention was made of the legal impediments to the 'provision of an environment . . . to mobilize all of Nepal'. John Mellor wrote that sentence on 31 August 1992. There is cause to wonder why a Cornell academic 'expert' in development planning did not know to ask what impediments existed to women's full participation in the APP.

In the draft paper 'Institutional Arrangements to Implement the APP', the lack of access to land by more than half the human resource component in agriculture was not identified in the long list of constraints. In the category of policies the government was not pursuing and should adopt, legal impediments to full participation by women farmers were not mentioned, despite the statement in the Women in Development Sector of the eighth five-year plan. While user-group participation, people's participation programmes and farming systems research were identified in this category, there was no suggestion that these specifically target women users, women participants and women's farming systems. Women's participation in agriculture, and the major data problems associated with this, was not mentioned as a concern.

Well, I thought, perhaps this is not highlighted as a concern here because they've got it on board in all their other papers. Silly ever-optimistic me!

In the draft paper on the 'Rural Financial Markets', while it was noted that 'a number of legal issues have constrained the supply of and demand for credit', the legal reforms suggested no reference to the major impediment to access to credit for the majority of farmers: the lack of women's access to property as collateral. This made Mellor's claims in his strategic view paper most embarrassing for him.

If land ownership were denied for even the 40 percent of farmers who are men, it would be perceived as an economic nightmare to project a twenty-five-year vision on this basis.

No perception of the myriad problems associated with data bases was evident in the draft paper entitled 'Measuring Growth: First Step to Increasing Efficiency'. The prospect for 'the needed comprehensive and reliable agricultural statistics' for planning would be incomplete without women's visibility, but this was not considered.

While poor management, a lack of inter-ministry horizontal linkages, time wastage and other logistical inefficiencies detailed in many project evaluation reports had led to an understandable reluctance by donors to pursue multi-sectoral projects, to ignore the linkages was grossly irresponsible. It was acknowledged, for example, that 'in the absence of an effective programme to slow population growth, all other poverty alleviation measures [and, I might add, most project goals] will be meaningless'.[46] The international experience now is that the fundamental key to slowing population growth is female literacy. In Nepal 83 percent of the economically active female population are pre-literate. In 1991, at the primary school level, girl enrollees were only 37 percent of the total enrolment figure, and the percentages declined at lower secondary and secondary schools. The numbers were considerably lower in rural areas.

So what relevance did this have to the APP? Simply, that if this plan mimicked the policies pursued to increase production in the rest of the region, forcing anaemic overworked women to double their farming workload, neither men nor boys increased their hours per day to assist. Mothers-in-law, sisters and, overwhelmingly, daughters are required to assist with the additional workload. For this they are withdrawn from school, and the cycle of non-literacy, overwork, poverty and anaemia is regenerated.

The strategic policy response would be to ensure, as the priority, that improvements in technology were intended specifically to relieve the time burden of women in their endless repetitive round of household and agricultural work. No reference to this key priority was found in the draft APP paper on technology.

The myopia continued in the papers on the environmental component, on poverty, on the agro-industry, and on energy in agriculture. The last noted the major dependence on fuelwood and biomass. The cost-benefit analysis and assumptions which followed were highly questionable. Not only are traditional fuels non-monetarised, but the marginal value of time taken by women and girls to collect them was assumed to be zero. A cost-benefit analysis purely on this basis would show that alternative energy (imported kerosene) was not affordable in most households.

In this context I consulted the energy strategy in the eighth five-year plan. It stated that all energy would be 'priced' to reflect its 'social cost'. Really! What could the authors of the plan have meant by this? Would that 'cost' reflect the time spent by women and girls in gathering it? Would it reflect the opportunity cost of a lost education, and all the by now well-documented aftermath of that? The APP paper did recognise the increased dependence on dung as a cooking fuel and the environmental consequences, but to propose imported expensive alternative cooking fuels was just not realistic.

The attitudes and opinions in the draft APP papers were not significantly different from the rhetoric of donors with whom I had the opportunity to talk. Let me emphasise that the candour and honesty with which we communicated on such occasions were enlightening, refreshing and most helpful. But some of the approaches were breathtaking. One major donor advised me: 'agricultural extension just doesn't work, I think it should be dropped altogether until it is managed and operated efficiently'. 'Well, thank you very much,' I said, 'but the other half – women as extension officers, women as junior technical assistants, women as farmer clients, haven't had a slice of the cake yet. They're written off because of male failure to perform.'

In the course of my investigations I called on the Nepal representative of the FAO, another donor participant in the APP. He had been in the FAO for many years, and at his post in Nepal for 18 months. 'I know why you're here,' he said, 'but I'm familiar with your point of view. I have three daughters, and I've been to a two-day gender awareness training course.' And how was he coping, I asked, in a country where the majority of food producers could not own land? 'Is that right?' he replied. 'I didn't know that.' No one had told him this, he had never asked, and obviously had never read any of the substantial number of available documents, including FAO publications, which contained that information.

The saga of Nepal's APP is a very typical example of development planning everywhere, and it is not peculiar to the agricultural sector. You do wonder, in the end, just what can possibly make a difference to male resistance. In more than twenty years of political experience and policy development, I have encountered only the occasional exception to the attitudes demonstrated in Nepal. I found one in a Muslim country in Asia.

The Secretary of the Department of National Planning there was responsible for the mission to mainstream women into the five-year plan. He was in his last year before retirement. He did not see this activity as a thing some middle-ranking bureaucrat on the 'women's desk' should take care of. He was totally supportive, interested, determined that all assistance would be given. He had sharp words for the Western-educated, neoclassical, male economists of his department, who were patronising and offhand about the mission's proposals. He wasn't interested in banal chatter about 'integrating women into development'. He had briefed himself on the international literature. He wanted strategic concrete proposals.

He might have been unique, but his Minister of National Planning was equally assiduous and attentive. He missed a Ravi Shankar concert, attended by the rest of the cabinet, in order to read the mission's final report the evening before chairing the meeting to receive it. He quickly silenced the ill-informed male critics at the meeting. He announced that, while the criticisms in the report were harsh, they were true. He accepted and endorsed the findings and the recommendations. The male United Nations Development Programme resident representative was amazed. 'He seldom comes to these meetings', he said. 'I can't understand it.'

I might not have understood either, if I had not spent some time earlier in the month talking to the wife of the secretary of the department. The couple had three daughters and had worked hard to give them the best possible education, all culminating in university degrees in the UK or the USA. Now each daughter refused to return home.

'They refuse to be treated as second-class citizens', the secretary's wife told me. The secretary was doing all he could in his last months at the post to change the government's approach to the treatment of all women.

The minister's wife, she said, had interests in a substantial cattle farm, and she personally planned and oversaw the genetic improvement programme, in a society where women of her class would not normally play such a role. Their only daughter had recently returned home. Just a few months into an arranged marriage, she had been subjected to habitual domestic violence in a country where laws offered her no protection. 'They are interested', the secretary's wife explained, 'because the inequities have come home. They cannot ignore them any more.'

In yet another developing country where I worked, the official in charge of agriculture in the Department of Planning cancelled four appointments with my mission team designing a project on women in agriculture. While I had been advised that the official liked to be taken to lunch at expensive hotels by women diplomats, I was not about to participate in that game. The official met with us only on the presentation of the project report, when the man from the headquarters of the donor UN agency arrived.

This man was as ignorant of the complexities of the issues as he was arrogant. (He had no daughters.) When his attention was drawn to information that rural women in his country worked longer days and at many more tasks than men did, he scoffed. His mother (from a family with significant estate holdings) was a farmer, he declared, and this was not true of her. The inference, therefore, was that it was not true of any rural women. Then he attacked the research in question, implying it was Western, biased and not about 'our women', at the same time making a mistaken assumption about my nationality. He looked particularly foolish, and the well-qualified national consultants whose own field work had provided the research findings were deeply embarrassed. Such episodes have no effect on international consultants like me, but they are very costly to economic progress, and to the official's reputation in his own country.

Now, why bother with such stories? What relevance do they have to this argument? Because, whether we like it or not, these are typical stories of the basis for policy decisions in key economic sectors. These are illustrations of the political approach, by men, to major economic questions concerning the roles and status of half a country's population.

Women in government bureaucracies have begun to leak similar findings in official documents. The initial report of the Republic of Korea on CEDAW acknowledges that 'In spite of the above mentioned advances, we cannot deny that it is difficult and thus time-consuming to eliminate completely the entrenched traditions of discrimination against women and also to realize fully the equal participation of women in every field.' In Western Samoa, the Ministry of Women's Affairs notes in project plans that, 'while women's unpaid work is a priority for . . . Women's Affairs, the topic may well be sensitive and its value questioned by others'.

NON-ORGANIC DAILY BULLSHIT

As we see, it is impossible to talk about women without talking about the processes occurring throughout an economy. Yet planners usually talk about the economy without talking about the specific effects on women. The direct discrimination against women is both overt and covert and exacts major economic costs. There are the opportunity costs, of ignoring constraints women face and of failing to provide women with improved opportunities to participate fully in the development process. There are the costs of gender stereotyping in major labour-market and home-maintenance activities. There are the costs of refusing to recognise women by claiming that the household is the unit of economic analysis, but then failing to analyse the household as a business enterprise of interdependent workers, contributing to two sub-systems of production with different skills, potentials, knowledge bases and rights to resources. There is the inefficient use of resources, poor targeting and malinvestment by men's deliberate obstruction of women's access to land titles, credit, knowledge, extension services, appropriate technology and a wide range of other services, all of which hinder a nation's development and growth statistics. And all the above accumulatively contribute to the inter-generational costs incurred through poor nutrition, overpopulation and poverty.

In such a context, women are not just another category to be met in macro-economic policy (though they are seldom considered in that context). Trade, trans-national corporations, commercial lending and aid are the four dominant channels through which international economic relations manifest themselves and affect national macro-economic policies. Usually, the policy strategy mix advocated to generate a high growth rate in the GDP increases poverty, inequality and unemployment. Low-income groups suffer the most, and women suffer more than men. When powerful macro forces are working against the poor, special micro measures such as a few income-generating projects will not bring about any significant improvement in the well-being of women.

Equity and efficiency are not mutually exclusive outcomes. Women are not a problem for the economy. On the contrary, meeting the challenges of survival depends more than ever before on women's organisational, management, ecological and productive skills. That women have been, through direct discrimination, denied both opportunities to influence the adjustment process and their share of benefits brought by structural change means that they are the least-dependent resource in the community. They are, therefore, the group most likely to respond to inputs leading to self-reliance.

It does not require years as a policy planner or a degree in economics to observe that an extremely effective way to increase the time women have available for income-generating or productive activity is to introduce appropriate technology to save their time spent in hours of repetitive drudgery necessary for the survival of the household. Simone de Beauvoir wrote in *The Second Sex*, 'Few tasks are more like the torture of Sisyphus than housework, with its endless repetition: the clean becomes soiled, the soiled is made clean, over and over, day after day.'[47] In fact, technology inputs in the name of economic progress, overwhelmingly directed at males, have frequently had the effect of increasing the working day of women even more. Studies by the International Rice Research Institute in the Philippines demonstrate conclusively that the increase in rice production in Asia increased the work traditionally done by women twofold, while the money from the twice-yearly harvests went to the men because the land was in male names. Labour-saving technology was applied to men's tasks (land clearing, ploughing), while women's planting, weeding, harvesting and storage work doubled with increases in crops and production.[48]

It should be noted that the female activities in this production arrangement constitute the bulk of the labour requirement for these crops. Regardless of such evidence, throughout the region men have higher levels of input in the early stages of agricultural production, such as field preparation, and monopolise most mechanical–technical inputs. Ploughing or threshing, by either animal- or fuel-powered machines, is done by men, while hand threshing is a female, labour-intensive activity. Driving tractors is reserved for men, and all the menial agricultural tasks of the region – seed preparation, weeding crops, transplanting rice, picking cotton or tea, raising silk worms and cocoon reeling – are overwhelmingly women's work, and have the fewest technological inputs.

I can think of countless similar situations in New Zealand. I always remember the breathtaking incompetence of the purchase by male farmers of that vast new machine, which was tax-deductible, that was supposed to save labour and time – meaning, for example, the hay would be harvested in a few hours less a year. The machines most in daily use, and most needed to free women's additional productive time – called automatic washing-machines or clothes dryers or dish-washers – were not of course tax-deductible, concerned as they are with the non-productive household and domestic service sector.

Consider, from a public policy viewpoint, the treatment of women's unpaid work in accident compensation. (The right to an action for damages in tort was abolished with the introduction of this scheme.) Recently I reread the Woodhouse report,[49] the original document setting out the philosophy of 'Compensation for Personal Injury in New Zealand'. The author makes it quite clear that he understood that no paid production whatsoever was possible without the unpaid production and consumption of those who were at home, namely housewives. The report suggested that, were an accident to occur to these unpaid workers, not only should their medical expenses be met, but that payment should be made to a responsible person to pick up that work during the period of recovery.

I remember the story of a constituent in Oparau who broke her leg just at the beginning of shearing, and had to be replaced by one farmhand, one rousie and one housekeeper. She was at that stage not a partner in the farm, nor was she (I don't like to say 'paid' in rural situations) a book entry for accountancy purposes and taxation deductibility, which tends to be how rural women's work is recognised. After a sustained argument with the Accident Compensation Corporation (ACC), we did have the additional farm worker and the rousie compensated but, because the women's mother became the housekeeper, ACC would not pay her at all. They were not interested in the replacement of the work, nor in the quality and nature of the work done, but said that it was an altruistic and community expectation that the mother should move in in an unpaid capacity and perform the work.

The problem does not lie with rural women's self-image. In a comprehensive study of farming women in New Zealand, Deirdre Shaw[50] found that 88 percent view themselves as being in the farming profession, seeing their role as physical, decisional, administrative, economic, supportive and organisational. Ninety-nine percent were involved in horticultural or stock work, yet felt that little was done to enable them to participate in discussion groups, field days and farm visits, due both to lack of childcare and, at times, to attitudes.

Women who have the opportunity or flexibility to make choices about their treatment by governments change their votes. And, in the marketplace, they deliver their judgements in an equally appropriate way. Forty-one percent of the women in the study make it clear that particular companies in the rural service industry will, and do, lose their business if the women are not treated as equal and knowledgeable partners. At the same time, interviews with people in the rural service industry revealed that 82.5 percent first thought of a farmer as being male. Less than half felt that a woman's role on the farm was a partnership, with one-third seeing women in a 'farmer's wife/support' role. It also revealed that, while the majority of men interviewed saw women as being in a partnership, they also considered women to be farmers only when farming on their own.

The market is as tardy as governments to respond. The New Zealand Agricultural Fielddays are held annually in the middle of winter at Mystery Creek, Hamilton. Billed as the largest single annual event in the country and attracting 140,000 people, they are seen by the suppliers of equipment, information and services to the industry as 'the window for our products for the year'. One hundred and twenty-six million dollars is reported to have been spent in four days on the product lines on display in 1994, and millions more is spent subsequently as a direct result of the visits of farmers to the event. For a number of years I lived directly across the road from the site, which was in my constituency, so I have had the opportunity to observe its growth and its shortcomings.

In New Zealand, women play an increasing role in the financial administration of farms. They are frequently the book-keepers, planners, data-entry specialists. There is evidence that they generally, in Australia perhaps more markedly than in New Zealand, have higher educational qualifications than their husbands. They furnish the accountants with the materials for taxation returns, pay the accounts, and are active partners in designing the cropping or breeding policies for the year and in setting the production targets. But all of this seems lost on the marketeers at this biggest event of the year. There is no provision of on-site quality childcare facilities. Equity questions aside, I consider this a major marketing blunder. No one can concentrate on making decisions about equipment worth thousands of dollars with a toddler demanding attention.

Whether or not markets or governments dominated by men can face it, the fact is that an increasing proportion of agricultural production, food security, environmental protection, nutrition and animal health depends on the efforts of women, who work the longest days, at the most activities, with the least financial rewards and minimal economic recognition.

The role and work of women on the planet are intimately related to the goal of comprehensive socio-economic and political development. This work is vital for the development of all societies and for the quality of life on our planet. The manner in which high growth-rate activities are pursued increasingly sees escalating import volumes, environmental plundering, repatriation of profits and little evidence that skills and technology are transferred, especially to rural women. In the key issue of agricultural trade in the Uruguay round leading to the GATT agreement, Asian members of the Cairns group, which included Indonesia, Malaysia, the Philippines and Thailand, had assiduously pursued the policy of restoring free trade to agriculture, with no evidence that any planning had been done to assess the socio-economic impact on the majority of the rural population, namely women and children.

The textbook World Bank and IMF formula for structural adjustment is argued frequently in the context of 'political stability'. The emphasis is on the deregulation of finance, capital and labour, and a reorientation towards exports, along with a downward adjustment of exchange rates. Throughout this period, the developed countries have manipulated the system of exchange rates in order to maintain favourable terms of trade for themselves.

These policies for 'political stability' have been policies for corruption, for unfair taxes and for food shortages. They have seen rural revolts over expropriation of land. They have threatened food security and, in their concentration on mono-cropping for export, have inflated basic food prices in the developing countries and vitally affected basic nutrition with the loss of land and resources for subsistence agriculture. A poor crop or harvest failure has not infrequently provoked armed conflict on a national or international level. Not only does food become a weapon of war, but the conflict causes extensive environmental degradation and population displacement – a most unstable situation.[51]

Throughout the world there are political movements of people concerned about their own impoverishment, social disadvantages, and the misuse of national resources. While they recognise the debts run up by former and present corrupt leaders, the despoliation of colonisation and the needs for economic restraint, they also notice, and speak boldly about, the connections between powerful foreign states, their political leaders and local elites. It is no accident that women's non-governmental organisations are frequently those calling attention to the hypocrisy of governments who voice concern about the loss of fisheries or forest resources while simultaneously signing agreements with foreign and local companies for exploitation of these resources.

Women's right to half of everything is not an extreme neocolonial Western feminist idea. (Indeed, many traditional societies were matri-lineal, to ensure proper land use and management, and conservation of natural resources.) It is a conscious struggle by women from all classes, castes and nations against their inequitable burdens, their exclusion from political power, the lack of autonomy over their own bodies and, for too many rural women, a struggle for the lives of themselves and their children. And it has not escaped the observation of these women that their subordination is continually imposed on them, willingly and unwillingly, by men in a multitude of guises and in a multitude of ways. Women understand 'agency', that they do not live as passive victims: that men have complicitly and explicitly denied their options.

The use of language to avert blame can be seen in relation to the environment, which shares with women an economic invisibility, as well as a fate to be 'managed and controlled' by men.[52] 'We' are not 'losing' forests. Multinational oil companies, timber firms, local elites, with the complicity, co-operation and corruption of specific govern-ment and security officials and international development agencies, are burning, clearing and clear-felling vast areas of tropical forests at a staggering rate for paper, power plants, mineral exploitation, timber and mono-cultural agriculture. Even when tropical rainforest is replaced, it is usually with mono-plantations of fast-growing trees for pulp paper. The passive voice obscures questions of agency, but political movements of people impoverished by such activity are not fooled.

THE MARKET INDICATORS

From time to time women's work has been recognised in traditional economic ways. As early as 1912 women's unpaid work was counted as 15 percent of Norway's national income. Men's work in this sphere was considered insignificant and was not counted, while paid and unpaid women workers were grouped together. Workers included maids, wives and all daughters in the household aged over sixteen. The estimates were based on the number of households and the value of wages, bed and lodging. Sixty percent of rural women were included in this sector, and the remaining 40 percent were recorded as working in agriculture. Until 1947, estimates were based on the 1930 census and increased over the years in accordance with increases in the total population and the cost of living index.[53]

Petter Jakob Bjere, who worked for many years in Norway's Bureau of Statistics, described his experiences to me when I met him in Oslo in 1990. In the Bureau of Information's preparation for claims for reparations against the Germans after the war, the household was included as a major sector. When I asked him why the sector was included, he replied that this was considered obvious and wasn't even discussed. The bureau was strongly influenced by the philosophy that national product was an indication of welfare, the flow of all goods and services. The *real* economy was important, he said.

By contrast, the prevailing post-World War II approach, led by Richard Stone, the original author of the UNSNA, was concerned with estimates of payments, therefore unpaid household work could not be included.[54] Bjere joined other Norwegian economists and statisticians in a meeting with Stone in 1946 and tried to explain to him the difference between the *real* economy and the *financial* economy, but their efforts were in vain. Stone's approach was recommended for international use by the Statistical Commission of the United Nations, and Norway's work was discontinued in 1947, although figures for unpaid household work were mentioned in a footnote in 1948.

Bjere recalled that the problems of international comparability, and data difficulties, were the reasons Stone gave for excluding the sector.

But he also recalled that economists and governments were preoccupied with trends and business cycle analyses, and a large household sector did not assist their analysis. 'International comparability cannot be a major argument for exclusion', he said. 'And, although our data collection and imputation methods were very crude, they were better than the current situation of exclusion.'

In 1988 a concerted effort by all the major women's organisations in Norway led the Bureau of Statistics to conduct a pilot study of unpaid work as a contribution to GDP. The study indicated that in 1981 household production amounted to 40 percent of GDP, with women contributing two-thirds of the total. (It is noteworthy that at the time Norway had the highest percentage of women parliamentary representatives in the world.)

In Australia in 1990, the Bureau of Statistics[55] suggested that the average homemaker would earn about A\$400 a week if he or she were paid at award wages. The bureau estimated married women not in paid work at an average of 95.5 unpaid hours a fortnight at A\$8.68 an hour. It is immediately obvious that the hours worked figure is wrong. And it is highly unlikely that the suggested hourly rate would pay for replacement labour. The figures were low compared with other studies done at a similar time. A national study by a firm of investment advisers put a price of over A\$800 a week on a homemaker's head. An insurance company estimated it would cost A\$903 a week to employ someone to do all the chores performed by the average housewife with small children.[56]

These hours of work and rates of pay can be compared with emerging court determinations on the value of unpaid work in the household. While the acknowledgement of any value at all is radical in judicial determinations, the figures are outrageously inadequate.

In a Canadian case, a Mrs Logozar was awarded C\$6552 for pre-trial loss of voluntary services, despite evidence that her housekeeping capacity had been reduced by more than 1300 hours a year for the five years between her injury and the trial (this was equal to C\$1 an hour's compensation over five years). The judge found that her housekeeping capacity had been reduced by eighteen hours a week, rather than the twenty-five hours claimed, and for a period of one year rather than five. The compensation was at the rate of C\$7 per hour rather than the C\$8.48 submitted by the family economist who testified at the trial.

Mrs Logozar claimed to do about forty-four hours of household work a week prior to her injury, including at least four hours a week tending an extensive vegetable garden and a flock of chickens, which provided her family with eggs and meat. According to Canadian time–use data, Alberta women with family and employment characteristics close to hers spend between 25 and 96 hours a week doing household work, so the plaintiffs reported that the weekly hours were not excessive.

In 1992, Saskatchewan home manager Verna Fobel won a landmark Canadian Supreme Court decision awarding her direct compensation for lost capacity to do unpaid work. Prior to that, compensation was typically awarded to a husband for loss of his wife's services. Even so, while the average wage for domestic services was C$7.54 an hour, the court reduced the rate to C$5.50 because it assumed that hiring by the week or month would be less. Since the replacement labour was set at fifteen hours a week, this was not logical.[57]

Canadian activists were quick to compare the judges' determinations with the going market rates. The Aitken job evaluation plan, a device used by human resource consultants, scored an unpaid housewife at the equivalent of a middle-level supervisory job or a senior specialist, which would have been C$32,000 a year. They also pointed out that the time spent on unpaid work doubled for women by the time they reached the age of twenty-five, and that this was work from which there was no retirement.[58]

Breastfeeding is a major reproductive activity carried out only by women, and this thoroughly confuses statisticians' and economists' production models. The reproduction of human life also seems conceptually beyond their rules of imputation. But bodies most certainly have market prices.

In 1991, the High Court in England awarded £130,000 to a woman who gave birth to a fourth child after a sterilisation operation went wrong. Damages were awarded against the regional health authority, which admitted liability.

In the US, the cost of reproducing another life can range from US$1800 for artificial insemination to US$36,000 for a surrogate mother to carry the child. This is the equivalent of US$5.35 an hour in a 280-day pregnancy. It can cost more than US$800,000 for six cycles of *in-vitro* fertilisation if the woman is over 40 and the male has a low sperm count.

If a US airline crashes on an international flight, the value of a life is limited to US$75,000, unless wilful misconduct on behalf of the airline can be proved. In 1993, compensatory damages for wrongful death in US courts covered a wide range. Women in general tend to receive smaller awards than men, but there are exceptions. The highest award was US$11.3 million, for a woman with two small children. Her car burst into flames after it was hit head-on, and the manufacturer of the defective fuel pump was found liable. The highest verdict for a man in 1993 was US$10 million, for a nineteen-year-old shot to death in the parking lot of an apartment complex that had failed to provide adequate security. The lows were US$62,987 for a 37-year-old father of two killed in a construction accident, and US$28,000 for a woman in her 60s who was killed when a driver failed to stop at a compulsory stop sign; the county was found negligent in failing to keep the sign visible.[59]

According to Jim Hogshire,[60] it might be more worthwhile to add up the sum of our parts. In India a healthy kidney is worth more than US$1500, whereas in the Persian Gulf it can fetch US$50,000. On the world black market a heart can make US$20,000. A liver is worth up to US$150,000 a slice, and the slice will regenerate. Bone marrow sells for US$10,000 a quart, lungs for US$25,000 and the range for kidneys is US$10–50,000. A woman's eggs are worth about US$2000 per harvest, and are frequently taken without permission by surgeons while doing other operations.

These are *ad hoc* market indicators. They may assist in demonstrating the lunacy of the current system, but they do not provide a constructive response as a basis for planning and policy alternatives. Finding a market equivalent wage for all unpaid productive and reproductive work is not the point.

So what can be done to illuminate the picture with such clarity that the glare forces the removal of patriarchal blinkers from the eye that is blind to what women do? Are there tools to explode the myths promulgated by one-dimensional economic statistics? The answer is yes, and the key is time–use surveys.

TIME–USE SURVEYS

Now, why are we interested in time? Time is the one thing we all have. We do not all have market labour-force activities. We do not all have disposable cash. Many of us do not trade on the basis of money, we trade our time. Our economics is about how we use our time. And, even though we frequently do not have a choice about how we use our time, it is the common denominator of exchange. So time is the one unit of exchange we all have in equal amounts, the one investment we all have to make.

Statistics Sweden comment that time–use surveys are well respected and reasonably common. Hours and minutes are a universal measurement and protected from inflation, deflation, changing exchange rates, etc.[61]

According to validity studies, the time-diary method produces for most activities data which is consistent with real behaviour and not subject to misunderstandings, recall problems or over- or under-reporting, apart from some highly sensitive activities.[62]

I have had many arguments with economists and statisticians on the difficulties with time–use surveys. I had one of the best with Jan von Tongeren, from the United Nations Statistical Commission. Finally, in desperation, he turned to me and said, 'This is all very well. I suppose you could do it in New Zealand. It's such a little country and of course the women there are literate. But what would you do with women who were illegal immigrant populations, what would you do about women in purdah, what would you do about pre-literate women?' (Actually, he said 'illiterate women', but every women would read if she were given the opportunity.)

Several years later I had the opportunity to respond to that challenge. Alexandra Stephens, who was the senior sociologist for the FAO in Asia and the Pacific, based in Bangkok, could clearly see the value of such data for her work and for that agency. Under her guidance, and working with women of the region, a workshop including statisticians, agricultural planners, field workers, academics, leaders of non-governmental organisations, aid donors and agency representatives was organised.[63] I have returned to the file notes of those days to reproduce them here, so our priorities, our conceptual framework and politics might be compared with the usual 'mainstream' agenda.

First we outlined our objectives. The first group of these read: to empower and conscientise women, to maximise women's potential, to meet women's needs, and to provide for grassroots strategising and networking. The list continued: to provide for better planning at national, regional and local levels; to identify target groups for new and existing policies and programmes; to provide for more focused agricultural research, for better extension packages, for better development inputs, for better use of human resources; to define who has access to and control over the factors of production; to identify sectoral problems and inter-sectoral relationships; to justify budgets; to set planning priorities; to analyse the divisions of labour, and the social structure implied by that information; to assess the distribution of benefits of projects and programmes, and to identify constraints to women's participation in them.

In identifying these objectives, we were looking to assist the practical participation of women, to better understand their role, and to evaluate the impact of development on their lives.

In order to give the research economic credibility, further objectives were: to assist in the assessment of women's contribution to national income; and to provide data for placing a market value on women's work.

We listed our priorities for a conceptual framework. These were:

1. to reflect what women actually do – the multiple roles, the sequence, frequency and duration of activities, where they were carried out and with whom;

2. to establish an accurate picture of this, and to eliminate all biases emanating from sex-role stereotyping or notions of what women should do instead of what they really do;

3. to establish indicators addressing the current voids in information about the majority of the world's farmers, namely women, and the majority of those who live in rural areas, also women;

4. to establish mechanisms to reflect priorities desired by women.

In accordance with our objectives, and on a budget of only US$10,000 for each country, pilot surveys were conducted. Members of a profiled group sample were individually followed for an entire day, recording every one of their activities, who they were doing it for, where they were doing it, why they were doing it and who they were doing it with.

Before the survey began we made some demanding rules for ourselves. First, the research team must not be officials of a government, both because we wanted the people to trust the research team and because we did not want the money to finish up in somebody's Swiss bank account. Second, every research team had to have men researchers following men. (You see, men get terribly affronted and suspicious if you're interested only in women; so we had to follow them as well. Of course, this would also give us comparable and generally less biased data.) Women would follow women. Third, the leader of every research team had to be a woman. This was fine in Malaysia, Thailand and India, but we were having real trouble with this in Pakistan until we secured as our field team leader a woman who had a younger brother. He was put in charge of the chaps, she was in charge of the whole team, and the men did what they were told. Finally, because of the intimacy of being followed for a day, we decided that only people who spoke the language, and also were known to those being surveyed, could be leaders of the survey teams.

Field data was gathered most successfully on the illegal immigrant populations of northern Thailand, an almost impossible population to survey. These people are constantly on the move, fleeing from both the Burmese military on one side and the Thai military on the other. In a Pakistani village in strict purdah, excellent results were also achieved.

The operational challenge remained of gathering information in a totally pre-literate village in India. I kept thinking of Jan von Tongeren and wondering how the team would solve this one. Then our wonderful extension worker in India said: 'Well, there is no problem, we will do it in the school holidays and the twelve- to fourteen-year-olds will follow their parents. That will be very much better because then we won't even get any change in behaviour from our respondents.' She was quite right. We got excellent data back from those young people.

The pilot surveys established the following instruments as the most accurate and effective for reaching the objectives. A village profile should be established, using national and local data, to include the following as a minimum: a. the number of families, broken down into individual members by gender, age, marital status, education and occupation; b. livestock per household; c. landholding per household; d. agricultural technologies per household. Complementing this, a village profile was to be elaborated identifying the total amount of surrounding land, the cultivated area, the types of crops grown, agricultural methods used, fertilisers, pesticides, the availability of machinery, transport and civil amenities.

The most preferred survey method was non-participant observation[64] for a minimum of 24 hours and a maximum per individual of three days. The survey should be conducted seasonally, preferably starting in combination with or at the same time as the census of agriculture or other census.

The traditional interview format was used to supplement the information gathered in the diaries. Specifically, interviews were to elicit

information about mobility within and outside the village for occupational and social reasons, the respondent's assessment of gender-specific
responsibilities in livestock and crop care, yearly time-use patterns and
activities, mutual assistance in the village, some idea of who made
what decisions in the household, and pregnancy and post-pregnancy
practices. However, the focus of the study should remain on productive
activities, and the quality of information collected on, for example,
health and pregnancies would not be of the same depth. (There is
always the problem that, since we have so little information on women,
any opportunity to collect significant economic data of use to women
sees an expanding wish-list trying to incorporate everything we can
think of.) Finally, a group meeting with women respondents supplemented by other women from the village or neighbourhood, could be
held. The aims were: a. to focus on critical aspects such as human and
animal health, water, agricultural practices, and to identify changes in
knowledge and practice over time; b. to identify sources of information,
to see whether these differed by gender, and to identify changes in
sources; c. to identify environmental changes; d. to enrich the raw data
by having the field team respond to women's questions about the
research, and to feed back preliminary findings.

This combination of instruments would capture the diversity of
farming systems in any country, and the sampling framework therefore
had to reflect different farming systems, different agro-ecological zones
and different ethnic-cultural groupings. The sampling framework
should also encompass as many of the following categories as possible:
rural women and men, land tenure, marital status, age, religion, socio-
economic status, ethnicity, household size and the operational head of
the household.

Operationally, we tried to conduct the research in an utterly feminist
way. We wanted all research copyrighted in the names of the villagers: it
belonged to the people.[65] Our procedure ensured that the full research
team met first with the villagers to explain exactly what was going on,
and then met again later to feed back the information. In one small
village in Pakistan, data was simply presented in a coloured bar graph,
so that everyone who saw it could immediately understand it. I wish I
could describe it properly. Every activity was represented by a different
colour. Every respondent's day was represented by one bar in the
graph. Orange was used for leisure and social activities, so that my first
key observation was that men had leisure and women did not. Then I

saw that men did far fewer activities in a day than women. Their bars generally had six or seven colours, the women's had twelve or more. Men didn't get interrupted when they engaged in their activities, unlike women, whose bar lines were constantly shifting in colour. Women got up earlier in the morning and retired later at night. They worked longer days than men, especially when we took into account those formidable leisure periods men enjoyed.

The researchers reported that, when data like this was presented and displayed on the village walls, they could see the excited body language and movement of the women. After each checked her graph line against her husband's, and then against her women neighbours', they got moving politically.

While presenting data like this might seem simple or unsophisticated to national statisticians, there was a plethora of information there. For example, if in a village the men wanted a bulldozer, the women would be able to demonstrate that it was taking them five hours every day to cook. It was not because they were inefficient cooks, but because their stoves were hopelessly inadequate. This simple time–use data was sufficient to place fuel-efficient stoves as top priority in that village. Similarly, this kind of data presentation could demonstrate immediately the major time-consuming tasks – for example, the hours taken every day getting water. In such cases the women did know that a new well was an overwhelming priority for the village, but they had never been empirically empowered in this way, owning the information to argue for political change.

All the pilot time–use studies (and similar micro studies in Australia and New Zealand) confirmed that women in rural areas of the region worked longer days than men, at a much larger number of tasks, with a simultaneity of two tasks for 60 percent of the time, and three or more tasks for 30 percent of the time. By comparison, men had long uninterrupted periods of doing one task at a time, a shorter working day, and much greater leisure time.[66]

On a national level, what can time–use data tell us? It can show what goods and services households produce, what the unemployed do with their time, how much additional work children in a household create, and whether equality in the distribution of household tasks has been achieved. The use of discretionary time by those in and out of the paid labour force can be analysed.

The data points to inefficiencies in the use of human resources by unnecessary fragmentation of time. In Vietnam, the provision of childcare for women farmers increased their productivity by 60 percent. The information also shows up which sex gets the menial, boring, low-status and unpaid invisible work, which in turn highlights oppression and subordination. In the rural areas, such surveys show seasonal variations, allowing identification of suitable time-slots for education and other programmes.

Time–use data also provides a measure of the interdependence of the activities of household members, and of how paid work, caring work, housework, community work, leisure and time spent on personal care are interrelated. This is vital for understanding how the impact of paid labour-force participation of women leads to growth in market activity to replace formerly unpaid activity in the home.

Time–use data also tells when activities are carried out. It assists in planning post-compulsory educational facilities, and in targeting hours and topics to match current and potential students' benefits, libraries, schools, community learning and private educational institutions.

The interdependence of market and non-market activity makes it necessary to measure both. Changes in non-market activity, such as childcare, affect the context within which market activity is measured, and can explain a lot of the changes in market activity.

The hours when various activities are carried out, and for how long, provide valuable tools for planners – for example, in electricity demand, opening hours of retail outlets, and broadcasting programming. Information on where the population will be and whom they will be with in the event of a disaster like a major earthquake allows informed civil-defence planning for different hours and days of the week.

French government agencies use the time–use patterns of women at different life-stages to predict the availability of skilled workers in years ahead. This allows tailored recruitment and training programmes to be implemented in time to overcome any shortfalls, or for implementation of retraining in times of excess. Travel and work patterns have been used in Norway to set the opening hours of businesses. Time–use diaries were influential in the Finnish government's decision to recommend shorter working days and flexible working hours for some population groups to allow family and community obligations to be met. And time–use data has been used in various countries to plan leisure and recreational facilities.

A major block to progress in the formal establishment of national time–use surveys is the determined, or unconscious, resistance to embracing the policy implications of acknowledging the economic value of what women do. In the current political climate, new initiatives from a bureau or department of statistics must demonstrate a need by policy clients – for example, other government departments, the banking and insurance industries, business, the labour movement, the media – for the information to be produced. Since the men in power are not disinterested, and do recognise that the implications of this data are a threat to their slice of the pie, there is little market demand for the information.

A clear example of this occurred in New Zealand. There had been considerable pressure for a long time to have a time–use survey. Statistics New Zealand finally designed and piloted a time–use survey in August 1990. It was in diary form and the women respondents had to fill it in every 10 minutes on selected days.

The survey had major problems. It did not ask respondents to address what are called 'secondary' activities. This I find a major conceptual problem. Picture Cathy at 17.15 hours. She is answering the telephone, supervising the homework, cooking the dinner, probably getting the washing in if it starts to rain, waiting for *him* to come home so she can do the counselling, and somebody's sitting there with a questionnaire saying, 'What is your primary activity?' At that moment Cathy is engaged in four or five activities, and every one of them is necessary, so she cannot tell you which is the primary activity. But the women who responded to the time–use diary had to decide from moment to moment what their primary activity was, to the exclusion of all others. Of course women have a conceptual problem with that, unlike most men, who generally do only one thing at a time (there are exceptions, I'm sure).

Nevertheless, the results showed that unpaid work would have a market valuation of up to 68 percent of GDP. About 68 percent of primary unpaid work was performed by women, and 90 percent was performed in the home.

The Cabinet paper of March 1992 putting the case for a time–use survey was sponsored by the Ministry of Women's Affairs. The ministry was required to specify how the project would be funded by other parties and/or what outputs might be discontinued to compensate. The pledges given by those interested in the survey results fell well short of the total survey costs and other government departments did not identify any outputs that could be withdrawn.

The Cabinet then ordered a 'strategic review of the information needs of those who develop, implement and monitor social [note, not economic] policies'.[67] These were public agencies and some voluntary agencies. How surprising, then, that the priorities identified were for initiatives in data on the labour market and the voluntary sector. In supporting the refusal to proceed with a time–use survey, the minister commented that his concern was that the resources used in public statistics should be directed at initiatives which have the most significant impact on the quality of public sector decision-making and the accountability of government.[68]

My final correspondence on the matter was to the point.

> Dear Marilyn
> Funding a full time–use survey is not high on the government's priority.
> Yours sincerely
> Jenny Shipley
> Minister of Women's Affairs.

The invisibility of women's work is criminal in the maldistribution of public sector resources. There is no question in my mind that this contributes to additional costs in public policy expenditure because of the failure to invest in support services in the area where the most work in New Zealand is done. This invisibility is universal and is now compounded by the fact that we are signatories to various UN resolutions which say that we must recognise it. Yet, as at September 1996, this country has no intention of making provision to do so.

What difference would such data make? Let us consider the failure to account for all the work that women do in the context of public health policy. If I were in charge of the transitions in the health sector in New Zealand at the moment, and my key concern was prevention, I would be looking to primary health care. I would stand back and ask, which people spend the largest amount of time in providing primary health care? The answer is untrained, unassisted, unsophisticated, invisible women, mainly called mothers. And sometimes called wives or daughters, sometimes women neighbours or relatives, sometimes grandmothers. Were I then to define how much time those practitioners spent in primary health care, I would find that up to two-thirds of all primary health care in the country was carried out by these women.

If it were then my concern, for example, to close a psychopaedic ward and have its patients returned to these health workers, my primary public policy objectives would be the immediate support of them with domiciliary care and laundry services, with psychopaedic nursing care, and to ensure that physiotherapists were available, that there was relief at weekends, that various forms of assistance were available for changes in home maintenance and structure, and that there was a payment which recognised that the state had been relieved of the burden of care for 24 hours a day, seven days a week.

What a terrifying prospect for men that would be, and particularly for the business of health care! But the resistance to data collection is never phrased in terms of the threat of such information to patriarchal power.

In early 1993, after major activism and activity from women across Canada (and internationally), Statistics Canada held a major international conference of economists and statisticians on unpaid work.[69] As background to the conceptual approach to this conference, it is useful to know that the *Canada Year Book* states that the 'census . . . has remained the single most comprehensive survey of information on the way Canadians live'[70] and is 'a principal source of information for measuring social and economic change, and for detecting those needs which necessitate the development and implementation of policies and programmes such as regional development, health and welfare programmes, educational facilities, immigration, low-income housing, and transportation networks'.[71] Yet Canadians performing unwaged productive and reproductive work are categorised as 'Not in the Labour Force'.

In 1986, the work of those 'Not in the Labour Force' comprised half the working time of all Canadians,[72] was worth almost twice the value of the manufacturing sector and occupied 62.5 percent of the working time of Canadian women.[73] In 1992, the value of unpaid housework in Canada would have been C\$319 billion a year at replacement labour estimates. The time expended in this work was 25 billion hours, and women performed 66 percent of it measured by time. For comparison, where this is the equivalent of 46 percent of Canada's GDP, the black market is estimated at about only 2.5 percent of the GDP.[74]

How anyone can claim that a census which omits this productive contribution is 'a principal source of information for measuring social and economic change' escapes me. The prospect that such a barren data base then detects needs in major economic policy planning sectors gives rise to major questions about the quality of those policies and their ability to respond to the real needs of the Canadian population.

There is no doubt that a considerable difference exists between the resources available in Canada to capture a true picture of the full working population and those in Nepal. Advanced development in Canada also means that logistical difficulties in survey work are insignificant compared with those in Nepal. But at the end of the day, the treatment and lack of recognition of womens' productive and reproductive work are directly comparable.

The emphasis of the 1993 conference was on statistics, valuation methods and definitions. The same old themes recurred consistently in presentations and discussions. The conference acknowledged that valuing unpaid work using paid work equivalents reinforces the low values placed on women's traditional occupations. (Conceptually such imputations have never addressed reproduction, whether it be biological reproduction, lactation or services such as counselling, as productive work, and so none of these economic activities is imputed into such figures either.) The conference did acknowledge that not all unpaid work activities have a parallel in paid work. The issue is further complicated by the inability of such a comparator to account for differences in quality, especially when considerations of care and nurture are considered.

The challenge of measuring simultaneous activities was mentioned, as was the problem of gendered responses to surveys, well known in the field in development projects. Men record more unpaid work because it is less ordinary to them, so it is noticed. Women, on the other hand, are notorious for under-reporting their activities.

The Canadian time–use survey is conducted by phone as part of the country's general household survey. The time allocated to it is 10 minutes. Canada has a 98 percent phone cover and Canadians are used to using the phone. Other populations, in Europe for example, may be more cautious about giving personal information over the phone, although Denmark conducts a phone time–use survey. (In many parts of the world whole populations, for good reason, fear giving personal information to any government agent for any reason.)

Many general census surveys have been extended to include time–use, but often only with voluntary work. This may be because the interface between voluntary agencies and the government is visible, because such work has major expenditure implications for governments, and because it is obvious that men are involved.

THE FULL-PICTURE INNOVATORS

There are dedicated insiders who understand the need for data and who will find some way to get it. Klas Rydenstam, of the Central Bureau of Statistics in Sweden, tells the story of the 20 years it took to collect time–use data. He organised the data collection one year when there was a little surplus money, then held the data for years, as no funds were available to have it coded. One winter, staff in another government department had a down time so he got them to code the data for him. He taught himself enough to run the data analysis on a personal computer. The first report raised procedural and conceptual questions, but it included basic time–use tables. Then Klas Rydenstam heard about an equal employment opportunities (EEO) proposal being developed by a woman he happened to know. He showed her his paper and she realised the value of time–use studies to EEO. A time–use survey became part of her proposal and was funded as part of the EEO package.

The Swedish time–use survey of 1990–91 provided figures on household production that demonstrated a doubling of time spent in production when added to the labour force survey figures. The largest single branch of production was domestic work, with a time input a third bigger than the time input in services, and more than double that of manufacturing.[76]

In Germany, denying the 'most users' scenario of the authors of the 1993 revised UNSNA, the demand for information on the contribution of women to the GDP, including unpaid work of households, was so enormous that the Federal Statistical Office received the financial resources to conduct a representative time–use survey. In 1992, in the former territory of the Federal Republic of Germany, the total hours worked in all activities in the national accounts were 47.7 billion. The total hours worked in unpaid household production were 76.5 billion.[77]

As a result of the pressures now being exerted by the women's movement and by unthreatened men who wish to use the data, enlightened by the survey findings in Norway, Sweden and Germany, and in recognition of the tireless work of individuals such as Luisella Goldschmidt-Clermont at the Organisation for Economic Co-operation and Development (OECD), pilot time–use surveys are to be conducted in Europe in 1996, and main surveys, covering all seasons, with proposed sample sizes of 5000 households in each country, are due in 1997. The data collected will cover primary and secondary activities, for whom the unpaid work is done, where it is done and with whom the time is spent.

The main objectives of the proposed European Time–Use Survey are: to improve national accounts, particularly to give data for satellite accounts of household production; to contribute to the formulation of policy for working time, for gender and family, and for senior citizens; to provide data on reasons for travel, for passenger transport and tourism; and to provide evidence on culture and leisure participation.[78]

This is all significant progress towards a real picture of the total economy, but the work I find most exciting is being done in Australia, led by economist Duncan Ironmonger. As you will recall, he defined the household economy as the system that produces and allocates trade-able goods and services by using the unpaid labour and capital of house-holds. The household economy transforms intermediate commodities provided by the market economy into final items of consumption through the use of its own unpaid labour and its own capital goods.[79]

Ironmonger was the first to adapt traditional input–output tables showing the internal structure of the formal business and government sectors of the economy to the household. The traditional measures he calls the gross market product (GMP). Household input–output tables show the internal activity structure of the informal household sector of the economy and present the uses of intermediate commodities, labour and capital in each type of productive economic activity undertaken in households by unpaid labour and own capital. This he labels gross household product (GHP). Gross economic product (GEP) is the total of GMP and GHP. These input–output tables can be prepared for different sorts of households, e.g. those with and without children. In addition to those developed in Australia, such tables have now been produced for Finland (1990), Sweden (1990–91), and Norway (1991).

Grossing up the 1987 time–use sample survey to reflect all Australian households, Ironmonger showed that 76 million hours a week were used in meal preparation, 63 million in cleaning and laundry, and 53 million in shopping. These were the three largest industries in the Australian economy, and compared with the three largest market sector industries, wholesale and retail trade with 49 million hours a week, manufacturing with 49 million, and community services with 41 million. Women did 70 percent of the unpaid work in household indus-tries; men did 67 percent of paid work in market industries. Overall, in the total economy women did 52 percent of all paid and unpaid work, in precise proportion to their being 52 percent of the population aged fifteen years or over.

Using the results of the national time–use survey conducted in 1992, Ironmonger found that Australians do about 380 million hours of unpaid household work each week, compared with 272 million hours in paid employment. The value of the unpaid work, according to Ironmonger, calculated at the average salary rate (including fringe benefits) of A$14.25 an hour, was A$283 billion in 1992. Add the contribution from household capital, i.e. A$25 billion for equipment and vehicles, and A$33 billion for the use of owner-occupied housing, and the gross household product was A$341 billion, while the gross market product was A$362 billion. Household production therefore accounted for more than 48 percent of total production.

Drawing on the work of other commentators, Ironmonger has demonstrated the interdependence of GMP and GHP. For example, investment in the US rose from about 33 percent of gross capital formation in equipment in market industries in 1900 to over 100 percent by 1950. In other words, by 1950 US residents were placing about as much new equipment in their households as they were putting into their business sector.[80] He also draws attention to the significant fall in the UK between 1954 and 1974 in the proportion of household expenditure devoted to the purchase of services from the market. This fall was offset by a rise in the proportion of household expenditure on capital equipment – cars, refrigerators, stoves, freezers, washing-machines, vacuum-cleaners, power tools, televisions, stereos and videos.[81]

In his classic *The Third Wave*,[82] Alvin Toffler described the wholesale movement of tasks from market to the household as having been driven by the opportunities to externalise the labour costs of market industries. Such tasks include direct toll dialling, automatic bank tellers, self-service petrol stations, customer selection of goods when shopping, with few sales assistants, and lots of do-it-yourself home maintenance, decoration and renovation.

Ironmonger comments that product innovation in the household economy has been, and will continue to be, a major source of economic growth for both the market and the household. Moreover, many of the new commodities will have a significant impact on the use of time. New economic models, which include a more realistic portrayal of household activities in both production and leisure, should help unravel these effects on the use of time. They should also improve understanding of the environmental resource impacts of household activities and how these can be minimised.[83]

To underscore his findings, Ironmonger contends: 'In regard to the business cycle fluctuations of Gross Market Product (GMP), it is my hypothesis that Gross Household Product (GHP) varies in a counter cyclical way so that Gross Economic Product (GEP) is relatively constant through the business cycle. I believe the trade off could be as high as 80 percent. This would mean that a $100 million rise in GMP would be balanced by a $80 million fall in GHP so that the cyclical effect on total economic output, GEP, is only a rise of $20 million.'[84]

A handful of market analysts are similarly concerned with the current myopic production statistics. The National Bank of New Zealand has stated that 'the extended measure would be a better guide to assessing production changes within the economy. We recommend that serious consideration be given to extending current national account statistics in this direction. We can then be a world leader not just in some of our economic policies, but also in our measures of production used to help assess the effects of those policies.'[85]

Finally, the political effects of his work are not lost on Ironmonger. He writes: 'The most numerous and ultimately influential decision making units in the economy are not governments, firms, or multi national corporations, but households which have different methods of organization, management and decision making . . . We are talking about a major change in our view of the world and a major change in what needs to be measured.'[86]

The poverty of the current tools for measuring economic activity, and the use of them as a basis for policy planning, are now thoroughly trashed. How much longer are we expected to give credibility to such selective data?

Perhaps the volumes that the statistics occupy could be converted to fuel to produce energy. If the real thing were not so valuable, I might be tempted to describe these official economic statistics as a heap of shit.

Hu(man) Rights

In January 1993, the Canadian Government granted refugee status to a Saudi Arabian woman persecuted on the grounds of her sex. The woman had tried to go without a veil, to travel alone, and to pursue a university education in the field of her choice. She was threatened with severe punishment if she persisted in her views on the status of women, to such an extent that she would have been 'in grave danger' if she returned to Saudi Arabia. She had been in hiding in Montreal for 21 months after the Canadian Immigration and Refugee Board turned down her initial request for asylum.

The appeal decision was a world first. The board recommended that the word 'refugee' include women who can demonstrate that their countries do not provide adequate protection from sexual abuse, domestic violence and genital mutilation, among other things. Canada led the world in extending the criteria for refugee status to 'sex' and adopting as government policy the position that a 'well-founded fear of violation' on the basis of sex constituted grounds for asylum.[1]

In July 1994, in accordance with the new guidelines, Canada granted refugee status to a Somali woman who fled her country with her ten-year-old daughter because the daughter faced ritual genital mutilation. The Immigration and Refugee Board ruled that the daughter's 'right to personal security would be grossly infringed' if she were forced to return to Somalia. The published decision explained: 'The panel is satisfied that the authorities in Somalia will not protect the claimant from the physical and emotional ravages of female genital mutilation, given the evidence of its widespread practice in that country.'

David Matas, president of the Canadian Council of Refugees, said the decision would 'help to redress the gender bias and capture the female experience of persecution. Until now the process has tended to use a largely male-dominated definition, of somebody politically active, involved in demonstrations and the like.'[2]

These changes in Canada's domestic policy were a culmination of growing global activism and awareness of 'human rights' as 'women's rights'. The networks from international conferences surrounding the United Nations Decade for Women, the activities of the women appointed to the UN Committee on the Elimination of Discrimination Against Women, the growing number of women lawyers with a feminist consciousness, turned the attention of women activists to the moral cornerstone of international law, 'human rights'.

Awareness of women's human rights was heightened by the reports of barbaric systematic detentions and rapes of women being used as a deliberate strategy of war in the former Yugoslavia, even though Susan Brownmiller's 1975 book *Against Our Will*[3] had chronicled war as a tacit licence to rape. It was not until the fourth Geneva Convention in 1949 that the modern rules of war and international law expressly forbad the sexual abuse of women civilians. This provided that women should be protected 'in particular' against 'rape, enforced prostitution, or any form of indecent assault'.[4]

In the 1970s and 80s, a host of feminist non-governmental organisations focused on activism on female human rights, in the absence of any commitment from Amnesty International to move outside the traditional male-defined sphere. Organisations as diverse as Women Living under Muslim Laws, the Sisterhood Is Global Institute and the International Women's Rights Action Watch worked on specific cases and causes alongside the women 'on the inside', such as Dorothy Thomas at Human Rights Watch. Writers and activists such as Charlotte Bunch, Lori Heise, Nawal el Saadawi and Robin Morgan spread the word among women, and lawyers such as Asma Jahingir, Catherine MacKinnon, Rebecca Cook, Shelley Wright, Hilary Charlesworth, Christine Chinkin and Kathleen Mahoney confronted the males and the sexism of their theories, concepts, principles and practices in human rights law.

None of this would have been possible without the women survivors with the courage to be the test cases, the women who had not been independence fighters or liberation poets or trade union leaders or shadows of the forms of male activism and resistance that you had to be to qualify, for example, for adoption as a prisoner of conscience by Amnesty International.

The cases in Canada had been preceded by one in France. Amanita

Diop fled to France from Mali in 1991 to escape female circumcision.[5] Amanita was sold into marriage when she was seventeen. Four years later, before her intended marriage, her family as well as her fiancé (with whom she had had a sexual relationship) and his family determined that she must undergo circumcision. When she arrived in France, she applied for the status of political exile as a refugee, on the ground that if she were to be returned to Mali she would have 'a well-founded fear of violation'. She would be subjected to torture and 'cruel, inhuman and degrading treatment[6]'.

Her arrival in France coincided with public political discussion about whether immigrant communities in France should be able to perform female circumcision, or whether the procedure should be allowed in French public hospitals. The argument was that 'if we don't allow these practices in the public hospitals they will be performed backstreet in immigrant communities'. Edith Cresson, as Prime Minister, was in charge of immigration policy. Immigration was a big issue in the local government elections. A major rise in the support of the right-wing nationalist movement, led by Jean-Marie Le Pen, coincided with an horrendous violent backlash against immigrants. This was the political climate in which lawyer Linda Weil Curiel took on the case of Amanita Diop.

An international letter-writing campaign was launched, drawing Cresson's attention to the international human rights instruments which France had signed in addition to the UN Convention Relating to the Status of Refugees. These included the International Covenant on Civil and Political Rights (ICCPR) (see Appendix 2), the UN Convention Against Torture and the UN Convention on the Elimination of All Forms of Discrimination Against Women (CEDAW) (see Appendix 3).

The 1951 UN Convention Relating to the Status of Refugees defines a refugee as a person who has a well-founded fear of being persecuted for reasons of race, religion, nationality, membership of a particular social group or political opinion (note that sex is not a category here), is outside the country of his/her nationality and who is unable or, because of his/her fear, unwilling to avail him/herself of the protection of that country. The Refugee Appeal Committee in France acknowledged that Amanita's refusal to undergo the mutilation was in part because (and this was substantiated) circumcision had caused the death of her best friend. Diop's fear, then, was reasonable and well-founded.

When Amanita fled Mali, the government there allowed female

mutilation to be done as a surgical operation in state hospitals and made no effort to halt the practice. In the stipulations of the UN convention, a country must have both legislative and practical, workable prohibitions against torture, and not condone the activity in any way. Thus the Appeal Committee found that female excision, even when it was passively tolerated by any authority, would constitute persecution of those women who sought to avoid it.

This was very significant. It was the first time anywhere that a judicial authority had held that female circumcision was torture. But the Refugee Appeal Committee also found that Amanita Diop did not demonstrate sufficient evidence of having sought police protection in Mali before fleeing to France. It does not require any imagination to know what seeking police protection in Mali for this kind of situation would mean. While evidence of the incidence of female circumcision in Mali had been submitted, the committee claimed that the sole testimony it had received on the specific circumstances surrounding attempts to have Diop circumcised 'lacked verisimilitude'. This submission was the oral testimony made by Diop's pre-literate mother to a scribe in a Mali village. Cultured, literate, privileged French authorities required that the legal burdens of proof to be offered by pre-literate Mali women in a French tribunal were to be of the standard expected of Parisian citizens.

The appeal for refugee status was refused. Within hours of the announcement of that decision, the French government granted Diop a work permit – mainly because of the international attention the case had aroused. It should be noted particularly that it was a woman politician and Prime Minister who was ultimately in charge of Diop's future well-being.

Linda Weil Curiel appealed the decision on refugee status to the highest court in France. Diop was safe, but the question of her status remained. And, even if this court refused to grant her refugee status, her remedies were not exhausted.

Under both the Geneva Conventions and the ICCPR torture is outlawed. If a country has signed the Optional Protocol to the ICCPR, individuals who have exhausted all their domestic legal remedies in respect of human rights protected by the covenant may approach the United Nations Human Rights Committee (UNHRC) for a further hearing. As France is a member of the regional human rights body, appeal was also open to the European Commission on Human Rights.

The UN Convention Against Torture and Other Cruel, Inhuman or Degrading Treatment was adopted by the General Assembly in 1984 and came into force in 1987. As of November 1992, it had been ratified or acceded to by 70 states. In addition, under Article 22 of the convention, 28 states, including France, had recognised the competence of the special Committee Against Torture to receive and consider communications from or on behalf of individuals subject to its jurisdiction.[7]

The term 'cruel, inhuman or degrading treatment' has never been defined by the General Assembly, but it is intended to provide the widest possible protection against abuses, whether physical or mental. Torture has a specific definition under the 1949 Geneva Convention: 'The deliberate, systematic or wanton infliction of physical and mental suffering by one or more persons acting alone or on the orders of an authority to force another person to yield information, to make confession, or for any other reason which is an outrage to personal dignity'.[8] The Committee Against Torture's interpretations and applications of this convention are also based on the assumption that the terms and concepts are independent of any particular domestic national legal system, and of all dictionary definitions.

While Western governments have signed the convention on refugees, and few have entered any caveats or reservations about it because of the increasing number of asylum-seekers, these same governments are assiduously legislating all around the margins of the convention. They are doing so despite the convention's most effective limit that there is no reciprocal duty on states to grant asylum to asylum-seekers.

The best way to stop refugees entering your country is to ensure that they never get there in the first place. First, you have really tough visa requirements. A visa is hard enough to acquire for somebody in political danger, but it is desperately difficult for a woman who needs a passport first but is not allowed to apply for one in her own right, because only her father or her uncle or her brother or her custodian can apply for it on her behalf – because she is not really a person.

Then there are carrier sanctions initiated by the British government. These are liabilities for the personnel and the carriers, usually airlines, who bring refugees from one country to another. (A Mali air hostess helped Amanita Diop get to Belgium, and she travelled from there by road to France.) Immigration control has been delegated to airline personnel, who ask you for your passport and check that you have an entry visa for your destination. If you do not, the airline is liable for carrying you, and to a huge fine, plus costs, if you land without valid entry documents.

The 1951 Convention Relating to the Status of Refugees categorically prohibits the return of an asylum-seeker to a place where he or she is in danger. It states: 'governments must not expel or return a refugee in any manner whatsoever to a country where his or her life or freedom would be threatened.' As a result, there is now a growing propensity for the so-called developed world (and the French treatment of Diop is one example) to grant a lesser status than refugee, with all its entitlements. The convention on refugees makes it quite clear that you are either a refugee or you are not. But in Scandinavia, for example, asylum-seekers are granted B or C status; in Germany, you are called a 'privileged alien'; in Britain, you receive 'exceptional leave to remain'.[9]

In January–February 1991, during the Gulf conflict, I remember flying home to New Zealand. There had been an increase in the arrival of asylum-seekers. A number had false passports. Others had destroyed their travel documents in transit on the aeroplane. On landing, nobody was allowed to move. Immigration officials entered the plane and every passenger had to produce their passports while they were still in their seats. Only then were we able to disembark. This was categorically in breach of New Zealand's undertakings in terms of the Convention Relating to the Status of Refugees. Any person seeking asylum has the right to have their case heard. These procedures not only denied individuals an adequate opportunity to rebut any allegations, but they made it appear as though the New Zealand government was arbitrarily considering anyone seeking asylum during the Gulf conflict as a security risk. In my many years of travelling and countless times of re-entry into New Zealand, this was the only time I had ever been held on a plane to produce documents before I could disembark.

In the light of these examples we can readily understand that, after the landmark ruling in Canada, Nurjehan Mawani, the chairwoman of the Canadian immigration board, said she did not expect a flood of claims to result. 'Refugee determination is always on a case by case basis. I expect we may see a few more cases, but certainly no floodgates. If you look at the overall worldwide situation, only 5 per cent of world refugees are able to claim refugee status in the West, and of these the proportion of women is abysmally small. Women do not have the same mobility as men.'[10]

HUMAN RIGHTS AND THE UNITED NATIONS

The phrase 'human rights' as a term of art and a discipline is very recent. There are few classical antecedents. 'Human rights' arrived in English as a translation from the French 'droits de l'homme' – the rights of man – and wherever I examine civilisations that have espoused the 'rights of man' that is precisely what was intended. Men who were slaves were excluded, as were men who were not citizens of that particular state or republic. Women were most definitely left out. The laws of ancient Rome guaranteed to a select group of men rights to participate in elections, in government, in the judiciary and the judging of their fellow citizens.

The male-centred human rights documents include the Petition of Rights in 1628, the American Declaration of Independence, the French Declaration of the Rights of Man and the Citizen, and the American Bill of Rights. These formed the domestic legislative background leading to the 20th-century consideration of human rights.

Traditional international law assumed that a state had the authority to treat its own nationals as it saw fit. The protection of oppressed or endangered groups by international treaty started in the seventeenth and eighteenth centuries in matters of religious liberty. In the nineteenth century, international treaties were used to protect ethnic and racial groups and to combat slavery and the slave trade. In the 20th century, these agreements came to prominence in order to improve labour conditions, most notably through the International Labour Organisation (ILO), and to enable supervision of the administration of mandated territories. To a limited extent, an individual became a subject with enforceable rights in international law independent of her/his citizenship of a particular state.

When the League of Nations was established in 1920 there was little discussion of human rights. The key players in the league retained power in many colonial territories, and human rights was not a subject they were eager to see discussed. Among the limited records I can find was an attempt by the Japanese (who were one of the few non-white members) to introduce a resolution opposing racial discrimination. It was quickly countered, particularly by Britain, South Africa and Australia.[11]

Traditionally, international and domestic law have been separate systems. The international legal system was a law of nations incorporating the rights and duties of states in the international community.

No sovereign body existed with universally accepted lawmaking or conflict-resolving authority. After World War II, a very different emphasis was given to human rights with the establishment of the new United Nations.

When we are dealing with issues where the UN has a lot to do or to say, we have to develop the ability to read a whole new language, UN-ese. When we read something like the United Nations Universal Declaration of Human Rights, although we may believe we understand terms such as 'equal', 'political' or 'civil', inside the UN they may have a completely different meaning, depending on which political bloc moved to have that word in any document. The initial debates on human rights in the United Nations were fraught with East–West bloc tensions. For many years in UN debates, civil and political rights were claimed as 'rights for communists' and social and economic rights were claimed as 'rights for democrats', and countries from one bloc would not sign covenants that the other bloc had promoted.

Despite this stand-off, since 1948 more than 70 international human rights instruments have been developed inside the UN framework. Now, we need a little demystification here. Instruments (this is part of 'UN-ese') is the generic term that covers declarations, conventions, covenants, protocols, and the UN Charter. Conventions are not large gatherings of political parties. Protocols are not culturally sensitive behaviour codes. In international law there is a different legal power associated with each of these terms. Some have the power of a treaty; others are supposedly endowed with universal moral force, whatever that might be. Some instruments (such as that on torture) have protocols. These establish special committees as the form of tribunal which is recognised by the countries who sign the protocol. We will get used to the jargon as we go on.

There are four instruments in particular which state the key international human rights standards. The Charter of the United Nations deals with human rights seven times. When countries (nation states) apply to join the UN, they are supposed to 'sign on' to the Charter. Since at the same time a country is expected to pay dues, I had assumed that such a signature might effect a contract, but that is not the case.

The UN is not a sovereign body. Its decisions are generally expressed in the form of resolutions. The text-books argue that these resolutions derive their legal force more from the voluntary consensus of member states than from any sense of legal obligation under the UN Charter.

Principal human rights provisions in the UN Charter are found in the Preamble and Articles 55c and 56. Article 55 calls for respect for the principle of equal rights and self-determination of peoples, for the UN to promote conditions of economic and social progress, for universal respect for and observance of human rights, and for fundamental freedoms for all without distinction as to race, language, sex or religion. Article 56 states: 'All Members pledge themselves to take joint and separate action in co-operation with the organisation to the achievement of the purposes set forth in Article 55.'

A leading expert in international law, Oscar Schachter, argues that 'pledge' in this context denotes a legal obligation. His research shows that this language was not accidental and that the technical drafting committee of the United Nations meeting in San Francisco attached particular importance to this point. The intention was to constitute a legal commitment on the part of the members.

He writes: 'This provision would not mean that the Organisation would have the right to interfere with the domestic affairs of its members. But it in no way implies that the Pledge in Article 56 is without legal force. It is a commonplace in international law that States assume duties of a legal character which are not enforceable by international organs.' He continues: 'In more than one resolution adopted by the General Assembly, it is clearly stated that members have made a legal commitment to respect and observe human rights.'[12]

Schachter argues that the major rules of legal interpretation, 'intent' and 'effectiveness', reinforce each other. When they are taken together, the inescapable conclusion is that the pledge in Article 56 constitutes a legal commitment on the part of members to take action in co-operation with the organisation to achieve respect for and observance of human rights and fundamental freedoms for all.

Whatever Schachter's opinion, the pledge has not operated as a legal obligation. Nowhere was this more apparent than when the UN Security Council intervened to 'restore democracy' in Kuwait, a member state where women are denied the right to vote.

Human rights are often called 'fundamental' and 'universal'. Since 'fundamental' would mean that there were no circumstances in which they could be denied, that is simply rhetoric. 'Universal' expresses an ideal. In view of the pledge of the UN Charter, I would expect to find some obligations somewhere. Yet it has been frequently claimed that the Universal Declaration of Human Rights, a resolution adopted by the UN General Assembly in 1948 without dissent, is not binding anyway. It is drafted in general terms and states objectives and policies. We have Eleanor Roosevelt and a handful of other women present at San Francisco in 1948 to thank for pressing to have the word 'sex' appear in Article 2 as an area of discrimination.

There are nation states which have never voted in favour of this declaration – for example, Saudi Arabia. The declaration has also been used in some famous human rights defences in courts of law, even when the nation state prosecuting is a pariah in the international community. Nelson Mandela quoted extensively from it at his trial before his imprisonment in South Africa.

Substantial parts of the Universal Declaration of Human Rights have now become part of customary international law binding upon all states. In 1968, the UN International Conference on Human Rights adopted the Declaration of Teheran, stating that 'the Universal Declaration of Human Rights . . . constitutes an obligation for the members of the international community'.[13] The politics of nation states change, and the host state of the 1968 conference, Iran, in its current domestic practices is patently in breach of a significant number of articles in the declaration.

From 1948 the UN Charter and the Universal Declaration of Human Rights were the sole international human rights instruments, but the international community was impatient with their vague nature. As a result, the objectives were translated into two covenants. These are binding on the countries that sign them, and considered relevant in human rights jurisprudence in countries that have not signed.

ECONOMIC, SOCIAL AND CULTURAL RIGHTS

The International Covenant on Economic, Social and Cultural Rights (ICESCR) (see Appendix 1) covers the right to work and to reasonable conditions of employment, the right to form and join trade unions, social security rights, protection and assistance to the family, with special protection for children, adequate standards of living, the right to health, access to education, and the right to take part in scientific and cultural life.

ICESCR has no enforcement mechanism. While there are internationally agreed guidelines for compliance and reporting for countries that have signed the ICESCR, countries are obliged only to fulfil it 'progressively' according to their 'maximum available resources'. There are no UN mechanisms for individuals or groups to complain if a country that had signed this covenant has not delivered. By 1995, 115 countries had signed this covenant.

The Limburg Principles on the Implementation of the ICESCR were agreed to in 1987 by the UN Economic and Social Council to assist states who signed the ICESCR in their preparation and presentation of reports. Part IA observes that 'human rights and fundamental freedoms are indivisible and interdependent. Equal attention should be given to the implementation, promotion and protection of both civil and political, and economic, social and cultural rights.' It continues: 'There is no single road to their full realization . . . States Parties must at all times act in good faith.'

Part IB deals with the 'Interpretative Principles specifically relating to the Covenant'. In respect of Article 2(1), 'to take steps . . . by all appropriate means, including particularly the adoption of legislation', the principles state: 'At the national level States Parties shall use all appropriate means, including legislative, administrative, judicial, economic, social and educational measures . . . Legislative measures alone are not sufficient to fulfil the obligations of the Covenant . . . States Parties shall provide for effective remedies.'

In commenting on the undertaking 'to achieve progressively the full realization of the rights', the principles require 'States Parties to move as expeditiously as possible towards the realization of the rights. Under no circumstances shall this be interpreted as implying for States the right to defer indefinitely efforts to ensure full realization . . . The obligation of progressive achievement exists independently of the increase in resources; it requires effective use of resources available.'[14]

It all sounds wonderful. There is just a large gap between the lofty rhetoric of the Limburg Principles and individual access to any machinery to guarantee these rights.

CIVIL AND POLITICAL RIGHTS

In theory, the International Covenant on Civil and Political Rights (ICCPR) is stronger. When a country signs this covenant, it guarantees that these rights are 'immediately enforceable' in its domestic jurisdiction. Article 2 requires 'Each State Party . . . to take the necessary steps . . . to adopt such legislative or other measures as may be necessary to give effect to the rights recognized in the present Covenant'.

The list of rights is extensive. Specifically protected are the right to equality and non-discrimination; the right to effective judicial and other remedies; the right to life, including restricting the death penalty to the most serious crimes, prohibiting the imposition of that penalty on persons who are younger than eighteen or on pregnant women, and the gradual abolition of that penalty; protection of the individual from torture or other inhuman treatment or punishment; protection from servitude or forced labour; the right to liberty and security of the person; protection from imprisonment for inability to fulfil a contractual obligation; freedom of movement; protection of the alien from arbitrary expulsion; fair and public hearings; presumptions of innocence; procedural guarantees in due process; protection from double jeopardy; the non-retroactivity of offences and punishments. Freedom of thought, conscience and religion; freedom of opinion and expression, of seeking, receiving and imparting information; freedom from war propaganda and protection from religious and racial hatred; freedom of assembly; freedom of association in forming and joining trade unions; the right to marry; the equality of rights of spouses; protection of the family and the right of the child to special measures of protection – all these are covenanted. The right to take part in the conduct of public affairs directly and through freely chosen representatives; the right to access on general terms of equality to the public service; the right of ethnic, religious or linguistic minorities in the community, with other members of their group, to the enjoyment of their culture, language or religion; and strict limitations on the kinds of rights from which derogations are permissible in times of emergency complete the subject list. One hundred and twelve countries have ratified this covenant since 1976.

THE OPTIONAL PROTOCOL

If signatories to the ICCPR want to go further, they can sign the Optional Protocol to this covenant. The UN Human Rights Committee (UNHRC), established in Part IV of the covenant, can receive and consider 'communications' from individuals who claim to be victims of violations of the ICCPR in their own country. The protocol means that individuals who have exhausted the domestic legal remedies in pursuit of their claim can have access to the UNHRC. Because this committee does not have jurisdiction inside a nation state, we cannot call it a tribunal, we cannot say that it handles cases, we cannot say that it delivers judgements. We 'communicate' with them, and they 'communicate' with us. Their findings do have judicial force in the different regional Human Rights Commissions.[15] Sixty-seven countries have signed the Optional Protocol to the ICCPR, effectively saying that they guarantee to their citizens the right to take cases to the UNHRC.[16]

Rules of procedure are established to provide protection to governments from investigations into allegations that are vexatious or without substance. The communication must come from either an individual who is a victim of an alleged violation of the covenant or her/his authorised representative. The Optional Protocol 'is not designed for wide attacks on state legislation or government policy without identification of particular individuals who are prepared to pursue the claim'.[17] Wide attacks can be made, but identified individuals have to take the case to Geneva. The process does not allow for any group claim or class action. Whatever the particular patriarchal reasons for this prohibition, and however many groups it impacts upon, it certainly disadvantages women.

The UNHRC cannot make abstract rulings on potential consequences of some government policy or legislation. An individual cannot allege that some government policy may affect her/him at some future date.[18]

Two elements are closely connected here. General claims on behalf of groups cannot be made owing to lack of personal standing. This means the only entity that has personal standing before the Human Rights Committee is an individual. But an alleged victim can authorise another person, including a non-government organisation, to act on his/her behalf.

Particular groups, such as indigenous peoples, prisoners, homosexuals, migrant women, cannot take a general case to test government policy. Christine Chinkin cites the rejection of the communication from a non-government organisation which had formed a group of associations for the defence of the rights of disabled and handicapped people in Italy, and of representatives of associations who claimed they were themselves disabled, handicapped, or parents of such people. The UNHRC found the petition inadmissible on the ground of a lack of personal standing. The claims made by representatives on their own behalf were admissible with respect to standing, but were rejected because they did not present substantiated claims of having been victims in violation of the covenant.[19]

The UNHRC has, however, accepted communications on the same issue from a number of individuals, provided that each one can substantiate a claim as an individual victim. Using this method, class actions are possible.

Where communications are submitted on behalf of a victim, the authority of the author to make the claim must be justified. This can be legally established by appointment of a legal representative, through power of attorney, or created by close family ties.

Applicants must have sought legal remedies in their own country. That is the basic test. The protocol says that the application of local remedies must not be unnecessarily prolonged and that it must be effective and available for particular situations. The UNHRC has frequently repeated its view that the availability of remedies which are not reasonably evident cannot be invoked by the government to the detriment of the author and proceedings under the Optional Protocol.

There is no international system of legal aid to take a case to the UNHRC. In many of the countries which have signed the Optional Protocol, substantial domestic law is not covered by legal aid either. The question must then be asked: in terms of basic human rights, do you have to pursue a legal remedy you cannot afford if legal aid is not available? What is the standard of reasonableness operating here?

The UNHRC receives thousands of 'communications' a year. They are sorted in the secretary general's office. The Centre for Human Rights receives the cases that might proceed. The centre seeks clarification on certain points in communications they have received, and decides which communications are 'mere contact letters' and which are to be registered as 'communications' under the Optional Protocol.

In the UNHRC itself, there is a working group of five members who decide whether or not a communication is admissible. If it is admissible, the government is sent the text of the complaint. The government then has an opportunity to respond.

Lawyers are not sent to represent complainants in Geneva. All communication is done in writing. An individual complaint is made. The government makes its response. Then the UNHRC makes its determination based on all the written information as well as other documentation. There are no oral proceedings. The UNHRC does not take field trips to look at cases. There are no issues of taking an oath, or cross-examination, or legal representation.

There is also a long time-frame. The UNHRC meets for three weeks three times a year to deal with all communications. It usually takes a year to decide whether a case is admissible. Investigation of the substance of the complaint can take another year or more before the final outcome.

The individual must show at least a *prima facie* case of violation of a provision of the covenant. The UNHRC finds the complaint substantiated unless the government in question supplies sufficient evidence to refute the allegations. The government cannot simply deny the basis of the complaint.

Regardless of the finding, a government is under no obligation to change anything. After signing the covenant and the protocol, every government has to report every five years. The UNHRC will take that opportunity to cross-examine a government's representatives on action taken as a result of any finding under the protocol procedure. In addition, the UNHRC has a Special Rapporteur who follows up on government responses to substantiated complaints.

WOMEN AND THE UN MAZE

Many women have had just cause to pursue their rights to equality through this maze. Article 3 of the ICCPR reads: 'The States Parties to the present Covenant undertake to ensure the *equal right of men and women* to the enjoyment of all civil and political rights set forth in the present Covenant' (my emphasis).

Article 26 reads: 'All persons are equal before the law and are entitled without any discrimination to the equal protection of the law. In this respect, the law shall prohibit any discrimination and guarantee to all persons equal and effective protection against discrimination on any ground such as race, colour, sex, language, religion, political or other opinion, national or social origin, property, birth or other status.'

While the Optional Protocol to the ICCPR provides for protection of human rights, exhausting the process in accordance with all its rules and procedures is such a marathon that it would be surprising if any woman had ever had the necessary financial and legal resources, or the courage and tenacity to use them.

On the very rare occasion that a relevant case on female human rights has come before the UNHRC, it has held to the principle of equal protection of the sexes and to protections within the family – that the protections must be equal and not discriminatory, and that any adverse distinction based on sex is a violation of basic human rights. It has been more concerned historically to respond to cases of direct discrimination – that is, disparate *treatment* – rather than indirect discrimination – that is, *outcomes*.

The case of *Aumeeruddy Cziffra et al* v. *Mauritius* raised the issue of the rights to citizenship of the foreign spouses of women who were Mauritius nationals. In such cases, the foreign-born wives of men were entitled to citizenship, but not the foreign-born husbands of women nationals. Mauritius was not the only country to practise this form of discrimination.

The UNHRC found that: 'Where the Covenant requires a substantial protection as in Article 23[20], it follows from those provisions that such protection must be equal, that is to say not discriminatory, for example on the basis of sex . . . it follows also in this line of argument that the Covenant must lead to the result that the protection of a family cannot vary with the sex of the one or the other spouse. Though it may be justified for Mauritius to restrict the access of aliens to their territory and to expel them for security reasons, the Committee is of the view that the legislation which only subjects the foreign spouses of Mauritian women to those restrictions, but not foreign spouses of Mauritian men, is discriminatory with respect to Mauritian women and cannot be justified by security requirements . . . The Committee therefore finds that there is a violation of Articles 2(1), 3 and 26.'[21]

The case of *Broeks* v. *The Netherlands* raised major issues of importance, especially in the relationship between the ICCPR and other UN human rights covenants. The substantive issues in the case were that Mrs Broeks was denied the right to an unemployment benefit because she was married. She claimed that were she a man, married or unmarried, the law in question would not have deprived her of the benefit. She claimed a violation of Article 26 of the ICCPR on the grounds of sex and status.

The procedural issues included the competence of the UNHRC to examine rights also set out under the ICESCR. The Netherlands contended that Article 26 of the ICCPR could not be invoked in respect of a right that was explicitly provided for under Article 9 of the ICESCR. Article 9 of the ICESCR reads: 'The States Parties to the present Covenant recognize the right of everyone to social security, including social insurance.'

In considering this question, the UNHRC 'perused the summary records of the discussion that took place in the Commission on Human Rights in 1948, 1949, 1950 and 1952 and in the Third Committee of the General Assembly in 1961 ... The discussions were ... inconclusive and cannot alter the conclusion arrived at by the ordinary means of interpretation . . . Article 26 does not merely duplicate the guarantees already provided for in Article 2. It derives from the principle of equal protection of the law without discrimination, as contained in Article 7 of the Universal Declaration of Human Rights, which prohibits discrimination in law and in practice in any field regulated and protected by public authorities. Article 26 is thus concerned with the obligations imposed on States in regard to their legislation and the application thereof.'

The UNHRC said that what was at issue was not the progressive establishment of social security in the Netherlands, but whether the legislation violated 'the prohibition against discrimination in Article 26 of the ICCPR, and the guarantee given there to everyone regarding equal and effective protection against discrimination'. In the Broeks case the committee found that there had been discrimination on the ground of sex that was not reasonable.[22]

LEAVING WOMEN OUT

That so few cases of sex discrimination have been tested by the UNHRC seems outrageous. In the context of these UN human rights instruments, the continuing substantive and conceptual neglect in the international community of human rights abuses against women is an unquestionable hypocrisy. Compare, for example, the actions of nation states against apartheid or racial discrimination with the inactivity against gender discrimination and sexual segregation in many parts of the world. Compare the efforts to outlaw torture with the lack of emphasis on rape, gender-specific torture, sexual surgery and genital mutilation. Compare the efforts in the international community to outlaw and condemn slavery with the inattention to the practice of trafficking in women, forced prostitution, forced marriages or sex tourism. There is great advocacy for fair trials and due process for all 'persons', but where are the calls for a woman's right to appear before a court at all, to bear witness on an equal basis with men, or to be a complainant for equitable treatment?

Some countries have adopted laws and procedures to prevent importation of goods made by forced labour or convict labour or where worker rights are violated, but where have any laws been established to forbid importing goods produced by women who suffer gross employment discrimination? At different times the US, the European Community and the Commonwealth have asked for curtailment of foreign aid or investment or military assistance to countries where there are gross violations of internationally recognised human rights. But where and when, and significantly in Kuwait, have women's basic rights been considered as part of this picture?

The excuses are the same old ones. First, they say these abuses are private, not public. It is the old split that once existed in law, in economics and in political philosophy, that women lead private lives and men lead public lives. Public lives are subject to scrutiny and legislation, not the abuses committed on women and children in the 'security' of their homes.

Then there is the excuse that says the state is not the active agent in most abuses. But the state does not have to be an active agent. Rebecca Cook writes: 'If a state facilitates, conditions, accommodates, tolerates, justifies, or excuses private denials of women's rights, the state will bear responsibility. The state will be responsible not directly for the private acts, but for its own lack of diligence to prevent, control, correct, or discipline such private acts through its own executive, legislative, or judicial organs.'[23]

The state just has to be acting in a permissive capacity. I was involved in 1992 in assisting a Fijian woman who was applying for refugee status in the US. She had a history of suffering domestic violence. She had a non-molestation order in force in Fiji, and a history of complaining to the police station and the police for not enforcing the non-molestation order when it was breached.

In such a case, the state is in complicity with the battery, since the state has tolerated and excused private acts that have been subject to judicial procedure, and has not prevented or controlled them when recourse to the state agents was sought. States are legally accountable for breaches of international instruments that are attributable or imputable to them. There are three distinct theories of government accountability: government agency, government complicity by failure to act, and government responsibility for the unequal application of the law. All three were at issue here.

A major excuse used to exclude abuses of women from the ambit of human rights instruments is that the practice is one of custom or religion. This was present in the Canadian and French cases cited at the beginning of this essay. Before these precedents, custom or religion was far more important than multiple abuses of women.

The final frequent excuse for excluding the reality of women's lives from the parameters of traditional human rights norms is that women have social and economic rights only, and not civil or political ones. This puts us right back in the Roman Empire, where we were simply not citizens. All of these kinds of excuses can be found in past debates by international jurists whenever the question or the specific illustration of female human rights has been raised.

Historically, the sources and evidence of international law have included treaties and conventions, custom, general principles of law recognised by civilised nations and, as subsidiary sources, judicial decisions and the teachings of qualified publicists and academics. But 'accelerating technological, economic, and political changes in the world community require speedier means for developing the law than traditional processes can supply. There has resulted a search for new methods of making international law less uncertain and more responsive to new needs and conditions.

'A contributory cause of this search has been the desire of many new nations of Africa and Asia to find ways to participate effectively in shaping and changing a body of norms in the creation of which they have no voice. In recent years, the search for new methods of clarifying and developing international law has centred on the role of international organizations, and particularly the United Nations General Assembly and its subsidiary organs.'[24]

It is important to recognise that changes are necessary for states who were not part of the drafting processes of treaties and other instruments to which they are now party. But I wonder how much that latitude would willingly be extended to women. A former judge of the International Court of Justice, Alejandro Alvarez has commented on the way a treaty or text acquires a life of its own once it has been established. In his view, treaties must always be interpreted within the context of contemporary life (rather than read by the intentions of those who framed them). But the courts, the tribunals, the UN committees of international law, and the representatives at the UN debating and signing and ratifying human rights instruments, are overwhelmingly men. What faith could any woman have that her 'contemporary life' would be paramount in interpretation?

Radhika Coomaraswamy writes that 'the barriers to the implementation of human rights are two-fold. The lack of proper implementation machinery to make rights real in the lives of women is an obstacle, as is women's lack of awareness of the rights machinery that would empower them. The more formidable barrier is the refusal to accept the values in and of themselves, an ideological resistance to human rights for women.'[25]

Justice Bertha Wilson of the Supreme Court of Canada acknowledged: 'It is impossible for a man to respond, even imaginatively . . . because it is outside the realm of his personal experience . . . [and] because he can only relate to it by objectifying it . . . The history of the struggle for human rights from the eighteenth century on has been the history of men.'[26]

We have come to expect comments from the rare women who make it to legal or political office such as that held by Bertha Wilson. It is so unusual for a man in a similar situation to make such comment that I do not expect it. I was delighted, then, to hear the Hon. Mr. Justice E. Dumbutshena, Chief Justice of the Supreme Court of Zimbabwe, speak at the ninth Commonwealth Law Conference. He remarked: 'It is time to question some of our male-defined legal principles, such as "rational", "objective", and "neutral". We all need a balanced legal consciousness. Abstract legal concepts, such as causation, duty and fault arise from concrete, recognizable human experiences. Law is socially constructed and can therefore alter social practices and policies that may have adversely affected a disempowered group such as women.' His key example in calling for the enforcement of the rights of women was the recognition of the value of all the productive and domestic work of women.[27]

I am not a one-way feminist. As a former politician I know that a diverse range of strategies is needed by women to secure any changes in the old order. I am not interested in any approach which pretends that legal instruments and procedures are the answer. There are activist political campaigns available to make a more significant impact on women's oppression than recourse to an international system which can apparently do little to ensure that the rights are enjoyed in practice. But I had to explore what use, if any, human rights jurisprudence might be to women's inequality in parliamentary representation, and to the invisibility of women's unpaid work.

A CONFERENCE WITH THE ACADEMICS

The General Assembly announced in 1989 that we are in the middle of the Decade of International Law. It is always an adventure to see if there is any expectation that women might get involved in such a decade. Unwittingly, I had already participated. In 1991 I attended a conference on 'The Role of Consent and the Development of International Law at the End of the Twentieth Century'. This was attended largely by male international lawyers, academics in particular. They were all from the West. No one representing the developing world was present. You could count the number of women giving papers on the fingers of one hand. It was an interesting experience, but my interest in it was very different from that of the male attendees. Following this three-day conference, and for just one day, the first conference on 'Feminist Approaches to International Law' was held. Some of the men stayed on for this conference, at which I had been asked to speak. It was a cathartic opportunity to voice the thoughts I had had at the 'men's' conference.

I began my speech as follows:

> I must for the sake of bridging the gap between the past three days' activities and today, when the word 'gender' is introduced to the equation, talk about the conceptual or methodological approach that might be brought to the study of international law to make it both rigorous and sophisticated. There has been debate this week, you will understand, that either you are rigorous or you are sophisticated, not both. And so I want to address myself to some of these matters as quickly as I can.
>
> It has not been unusual this week to hear international lawyers say, 'Oh but that is a question of politics'. There has been an insinuation that international law exists in a vacuum. That these academics serve most of their lives in an oxygen tent. To say or even to suggest that international law is unsullied by politics is a characteristic that can only be declared by those whose interests are totally guided by those in power. Only those people have the luxury of suggesting they need not have a concern for politics. I would be extraordinarily distressed (for it would be a statement of disturbing alienation) to hear any women, or any male other than a white man from the developed world, speak in such a way.
>
> As I've sat through papers and in the question and answer sessions that followed, I've heard that 'law is a digester of social reality', that 'we would not want to assimilate law to social reality, that law is part of social reality'. All of this took place with the analogy of a soccer field

you understand. About whether or not we were backs or forwards or offside or in the crowd. I took the liberty of asking a question that came from right outside the stadium which was, 'What was actually meant by social reality?' And in a characteristic dismissal, which I recall as being typical of my treatment as a first-year law student, I was advised that I should ask a sociologist. That was the full extent of the response. [28]

I noticed, and I listened, and one of the tricks of the questions of gender and international law was to hear what was in the silence, because international law and the law of human rights on gender is about silences. That was what I was listening for. And silences were overwhelmingly what I heard in that week.

The introduction of a gender perspective to international law requires asking all the fundamental questions all over again: looking carefully at language, making connections, not making assumptions, and taking great care to see clearly what is said or written. It requires a view from outside the cocoon of patriarchy.

From a gender perspective, then, the questions are not about the role of consent, but about its very nature, the presumption involved in assuming that the majority of the world's population, unasked, not referred to, invisible, taken for granted, have 'consented' to anything. It does involve asking just what is the nature of justice, of political power and of society.

Academics are certainly familiar with Denis Lloyd's description of 'norms' as 'regulations setting forth how *men* are to behave'[29] (my emphasis), and in international law that is precisely what norms describe: how *men* are to behave. The Universal Declaration of Human Rights makes this absolutely clear in Article 1: human beings should act towards one another in a spirit of *brotherhood*. More than half the people on the planet are physically incapable of that particular spiritual relationship.

The concepts at issue are not just a matter of 'add women and stir'. Nothing alters in the power dynamic of who chooses, who judges, who defines, who rules, who imposes, until the whole is exposed to questioning at the most basic levels. It invites a new vision with which to read any sentence that might hitherto have appeared non-controversial.

Even if we consider practice, and look to reality to see whether general principles about human rights come from there, I am nervous about whose reality we are describing. In one discussion session,

Prof. Oscar Schachter pressed this approach, saying that he could be ecumenical about principles and that he found them in the church or the mosque or wherever. His examples were all patriarchal institutions. You will not find my principles in any such institution. You might find my principles gathering water at the well, you might find my principles sitting in a circle around the water hole doing the laundry, you might even find my principles at the check-out counter in the supermarket, but you will not find my general principles about human rights in a patriarchal institution, as ecumenical as you want to be.

Professor of international law Hilary Charlesworth recalls: '[The men] listened to papers on a wide range of topics. Some papers ignored the academic conventions of detached analysis, they were angry, passionate and emotional. Worst of all they were personal. The sprinkling of men in the room no doubt felt rather vulnerable, atypically surrounded by women and having their discipline . . . attacked in an ungentlemanly fashion. A day after the conference one of our colleagues remonstrated that while he was all in favour of academic debate on serious issues, the worst aspect of the proceedings was that they had managed to estrange and upset our eminent guests. In particular we had alienated Oscar.'[30]

I remember Oscar Schachter sitting with his wife in the centre forward position of the main body of the hall throughout that day and listening attentively. I remember being approached by his wife over several comments I had to make, and being asked for references. Neither person seemed estranged or upset.

Perhaps some of these highly qualified academics were as insulted by the feminist perspectives and approaches as we had been for the previous three days by patriarchy. But I did learn a lot from listening to them, and I wanted to put it to good use. In 1992, I started to investigate international human rights law from the stand-point of our inequality in Parliament. In terms of my own country's obligations in international law, I had to discover what was and what was not applicable.

'ON EQUAL TERMS WITH MEN' – A CASE STUDY

Article 38 of the Statute of the International Court of Justice sets down three major and two subsidiary sources of international law. The three major sources are international conventions, international custom as evidence of general practice accepted as law, and general principles of law recognised by civilised nations. The two subsidiary sources of international law are judicial decisions of the domestic courts and the teachings of the most highly qualified publicists of the various nations. These sources are described, in an irony that is not lost on me, as 'hard' and 'soft' law. Just as in pornographic material, 'soft' law establishes custom and is generally described as a 'norm'.

New Zealand had signed the key conventions (ICCPR and CEDAW). It was not difficult to locate those paragraphs in different articles that would be under contention in any challenge. In addition to the equality guarantees of Articles 2(1) and 26, Article 3 of the ICCPR (see Appendix 2) requires the states parties to 'undertake to ensure the *equal right of men and women* [my emphasis] to the enjoyment of all civil and political rights set forth in the present Covenant'.

Article 25 requires that 'Every citizen shall have *the right and the opportunity, without any . . . distinctions . . .* [including distinctions on the basis of sex] . . . *and without unreasonable restrictions* [my emphasis]:

a) To take part in the conduct of public affairs, directly or through freely chosen representatives

b) To vote and to be elected at genuine periodic elections . . .

c) To have access, on general terms of equality, to public service in his [*sic*] country.'

The convention articles are one thing, interpretation of them is another. For the moment, while I am pursuing the sources of international law that might apply to this question, I will assemble the sources before turning to interpretation.

Not surprisingly, several articles of the Convention on the Elimination of All Forms of Discrimination Against Women (CEDAW) are relevant (see Appendix 3). Article 1 states: 'For the purpose of the present Convention, the term "discrimination against women" shall mean *any distinction, exclusion or restriction* made on the basis of sex which has the effect or purpose of impairing or nullifying the recognition, enjoyment or *exercise by women . . . on a basis of equality* [my emphasis] of men and women, of human rights and fundamental freedoms in the political . . . field'.

In Article 2(d) states parties undertake: 'To refrain from engaging in any act or practice of discrimination against women and to ensure that public authorities and institutions shall act in conformity with this obligation'. Both local and central government and their elected representatives are 'public authorities and institutions'.

Article 3 guarantees that: 'States Parties shall take . . . in particular in the political field, all appropriate measures, including legislation, to ensure the full development and advancement of women, for the purpose of guaranteeing them the exercise and enjoyment of human rights and fundamental freedoms *on a basis of equality with men*' (my emphasis).

Article 4 is in effect the affirmative action clause. It reads: 'Adoption by States Parties of temporary special measures aimed at accelerating *de facto* equality between men and women shall not be considered discrimination'.

Article 7(b) reads: 'States Parties shall . . . in particular . . . ensure to *women, on equal terms with men, the right* [my emphasis] . . . to partici-pate in the formulation of government policy and the implementation thereof and to hold public office and perform all functions at all levels of government'. This article is particularly important to us in the context of the communication from the UNHRC in *Broeks* v. *The Netherlands*, namely that the rights guaranteed in CEDAW were effectively details of the rights guaranteed in Articles 2 and 26 of the ICCPR.

For good measure I include Article 8 of CEDAW: 'States Parties shall take all appropriate measures to ensure to women, on equal terms with men and without any discrimination, the opportunity to represent their Governments at the international level and to participate in the work of international organizations.'

As a source, whatever the debate about meaning, the covenants are concrete. Other sources of international human rights law have both a selective and an illusive quality. In customary international law, states are seen to consent to the creation and application of international legal rules in terms of their general practice. Customary consent is not usually explicit, but evidence includes resolutions and recommenda-tions of international conferences and public interest organisations, and the declarations of states. This sounds all very well, but it soon becomes obvious that there is a hierarchy operating in human rights issues, and that decades of consents to recommendations on ending sexism are not ranked highly on the patriarchal nation state agenda.

What is more, the 'customary' behaviour of men towards women in a religious, ethnic or 'normal' context is generally used to defeat any calls for women's human rights that would inconvenience 'custom-ary', 'normal' male behaviour, whether of individuals or collectively protected by the patriarchal state. Andrew Byrnes comments:

A failure to be aware of and raise issues of gender can result in a distorted picture of patterns of human rights abuses, and can lead to an androcentric definition of substantive norms ... Quite simply, if you are not looking for something (or at least aware that it might exist), then your chances of finding it are significantly reduced. The importance of being aware that sex and gender may be significant, asking what the position of women is and whether that is reflected in universal norms and taken into account in designing responses to human rights abuses, has been demonstrated time and time again. However, it appears that too often, this dimension of a situation is not explored thoroughly, and such examination as there is limited to relatively formalistic invocation of androcentric standards of non-discrimination.[31]

Then there are the subsidiary sources of international law. In terms of Article 38 of the statute outlining sources,[32] just what are 'general principles' of international human rights law, and who decides what they are? Who are these 'most highly qualified publicists' to be consulted, and how many of them have ever been women? And just what is the relationship between a custom and a principle and a norm? Is one more important than another? And who decides when one of them changes from one category to another?

This was getting to be a little confusing, and more than a little ridiculous. I thought I would seek some clarity by consulting one of the most 'highly qualified publicists' of international law, Oscar Schachter. I figured that 'alienated Oscar' might be able to unravel the indeterminate boundaries of international law for me.

No such luck. He wrote: 'The two principal categories – law-making treaties and general custom – have become entangled with each other and with a variety of normative declarations that do not fall into either category ... Apart from these, there are the multitude of international resolutions, recommended standards, memoranda of understandings, gentlemen's agreements, codes of conduct and parallel declarations ... calling for compliance by governments in question. Whether or not such texts are entitled to be regarded as international law or as some near relative has given rise to a considerable body of writing and a variety of views. However labelled, these international texts and instruments are part of, or closely related to, the law-making processes (and cannot be ignored) even if they do not fit comfortably into the categories of Article 38 "sources".' Of these 'norms', Schachter writes further: 'Governments could vote for them (in the past) on the comforting assumption that their non-obligatory character left compliance entirely to government discretion. Their "consent" in such cases was quite different from consent to a treaty.'[33]

According to Prof. Rosalyn Higgins, 'what one identifies as international law will be closely dependent upon what one believes to be the basis of legal obligation'.[34] Alain Pellet debates this strongly: 'Law is not as simple as that. There is no doubt that binding obligations are part of law, but law also includes permissions, recommendations, incentives, orientations etc.'[35]

Now, of course, once I was into this literature it became fairly obvious that the 'highly qualified publicists' vaunted by the International Court in Article 38 as being among the sources for international law could not agree on what does and does not qualify. So I thought I would look at the question from the point of view of the practices adopted by my country in dealing with so-called 'soft law'.

If we are interested in expanding on the key source – for example, an article in a legally binding covenant – and if 20 years of soft law on an issue is consistently supported, a formidable case can be established.

We can argue the soft law approach because, in nearly all of these bodies where 'resolutions, recommended standards, memoranda of understandings, gentlemen's agreements, codes of conduct and parallel declarations' are made, a quasi-parliamentary procedure is operating. Any member state which wants to speak can speak. Amendments are tabled, debated and voted on. There is a majority voting procedure, just as in a parliamentary law-making body, and this replicates the General Assembly's voting procedure in passing covenants.

Some governments vote for these declarations and resolutions in a cynical and cavalier fashion, because they are seemingly non-obligatory. This is not the approach of the New Zealand government. I have been fortunate in a number of forums to have had the experience of representation, and to watch the process for myself. If New Zealand does not agree with a paragraph, it does not vote for it. If it does not agree with a platform of action or proposal at any stage, it enters reservations on specific paragraphs, or rejects the whole. Its behaviour in international forums is consistent, no matter how soft the resulting resolutions or communiqué might be, and regardless of the nature of the forum.

A review of soft law over 20 years also demonstrates a changing emphasis and often a changing interpretation. Established law, especially international human rights covenants, can scarcely be said to be regularly updated, either by amendments or through judicial precedent.

The Restatement of the Foreign Relations Law of the United States makes this comment: freedom from 'gender discrimination as states' policy . . . may already be a principle of customary international law'. The restatement is careful to note that customary international human rights law continues to develop and that the list of customary human rights laws 'is not closed'.[36] It might then well be argued that the resolutions of 'soft law' are the significant updating exercises.

So what has New Zealand accepted in soft law? There are now two decades of resolutions, recommendations and platforms of action from UN World Conferences for Women in Mexico City (1975), Copenhagen (1980), Nairobi (1985) and Beijing (1995). Typical of the language of these documents is paragraph 86 of 'The Nairobi Forward Looking Strategies for the Advancement of Women': 'Governments and political parties should intensify efforts to stimulate and ensure equality of participation by women in all national and local legislative bodies and to achieve equity in the appointment, election and promotion of women to high posts in executive, legislative and judiciary branches in these bodies.'[37]

At its 39th session in New York in 1995, the UN Commission on the Status of Women addressed the issue as a first priority in 'Critical Areas of Concern'.[38] Key passages in the report of the secretary general read: 'the advancement of women in other areas will be jeopardized if equality in political participation and decision making is not achieved. Reference was also made to the close reciprocal relationship between the general advancement of women and the participation of women in politics . . . therefore, the advancement of women should be considered a priority in terms of national decision making, and women should participate as full partners in all those decisions . . . '

'The main trend in the foreseeable future is the continuing lack of equitable participation by women in political decision making. It deprives women of important rights and responsibilities as citizens. Therefore, women's interests and perspectives cannot influence key decisions, which has consequences for society as a whole and for future generations – for example, on national budgets and major reforms or socio-economic models to be followed. This situation is not only discriminatory to women but is also disadvantageous to society, which is deprived of women's skills and their distinct perspectives.'[39]

This language is not limited to the women's conferences and commissions. The UN World Conference on Human Rights in Vienna in 1993, the UN Social Development Conference in Copenhagen in 1995, and the UN Conference on Environment and Development (or Earth Summit) in Rio de Janeiro in 1992 produced similar statements. In the objectives proposed for national governments, the Earth Summit endorsed the following: 'To increase the proportion of women decision makers' and to take active steps to implement 'policies and establish plans to increase the proportion of women involved as decision makers'.[40]

The Vienna Declaration and Programme of Action of the World Conference on Human Rights, 'deeply concerned by various forms of discrimination and violence, to which women continue to be exposed all over the world', stated that 'the full and equal participation of women in political, civil, economic, social and cultural life at the national, regional and international levels and the eradication of all forms of discrimination on the grounds of sex are priority objectives of the international community'.[41]

In a vicarious manner, this soft law is endorsed in further international forums – in the Harare Commonwealth Declaration of 1991, for example, or at the Commonwealth Heads of Government Meeting in New Zealand in 1995, where the communiqué 'urged member governments to adopt legislation and develop national strategies to promote the advancement of women in accordance with the strategic objectives, actions and priorities adopted by the United Nations Fourth World Conference on Women, held in Beijing'.[42]

The latest Inter-Parliamentary Union report states that the number of female parliamentarians has actually fallen from a high of 14.8 percent in 1988 to 11.3 percent worldwide in 1995. The report commented that 'women remain sidelined at all levels of decision making, especially in politics'.[43] In September 1995 politicians from 57 nations signed a declaration urging governments to lift the number of women in elected and appointed bodies to at least 50 percent by the year 2005.[44] New Zealand legislator Lianne Dalziel commented: 'How can Parliaments be representative of the population if they don't really represent the gender balance of our societies?' Her colleague Christine Fletcher added: 'Parliaments need to change to accommodate the woman legislator because, at present, you've got to be a masochist to be a legislator.'[45]

Key domestic judicial institutions have reported on the effects of such inequality. The Law Reform Commission in Australia stated: 'The equal participation of women in political institutions and the legislative process is clearly essential if laws are to give equal weight to the concerns, needs and perspectives of women. Not only does the relative absence of women from positions of political power help undermine the serious consideration of women's claims to equality, but legislation is the only means of effecting change in the law quickly and directly.'[46]

Heads of the major UN agencies have stated their opinions. UN Development Programme Administrator, James Speth, told the Beijing conference: 'The doors to economic and political power for women are barely open. Today it is a man's world instead of a woman and man's world. Specific targets must be set for moving women into positions of decision-making power [because] in most of the world's countries, women are virtually excluded from lofty realms of political power . . . Men literally call the shots.'[47]

Now I would be very interested to know whether James Speth would ever be deemed a 'highly qualified publicist' in the terms of Article 38 of the Statute of the International Court of Justice. Would the Chief Law Commissioner of Australia qualify? (That's a trick question, really, because at the time of the research and publication of the report quoted above, the Chief Law Commissioner was Elizabeth Evatt, former chair of CEDAW, and member of the UN Human Rights Committee.) Does the Secretary General of the United Nations qualify, or the Secretary General of the Commonwealth, or is it only professors of law such as those I met and listened to in Canberra?

If the United Nations Development Plan is regarded as reflecting principles, customs or norms in international human rights, then the situation is not one of equality. The 1995 Human Development Report states: 'the free workings of economic and political processes are unlikely to deliver equality of opportunity because of the prevailing inequities in power structures. When such structural barriers exist Government intervention is necessary both through comprehensive policy reforms and through a series of affirmative actions.' It notes: 'in no society today do women enjoy the same opportunities as men. Women continue to be denied equal opportunities for political and economic participation.' Later it states: 'political space belongs to all citizens but men monopolise it'. It concludes: 'equality is not a techno-cratic goal. It is a wholesale political commitment.'[48]

Many similar comprehensive documents might be quoted, but these examples will have to suffice if we are to move on in our enquiry. All the words are very well, but just what do they mean in international human rights law, and how might they apply in a domestic context. What options are available to test a nation state's pledges and obliga- tions in respect of all the votes and signatures registered over the years?

TESTING THE SYSTEM

Nations differ substantially in their constitutional arrangements and their domestic legal procedures. New Zealand has no formal consti- tution, no Charter of Rights such as the Canadians have. The New Zealand Bill of Rights does not override other legislation, and the Human Rights Commission has recommendatory power only. Since 1893, the Electoral Act has given all citizens the right to vote and to stand at elections. That was the formal equality. But when have we ever been represented 'on equal terms with men'?

I sought advice from a range of lawyers. There was no equality or electoral legislation which appeared clearly able to be tested before the courts, even in seeking a declaratory judgement. The procedure I decided to pursue was to petition the New Zealand Parliament. After all, successive governments had signed the international human rights documents. Petitioning Parliament was undoubtedly a domestic legal procedure.

There was another strategic reason for choosing this course. Rule 408 of the then Standing Orders of the House of Representatives stated that the House would not receive or consider any petition from a person who had not exhausted his or her legal remedies. The receipt of the petition and a hearing would eliminate any argument as to whether or not legal remedies had been exhausted.

The timing was significant. There was to be a referendum on the voting system at the 1993 general election.[49] It would mean that the issue of political representation would be legislatively before Parlia- ment for a year or more. In addition, in 1993 New Zealand commemo- rated 100 years of women's suffrage, a most appropriate time to address the subject.

I contacted two friends and political activist colleagues, Georgina Kirby, former president of the Maori Women's Welfare League, and Jocelyn Fish, former president of the National Council of Women, who willingly agreed to be co-petitioners. We met and drafted the petition 'prayer'. It read: 'to redress the imbalance of 1126 men and only 36 women on the roll of the New Zealand House of Representatives, and to establish a truly representative democracy, we request a change in the Electoral Act 1956 to ensure equality of, and parity in, gender representation in New Zealand's elected representatives.'

The petition was launched on 8 March 1993, International Women's Day, and tabled in the New Zealand Parliament in September 1994 by women parliamentary representatives of all parties at that time. While signatures were being collected, I began work on a brief for the team of lawyers who had agreed to assist us in our submission.[50]

The two key terms for investigation were 'equality' and 'discrimination'. The *Concise Oxford Dictionary* entry on 'equality' states: 'equal: the same in number, evenly balanced. M.E. f. L. aequalis (aequus even): equality: condition of being equal.' Equality in the Aristotlean tradition, and adopted in law, has been 'formal equality'. Formal equality involves gender-neutral treatment, the principle of treating everyone the same. Discrimination is overt, such as denying women the right to vote or to stand for public office, or excluding them from entry into different professions.

Paul Hunt explains:

> Formal equality has serious limitations, it assumes that by removing gendered legal barriers, men and women of similar talent and motivation will enjoy the same opportunities and achieve the same successes. Further, formal equality treats discrimination as if it were an aberration which can be eliminated by extending the same rights and entitlements to all. Formal equality is blind to entrenched structural inequalities, it ignores actual social and economic disparities between groups and individuals. By constructing standards which appear to be neutral, it embodies a set of particular needs and experiences which derive from a socially privileged group. In this way formal equality may actually reinforce inequality.[51]

The model of formal equality uses a male standard of equality and renders women copies of their male counterparts. Thus women are forced to argue either that they are the same as men and should be treated the same, that they are different but should be treated as if they were the same, or that they are different and should be accorded special treatment.[52]

Hilary Charlesworth argues[53] that the norm of non-discrimination contained in both the human rights covenants is to place women in the same position as men in the public sphere. The activities of the

Commission on the Status of Women have generally been informed by the same approach. Thus the international prohibition on sex discrimination promises equality to women who attempt to conform to a male model, and offers little to those who do not. Hilary Charlesworth contends that the measure of equality in Article 1 of CEDAW is still a male one. And the discrimination it prohibits is confined to accepted human rights and fundamental freedoms. If these rights and freedoms can be shown to be defined in a gendered way, access to them will be unlikely to promote any real form of equality.

If our submission was to be confined to the language of the covenants, that might have been the end of the argument. But they are, as I have demonstrated, the coat-hangers for further articles of human rights garb. The UNHRC is authorised to make general comments under Article 40(4) of the ICCPR. It has used this power to develop a jurisprudence of the ICCPR articles and to improve the quality of reporting under it. General comments are perceived by the UNHRC to be a source expanding on and clarifying the protections of the covenant.

The UNHRC general comment on discrimination in 1989 refers to CEDAW Article 1 and adopts the same concept. 'The Committee believes that the term discrimination as used in the Covenant, should be understood to imply any distinction, exclusion, restriction or preference on the grounds of sex etc. which has the purpose or effect of nullifying or impairing the recognition, enjoyment or exercise by all persons on an equal footing of all rights and freedoms.'[54] In 1990 the chairman of UNHRC, Justice Rajsoomer Lallah, described the general comments as 'gradually acquiring an authoritative character as representing generally acceptable standards'.[55]

On non-discrimination, the UNHRC stated that:

> The principle of equality sometimes requires States Parties to take affirmative action in order to diminish or eliminate conditions which cause or help to perpetuate discrimination prohibited by the Covenant. For example, in a State where the general conditions of a certain part of the population prevent or impair their enjoyment of human rights, the State should take specific action to correct those conditions. Such action may involve granting for a time to the part of the population concerned certain preferential treatment in specific matters as compared with the rest of the population. As long as such action is needed to correct discrimination in fact, it is a case of legitimate differentiation under the Covenant.

In respect of Article 2(2), the UNHRC stated that the grounds of discrimination mentioned 'are not exhaustive'. It continued: '*De facto* discrimination occurring as a result of the unequal enjoyment of economic, social and cultural rights, on account of a lack of resources or otherwise, should be brought to an end as speedily as possible.'

'Special measures taken for the sole purpose of securing adequate advancement of certain groups or individuals requiring such protection as may be necessary in order to ensure to such groups or individuals equal enjoyment of economic, social and cultural rights shall not be deemed discrimination, provided, however, that such measures do not, as a consequence, lead to the maintenance of separate rights for different groups and that such measures shall not be continued after their intended objectives have been achieved.'

Finally, the UNHRC general comment describes systemic discrimination as 'a complex of directly and/or indirectly discriminatory (or subordinating) practices which operate to produce general . . . disadvantage for a particular group'.[56] The UNHRC also directs that 'when reporting on Articles 2(1), 3 and 36 of the Covenant States Parties usually cite provisions of their Constitution or Equal Opportunities Laws with respect to equality of persons. While such information is of course useful the committee wishes to know if there remain any problems of discrimination in fact which may be practised both by public authorities, by the community or by private persons or bodies. The committee wishes to be informed about legal provisions and administrative measures directed at diminishing or eliminating such discrimination.'[57]

Overall, this UNHRC general comment makes it clear that a discriminatory intention is not necessary to establish direct or indirect discrimination. It does not matter whether discrimination is conscious or unconscious, intended or unintended.

The expert commentators in international law agree that meanings do evolve, and the meanings of 'equality' and 'discrimination' are no exception. Through the general comments of the UNHRC we have now been introduced to indirect or systemic discrimination. CEDAW has no specific reference to systemic discrimination, but it does recognise the political environment providing for it. Article 5(a) obliges signatories to take appropriate measures to 'modify . . . the social and cultural patterns of conduct of men and women, with a view to achieving the elimination of prejudices and customs and all other practices which are based on the idea of the inferiority or the superiority of either of the sexes or on stereotyped roles for men and women'.

The Australian Law Reform Commission has written that 'gender bias should be regarded as a form of discrimination, systemic in nature, which prevents women from enjoying full equality before the law, equality under the law, equal protection of the law and equal benefit of the law'.[58] Further, it explains: 'The concept of equality must be able to promote understanding of how the disadvantages suffered by women are created and maintained. It must be capable of exposing the relationship between social inequality and the law.'[59]

This concept of equality is known as 'substantive equality'. Substantive equality demands an examination of the actual conditions experienced by groups and individuals, and requires the elimination of discriminatory structural barriers. In our parliamentary submission, Paul Hunt illustrated the difference with a very clear example: 'The difference between formal and substantive equality is neatly illustrated by the removal of the apartheid laws in South Africa. Formal equality requires nothing more than the repeal of apartheid's discriminatory laws and the prohibition of direct discrimination on the grounds of race. It ignores actual social and economic conditions which continue to structure land, education and so on, on a racial basis. In contrast substantive equality mandates the removal of apartheid's discriminatory laws, the prohibition of direct discrimination and the eradication of social, economic and political barriers impeding access to land, education and other services.'

Key 'subsidiary sources of international law, the judicial decisions of domestic courts' contain judgements on the issue of substantive equality. Here again we find theoretical dispute among the expert commentators about the status of international and domestic law. In New Zealand, we find an evolution and transition in practice. The dualist theory in law envisages domestic law in the national legal system as being superior to international law, which can be enforced only if it is incorporated into the domestic law. According to the monist theory, both are binding and arise out of one system of law, but international law is superior.

In the Netherlands, covenant provisions are frequently invoked before the domestic courts. As early as 1982, there were 34 judgements by the courts referring to covenant provisions. That figure grew to 45 in 1984 and 58 in 1986. In Norway and Sweden, the covenants regularly provide a legal standard for the courts. They are used to fuel legal arguments and support decisions before the courts, which have cited covenants to guide interpretations of domestic statutes.

In New Zealand, covenants have finally been used to determine the application of a domestic statute.[60] This took some time. The general theoretical position had been that international *treaty* standards were not directly enforceable in New Zealand courts, while customary international law was part of the common law and therefore 'directly enforceable'. This applied particularly where the terms of the statute which were in conflict with the international treaty standards were clear and unambiguous. In 1981 the New Zealand courts declared: 'if the terms of the domestic legislation are clear and unambiguous they must be given effect in our courts whether (or not) they carry out New Zealand's international obligations'.[61]

This basic position was reaffirmed in 1991. However, the court commented that it was increasingly recognised that, 'even though Treaty obligations not implemented by legislation are not part of our domestic law, the Courts, in interpreting legislation, will do their best to conform with the subject matter in the policy of the legislation to see that their decisions are consistent with our international obligations'.[62]

The case of *Tavita* v. *Minister of Immigration* in May 1994 did not concern the interpretation of a domestic statute. The appeal focused on New Zealand's obligations under the Convention on the Rights of the Child. The signatory state's obligations to Tavita's child as a New Zealand citizen meant that the deportation of an overstaying father, who had a child born in New Zealand, would be in breach of international human rights laws.

The government's main line of argument was that the minister and the department were entitled to ignore the international instruments. The judgement said:

> That is an unattractive argument, apparently implying that New Zealand's adherence to the international instruments has been at least partly window dressing . . . The law as to the bearing on domestic law of international human rights and instruments is undergoing evolution . . . The Balliol Statement of 1992 [has a] reference to the judiciary to interpret and apply national constitutions, ordinary legislation and the common law in the light of the universality of human rights . . . New Zealand's accession to the Optional Protocol . . . is in a sense part of this country's judicial structure, in that individuals subject to New Zealand jurisdiction have direct rights of recourse to it . . . Legitimate criticism

could extend to the New Zealand Courts if they were to accept the
argument that, because a domestic statute giving discretionary powers
in general terms does not mention international human rights norms
or obligations, the executive is necessarily free to ignore them.[63]

For the purposes of our petition, the status of covenants in New
Zealand domestic law was clarified. In reference to our next source, we
were fortunate that decades of precedents had established the relevance
of decisions on the concept of 'equality' from jurisdictions similar to
that in New Zealand. The most important of these judgements, from
the Canadian legal system, became a key reference in our submissions
on parliamentary equality.

The equality provisions in the Canadian Charter of Rights and
Freedoms are designed to protect those groups who suffer social,
political and legal disadvantage. *Andrews* v. *Law Society of British
Columbia*[64] contested section 15 of the Canadian Charter: 'Every individual is equal before and under the law and has the right to the equal
protection and equal benefit of the law'. In addition to the meaning
of equality, the court examined what was meant by non-discrimination.

First, the court established that, if a barrier is affecting certain groups
in a disproportionately negative way, it is a signal that the practices
which lead to the adverse impact may be discriminatory. Second, the
court defined discrimination as 'a distinction whether intentional or
not, but based on grounds relating to personal characteristics of an
individual or group which has the effect of imposing burdens, obligations or disadvantages on such an individual or group not imposed
upon others or which withholds or limits access to opportunities, benefits and advantages available to other members of society'. This was
more than a question of formal equality.

In this concept, equality is 'ameliorative', looking to the reality of
people's lives and what discrimination actually does to them. It does not
matter whether it is the result of innocently motivated practices or
systems. The outcome, not the intention is the point.

The Canadian Women's Legal Education and Action Fund (Leaf)
made submissions to the court in *Andrews*. Leaf argued that under
section 15 equality should be understood as a matter of socially created,
systematic, historical and cumulative advantage and disadvantage.
Women suffer from social subordination, systematic abuse and deprivation of social power, resources and respect, because we are women.
Owing to social inequality, women are not in the same situation as

men. We cannot be treated as identical.

Justice McIntyre, writing for the majority in the judgement, noted that identical treatment may frequently produce serious inequality. 'To approach the ideal of full equality', the judgement says, 'the main consideration must be the impact of the law on the individual or group concerned. Consideration must be given to the content of the law, to its purpose and its impact upon those to whom it applies and also upon those whom it excludes from its application.' It continues: 'the promotion of equality entails a promotion of a society in which all are secure in the knowledge they are recognised at law as human beings equally deserving of concern and respect and consideration. It has a large remedial component.'[65]

The test adopted by the court in *Andrews* determines discrimination in terms of disadvantage. If a person is a member of a persistently disadvantaged group and can show that a law, policy or behaviour maintains or worsens that disadvantage, it is discriminatory. No comparator is needed. The requirement is to look at women as they are in the real world to determine whether any systemic abuse and deprivation of power they experience is due to their place in the sexual hierarchy.

When a policy or action appears gender neutral but has different effects on men and women that are unreasonable, the result is gender discrimination. Indirect discrimination is disguised in policies and practices which appear to apply to all people equally.

Let us return to the covenant guarantees. Article 3 of the ICCPR requires New Zealand 'to undertake to ensure the equal right of men and women to the enjoyment of all political rights'. Article 7 of CEDAW requires New Zealand to 'ensure to women, on equal terms with men, the right . . . to participate in the formulation of government policy and the implementation thereof and to hold public office and perform all functions at all levels of government'.

In the context of Article 1 of CEDAW and the UNHRC general comment on discrimination and all the sources referred to, as well as New Zealand's practice in the soft law forums, I do not believe that an argument confining the definition of equality to formal equality can be sustained. If there continues to be, in the numbers of women elected to political office, distinctions, exclusions, restrictions and preferences on the ground of sex, the effect of which is to nullify or impair the recognition, enjoyment and exercise of all rights and freedoms by all women, there is an active discrimination. This is called systemic discrimination.

We can apply the test suggested by Leaf to the situation in New Zealand. Can the lack of representation of women in Parliament be understood as a matter of socially created systematic historical and cumulative advantage and disadvantage? Has there been an historical philosophy and experience of politics as an interaction and competition between men, with men cast as the rational political actors with the masculine qualities of leadership? Yes. Is a well-developed body of intellectual opinion and literature advocating women's participation in decision-making lacking? Yes. Is there evidence of institutionalised gender discrimination in public policy? Yes. Is there an implicit discrimination within the dominant male culture of established political parties? Yes. Are there traditional male assumptions regarding the selection system, the electoral system, constituency work, the timing, duration and location of meetings? Yes. Is there a patronage system in government appointments? Yes. Is there sexist language and behaviour in the House? Yes. Are women politicians treated differently from their male colleagues in the media? Yes. Are women disadvantaged by their dual roles? Yes. Have women ever held political office on equal terms with men? No.

The question our petition tests, then, is: can international human rights law, in particular ICCPR and CEDAW, support and deliver *substantive* equality? The answer must be yes, if the test is based on powerlessness, exclusion and disadvantage, rather than on sameness and difference.

The important point is that it is the government's responsibility to solve the breach. Where the UNHRC issues general comments, CEDAW issues general recommendations in its annual report. General Recommendation No. 5 states: 'Taking note that . . . there is still a need for action to be taken to implement fully the Convention by introducing measures to promote *de facto* equality between men and women, . . . the Committee recommends that States Parties make more use of temporary special measures such as positive action, preferential treatment or quota systems to advance women's integration into education, the economy, politics and enjoyment'.[66] Every article of the key documents on human rights begins with the words 'States Parties' and then describes the obligation imposed on the state. However, if the states' actors are always overwhelmingly men, this presents major obstacles in giving effect to those rights.

Prof. Elisabeth G. Sledziewski has written: 'Modern doctrine attributes . . . the universal and abstract nature of [human] rights . . . to man and woman indifferently . . . This refusal to sexualize the definition of the citizen also confirms the latent power of a sexist scheme of things, which automatically masculinizes all social and political responsibilities.' She argues that no real democracy is possible if the question of equality is not posed as a political precondition. 'Only the introduction of participation quotas imposing equal representation of the sexes in all decision-making authorities can make women's active participation in the polis effective and irreversible. If democracy is to acknowledge the difference of the sexes, it has no other response to suggest than this: the human race is twofold, debates and decisions must be the acts of men and women, otherwise they cannot be the acts of the human race as it is.'

This implies recognition of the differences between men and women 'in order to prevent them from the outset from working in favour of inequality. This is precisely what quotas . . . seek to achieve, as their purpose is to disarm all forms of discrimination'. Such provisions 'are envisaged in the very name of the principle of equality.

'The advent of democracy based on equal representation will mean . . . a turning point in the democratic construction process. Equal participation by female citizens in the affairs of the polis will henceforth be considered a *sine qua non* of the completion of democracy. A democracy without women will no longer be seen as an imperfect democracy, but as no democracy at all.'[67]

Our petition was tabled in Parliament in September 1994. The parliamentary select committee hearing was on 23 November 1994. In June 1995 I enquired of the Committee Clerk what progress had been made; the Electoral Law Committee intended to make a decision on the petition when it had finished its consideration of the Electoral Reform Bill, which it did in October 1995. On 19 December Lianne Dalziel asked a question in Parliament. The committee chairman replied that the select committee would give the petition further consideration in the new year. In my experience, this is a very long time for petitioners to wait for a reply.

In the new year, the Electoral Law Committee referred the petition to the government for 'most favourable consideration'. While this is the 'highest' recommendation a petition can obtain, it is a non-debatable motion. Finally, on 21 May 1996 the government provided a response via the Minister of Justice. It read:

> The Government agrees that the greater representation of women in the House of Representatives is highly desirable. One of the advantages ascribed by the Royal Commission on the Electoral System to an MMP electoral system was that political parties would have an incentive to select party lists that fairly represented the electorate. Section 264 of the Electoral Act 1993 provides for the appointment of a select committee in 2000 to review various aspects of the electoral system including the provisions of the Act dealing with Maori representation. The House of Representatives might consider inviting this select committee to also examine the extent to which party lists have resulted in the better representation of women in the House and what changes, if any, to the electoral system might appropriately be made to further enhance the representation of women. For more immediate attention to be given to the issue, the House of Representatives might also consider inviting the select committee charged with reviewing the conduct of the 1996 General Election to examine the extent to which party lists have resulted in the better representation of women in the House.

How magnanimous! How patronising! The government seems to have missed the point. If the government accommodates, tolerates or excuses women's lack of access to political office 'on equal terms with men', the government, not political parties or select committees of Parliament, must accept responsibility.

Government agency, government complicity by failure to act and government responsibility for the unequal application of the law, resulting in disparate outcomes, are all at issue here. The government has not heard the last of the petitioners. And we have now, formally, exhausted all our domestic legal remedies.

BACK TO WORK

Yet with this experience it seemed to me that UN covenants offered the opportunity to pursue another of my political interests in the human rights field. While waiting for Parliament to find the time to deliberate on our petition, I decided to investigate the non-recognition of unpaid work, particularly that done by women as mothers and home-makers, as a fundamental breach of human rights.

In the second essay in this book I discussed some definitions of work, and I have previously written at length on this conceptual problem.[68] When I investigated how, in my 'culture', the words of concern to us are 'normally' used in debate, I found this. For 'work', the *Concise*

Oxford Dictionary listed: '1. expenditure of energy, striving, application of effort to some purpose; 2. task to be undertaken; 3. employment'. Under 'labour' I found: '1. bodily or mental toil, exertion; toil tending to supply wants of community; 2. task; 3. pains of childbirth'. '3. employment' was defined as 'one's regular trade or profession' and 'occupation' as 'what occupies one, means of fulfilling one's time, temporary or regular employment, business, calling'. Turning to *Roget's Thesaurus* I found that alternatives for the word labour included work and housework. A 'job' might be work, labour, employment, or occupation. But in my 'culture' the way we 'normally' use words is not necessarily the concept applied in law.

For many years I had intended to pursue the possibility of a human rights challenge on the question of unpaid work. I had discussed it with activists in Canada and Norway. I had strategised with individual women friends, usually parenting alone, who had just been dealt another discriminatory blow on the basis of their status as mothers and homemakers in unpaid work. The needed combination of passionate energy, time and resources had eluded me.

A synchronicity of events made a combined effort possible. I heard a radio interview with an organiser of a lobby group called Women As Mothers (WAM). I called her. We met. At the same time my university department needed to offer a new third-year applied paper in social policy. The students, with one exception, were mature women. The majority were mothers, and sole parents. There was a wealth of combined experience in custody, maintenance and matrimonial property battles. There was the shared experience of struggling to retrain while being called welfare beneficiaries. I offered the course. WAM offered the names for in-depth case studies. The students chose a specific area for study, where the impact of the law, policy and practice resulted in disparate outcomes for women who had spent most of their working hours in unpaid and unrecognised economic activity. Their subjects included government censuses, superannuation, home schooling, levels of benefit payment, matrimonial property divisions, breastfeeding, the care of the totally dependent, including the elderly and those with various disabilities, accident compensation insurance and payments, and paid maternity leave.

There was no obvious statute to test before the New Zealand courts. The Human Rights Commission and its legislation offered an alternative route this time in pursuit of domestic legal remedies. The grounds for opposing discrimination in the Human Rights Act 1993 included sex and other grounds which might be cumulatively useful, marital status and family status. The definition of 'employment status' in the Act included being a voluntary worker or a 'beneficiary'. 'Employer' was defined as being the person for whom work is done by a paid and unpaid worker, and 'employment' was deemed to have a corresponding meaning.

After a formal complaint had been made, the legislation allowed the commission to take a number of steps. It could enquire generally into legislation claimed to be in breach of human rights guarantees in domestic and international law. It could report to the Prime Minister on the desirability of better legislation. It could investigate the specific cases of complaint contained in each student's submission. I was particularly attracted by the commission's power to instigate a declaratory judgement, so that what was and was not 'work' might be clarified.

The case would again have to be assembled from the sources in Article 38 of the Statute of the International Court of Justice. We would begin again with the ICCPR Article 2 ('Each State Party . . . undertakes . . . to ensure to all individuals . . . the rights recognized in the present Covenant, without distinction . . . such as . . . sex . . . or other status'), and Article 26 ('All persons are equal before the law and are entitled without any discrimination to the equal protection of the law. In this respect, the law shall prohibit any discrimination and guarantee to all persons equal and effective protection again discrimination on any ground such as . . . sex . . . or other status').

I hesitate to introduce ICCPR Article 8 into the discussion at this point, because of the emotional response provoked by the suggestion of its relevance to the case. But it is very important. The key phrases read:

> 1. No one shall be held in slavery; slavery and the slave-trade in all their forms shall be prohibited.
> 2. No one shall be held in servitude.
> 3. (a)No one shall be required to perform forced or compulsory labour;
>   . . .
>   (c). . . the term 'forced or compulsory labour' shall not include: . . .
>   (iii) Any service exacted in cases of emergency or calamity threatening the life or well-being of the community [or]
>   (iv) Any work or service which forms part of normal civil obligations.

The term I am particularly interested in is 'servitude'. In the *Oxford*

English Dictionary (*OED*) 'servitude' is defined as 'the condition of being a slave or a serf or of being the property of another person, absence of personal freedom'. In the first definition the *OED* notes that it usually carries the additional notion of subjection to the necessity of excessive labour. The second major definition is 'the condition of being a servant, service, specially domestic service'. We are informed that its use in this context is now rare or obsolete.

Whenever the International Court of Justice seeks the origin of a specific challenge in international human rights law – for example, where or how did this issue first arise, what might a word mean, what was the intention of the drafting committee – it traces back through documents and deliberations that led to the final text of recommendations or resolutions or covenant articles. Whether the question concerns rights to continental shelves, rights to fish species, where exactly a country's border was, the nationality of a people, the court weaves its way back through old documents so that the sources of the original debate, and frequently the sub-committee notes of some rapporteur, are examined. We have seen evidence of this process in examining how the UNHRC reached its general comment on discrimination.

Andrew Clapham reports that in the debates on the drafting of the ICCPR,

> in discussing paragraph 2 [of Article 8], it was pointed out that 'slavery,' which implied the destruction of the judicial personality, was a relatively limited and technical notion, whereas 'servitude' was a more general idea conveying all possible forms of man's domination over man [*sic*]. While slavery was the best known and the worst form of bondage, other forms existed in modern society which tended to reduce the dignity of man. A suggestion to substitute the words 'peonage' and 'serfdom' for servitude was rejected as those words were too limited in scope and have no precise meaning. A proposal was also made to insert the word 'involuntary' before servitude in order to make it clear that the clause dealt with compulsory servitude and did not apply to contractual obligations between persons competent to enter into such obligations. The proposal was opposed on the ground that servitude in any form, whether involuntary or not, should be prohibited. It should not be made possible for any person to contract himself into bondage.[69]

Richard Lillich believes that there is no doubt that customary international law now prohibits slavery and servitude. In relation to 'normal civil obligations',[70] he comments, 'what is meant here is primarily the obligation of citizens to undertake joint efforts in the common interest on a local level, such as taking part in fire brigades or similar measures against other calamities. It cannot be translated into a general subjection to direction of labour for economic purposes.'[71]

The linkage of women and Article 8 is rare indeed in UN reports. In 1982 a report on slavery to the Commission on Human Rights indicated that women were 'among the victims' of institutions such as slavery. A special rapporteur noted 'new forms of servitude and gross exploitation', and recommended that 'at a proper time the UN might find it convenient to consider a consolidated convention aimed at eradicating all forms of servile status'. The revision of this report contained a whole section on slavery-like practices involving women. It is worth quoting at some length.

> A considerable corpus of evidence relates to slavery-like practices of which women are the particular victims. Mary Wollstonecraft and John Stuart Mill compared the unjust power of men and their attitudes to women with those of slave masters, and Gunnar Myrdal has pointed out that the ninth commandment in the Old Testament of the Bible, which links women with servants, mules and other property, was used to justify slavery . . . Mary Astell said in 1700: 'If all men are born free, how is it that all women are born slaves? As they must be, if being subjected to the inconstant, uncertain, unknown, arbitrary will of men be the perfect condition of slavery.' Janet Radcliffe Richards, more recently and specifically, has pointed out: 'Slavery can be not only enforced unpaid labour, but also underpaid work into which people are coerced by the unfair power of others. This description can apply to a great number of women, especially housewives and even mothers: but it can also be extended to the situation of many others.' Simone de Beauvoir and others have described 'the colonisation of women' which is equally so profitable to men. Certainly in this sense, virtually every society oppresses women, albeit in different ways and guises.
>
> 'Human rights' must not be diminished into being merely 'the rights of men'. There should therefore be no feeling of cultural sensitivity or sectional solidarity when looking at such problems . . . In the present report it is right to consider only certain of the most extreme forms of exploitation and abuse, although too often these would appear to be merely the most dramatic symptoms of a wider cultural malaise compounded of unjust and often violent male psychology, which needs to be remedied by a comprehensive change in social and educational attitudes.[72]

The subjects of my students' cases spoke consistently of their unpaid work being in the service of others, and leading to a restriction, if not an absence, of personal freedom. There was no question that this unpaid work was economically exploited by partners, family, the community and the state.

In respect of the rights of these unpaid workers, the next source to be consulted was the ICESCR (see Appendix 1). Article 2 guarantees 'that the rights enunciated in the present Covenant will be exercised without discrimination of any kind as to . . . sex . . . or other status'. While there is no clear consensus among legal critics as to the breadth of the obligation imposed by the term 'or other status', when the phrase was discussed in the drafting of the ICCPR it was regarded as all-inclusive.[73] Any argument that the phrase was to have a different meaning in the ICESCR would be extraordinary. On accepted rules of international law, the view held by the draftees of covenants should be applied. Its relevance and importance to this case will become clear as we proceed for, in addition to being a woman, clearly encompassed by 'sex', 'other status' might include being pregnant, being a mother, lactating or being an unpaid worker.

Article 3 undertakes 'to ensure the equal rights of men and women to the enjoyment of all economic, social and cultural rights set forth in the present Covenant'. There is no question about the relationship between CEDAW and the ICESCR and the guarantees of women's equality. The Limburg Principles state: 'In the application of Article 3 guaranteeing equal rights for men and women, due regard should be paid to the Declaration and Convention on the Elimination of All Forms of Discrimination Against Women and other relevant instruments and the activities of the supervisory committee [CEDAW] under the said Convention.'[74]

The relevance of the next group of ICESCR articles is contingent upon the universal and unpaid work of women being categorised as work. It is perfectly obvious, despite the rhetoric of the UNSNA, that women are not 'at leisure', economically inactive or unproductive when engaged in the activities discussed extensively in my second essay. Neither are they unemployed. That seems to me to leave two options: either these women work, or they are in servitude. If their unpaid production, reproduction and service provision is recognised as work, several other articles in the ICESCR apply.

Article 6 reads: '1. The States Parties to the present Covenant recognize the right to work, which includes the right of everyone to the opportunity to gain his living by work which he freely chooses or accepts, and will take appropriate steps to safeguard this right.

'2. The steps to be taken by a State Party to the present Covenant to achieve the full realization of this right shall include technical and vocational guidance and training programmes, policies and techniques to achieve steady economic, social and cultural development and full and productive employment under conditions safeguarding fundamental political and economic freedoms to the individual.'

Article 7 is particularly important. If what women do for hours a day in an unpaid capacity is defined as work, states parties are to

> recognise the right of everyone to the enjoyment of just and favourable conditions of work which ensure, in particular:
> (a) Remuneration which provides all workers, as a minimum, with:
>   (i) Fair wages and equal remuneration for work of equal value without distinction of any kind, in particular women being guaranteed conditions of work not inferior to those enjoyed by men, with equal pay for equal work;
>   (ii) A decent living for themselves and their families in accordance with the provisions of the present Covenant;
> (b) Safe and healthy working conditions;
> (c) Equal opportunity for everyone to be promoted in his employment to an appropriate higher level, subject to no considerations other than those of seniority and competence;
> (d) Rest, leisure and reasonable limitation of working hours and periodic holidays with pay, as well as remuneration for public holidays.

These are the entitlements of *all* workers.

Earlier I discussed the Limburg Principles, which act as the guide on implementation and reporting on the ICESCR. The principles also outline the circumstances in which a state party would be deemed to have violated the covenant. Caveats apply. 'In determining what amounts to a failure to comply', a state party has 'a margin of discretion in selecting the means for carrying out its objects, in that factors beyond its reasonable control may adversely affect its capacity to implement particular rights.'[75]

Of particular relevance to our debate, a state party

> will be in violation of the Covenant, inter alia, if
> (a) it fails to take a step which it is required to by the Covenant;
> (b) it fails to promptly remove obstacles which it is under a duty to remove to permit the immediate fulfilment of a right;
> (c) it fails to implement without delay a right which it is required by

the Covenant to provide immediately;

(d) it applies a limitation to a right recognized in the Covenant other than in accordance with the Covenant;

(e) it deliberately retards or halts the progressive realization of a right, unless it is acting within a limitation permitted by the Covenant or it does so due to a lack of available resources or *force majeur*.[76]

This should make it clear that patriarchal ideology and political expediency are not excuses for non-compliance with rights guaranteed by the covenant.

Article 18 of the ICESCR and Article 6 of the implementation procedures allow the specialised UN agencies to submit reports, along with the reports of signatory states. The International Labour Organisation (ILO) has been given the task of preparing these reports for the ICESCR Committee of Experts (always, to date, overwhelmingly men) who monitor country performance under ILO standards.

MEN LABOUR – WOMEN WORK

Article 3 of the ILO Constitution includes this: 'The meetings of the General Conference of representatives of the Members shall be held . . . at least once in every year. It shall be composed of four representatives of each of the Members, of whom two shall be Government delegates and the two others shall be delegates representing respectively the employers and the workpeople of each of the Members. Each delegate may be accompanied by advisers, who shall not exceed two in number for each item on the agenda of the meeting. When questions specially affecting women are to be considered by the Conference, one at least of the advisers should be a woman . . . Advisers shall not speak except on a request made by the delegate whom they accompany and by the special authorization of the President of the Conference, and may not vote.'[77]

In a generous moment at its 60th session, in 1975, the International Labour Conference asked in a resolution that women be appointed to delegations on the same basis and by the same standards as men.[78] It will not be a surprise to readers that there has been little improvement in the numbers of women representing governments, the employers or the 'workpeople' in delegations in the past two decades. From its beginning, the ILO has been preoccupied with male concerns. In such a context, it is of considerable concern that the ILO is the specialised agency reporting on the ICESCR.

Where the ICESCR speaks of 'work', the ILO is preoccupied with 'employment' and 'occupation', with exclusionary definitions. For example, the 1958 ILO Convention on Discrimination in Employment and Occupation defines the terms 'employment' and 'occupation' to include access to vocational training, access to employment and to particular occupations, and terms and conditions of employment, but does not include the bulk of women's work on the planet. While such conventions clearly exclude unpaid household production, reproduction and services from consideration, I do not believe it is possible to sustain any argument which limits the meaning of 'work' in Articles 6 and 7 of the ICESCR to the narrow conceptions of employment and occupation used by the ILO.

You will remember, too, the definitions of 'economically active' and 'subsistence workers' used by the ILO, as outlined in my second essay. The demarcations depend on work being 'an important contribution' to the household or an 'important basis for livelihood'. Again the gulf between rhetoric and reality takes my breath away. Just how the rest of the world thinks it would survive without women's unpaid contribution to their livelihood is beyond me.

There are claims that the ILO is shifting its ground on these questions. I have heard informally through the feminist network that a Housewives Union was admitted to the ILO as a member in 1995. In the plenary address to the Fourth World Conference on Women in Beijing, the ILO representative announced 'we want to emphasise that all women are working women whether engaged in market or non-market activities'. The statement claimed: 'the organisation has vigorously promoted the principle of equality of opportunity and treatment between women and men as a matter of human rights, as a matter of social justice and as a matter of economic efficiency and sustainable development'. It continued: 'the unequal sharing of family responsibilities between men and women continues to impede the reconciliation of work and family responsibilities. Women workers still have to juggle numerous roles with considerable difficulty and stress.'[79] Unless the ILO defines housework as servitude, however, there has never been an ILO convention protecting the rights of 'all women working in non-market activities'.

WHAT WOMEN SAY

Thankfully, in our pursuit of the non-recognition of unpaid work as a human rights violation, CEDAW is of major importance. Since 1982 62 experts from 50 countries have served on the committee. All of the CEDAW candidates except one have been female, and they have included doctors, politicians, psychologists, economists, sociologists, eductionalists and diplomats.

The UNHRC general comment on discrimination and the Limburg Principles have established our justification for reading CEDAW in conjunction with the ICCPR and the ICESCR. Article 2 of CEDAW establishes the full ambit of government responsibilities.

> States Parties . . . agree to pursue by all appropriate means and without delay a policy of eliminating discrimination against women and, to this end, undertake:
>
> (a) To embody the principle of the equality of men and women in their national constitutions or other appropriate legislation . . . and to ensure, through law and other appropriate means, the practical realization of this principle;
>
> (b) To adopt appropriate legislative and other measures, including sanctions where appropriate, prohibiting all discrimination against women;
>
> (c) To establish legal protection of the rights of women on an equal basis with men . . . ;
>
> (d) To refrain from engaging in any act or practice of discrimination against women and to ensure that public authorities and institutions shall act in conformity with this obligation;
>
> (e) To take all appropriate measures to eliminate discrimination against women by any person, organization or enterprise;
>
> (f) To take all appropriate measures, including legislation, to modify or abolish existing laws, regulations, customs and practices which constitute discrimination against women;
>
> (g) To repeal all national penal provisions which constitute discrimination again women.

Here we see that this convention obliges states parties to eliminate discrimination not only in public but also in private life. This is a major difference from what has always been understood as human rights territory, because of CEDAW's 'recognition of discrimination outside the public sphere and particularly within families and the obligation of the state to ensure its elimination' there. A further dynamic feature of the convention is its recognition that the formal prohibition of discrimination is insufficient to redress its inherited consequences. The CEDAW committee has reported: 'Perhaps the most important obligation of state parties under the Convention is the achievement of *de facto* equality for women. These obligations are clear from the terms of the Convention. Also apparent are their obligations to ensure that women enjoy this equality in fact.'[80]

Article 11 of CEDAW reads:

1. States Parties shall take all appropriate measures to eliminate discrimination against women in the field of employment in order to ensure, on a basis equality of men and women, the same rights, in particular:
   (a) The right to work as an inalienable right of all human beings;
   (b) The right to the same employment opportunities, including the application of the same criteria for selection in matters of employment;
   (c) The right to free choice of profession and employment, the right to promotion, job security and all benefits and conditions of service and the right to receive vocational training and retraining, including apprenticeships, advanced vocational training and recurrent training;
   (d) The right to equal remuneration, including benefits, and to equal treatment in respect of work of equal value, as well as equality of treatment in the evaluation of the quality of work;
   (e) The right to social security, particularly in cases of retirement, unemployment, sickness, invalidity and old age and other incapacity to work, as well as the right to paid leave;
   (f) The right to protection of health and to safety in working conditions, including the safeguarding of the function of reproduction.
2. In order to prevent discrimination against women on the grounds of marriage or maternity and to ensure their effective right to work, States Parties shall take appropriate measures: . . .
   (b) To introduce maternity leave with pay or with comparable social benefits without loss of former employment, seniority or social allowances;
   (c) To encourage the provision of the necessary supporting social services to enable parents to combine family obligations with work responsibilities and participation in public life, in particular through promoting the establishment and development of a network of child-care facilities;
   (d) To provide special protection to women during pregnancy in types of work proved to be harmful to them.

3. Protective legislation relating to matters covered in this article shall
   be reviewed periodically in the light of scientific and technological
   knowledge and shall be revised, repealed or extended as necessary.

In recalling the descriptions of shitwork in my second essay, Article
14 is of major importance: 'States Parties shall take into account the
particular problems faced by rural women and the significant roles
which rural women play in the economic survival of their families,
including their work in the non-monetized sectors of the economy,
and shall take all appropriate measures to ensure the application of
the provisions of the present Convention to women in rural areas.'

In addition to the convention, the CEDAW committee has released
general recommendations directly related to the question of women's
unpaid labour. General recommendations are addressed to states
parties. You will remember that the general comments of the UNHRC
are deemed to be a source expanding on and clarifying the protections
of the covenant, and 'acquiring an authoritative character as representing generally acceptable standards'. It should then follow that the
CEDAW's committee general comments should carry the same weight in
international jurisprudence.

It should follow, but it will not necessarily do so. Hilary Charlesworth
reports that 'the structure and institutions of women's international
human rights law are more fragile than their apparently more generally
applicable counterparts: international instruments dealing with women
have weaker implementation obligations and procedures; and the
institutions designed to draft and monitor them are under-resourced
and their roles often circumscribed compared to other human rights
bodies'.[81] However, we will proceed on the basis of 'equality of
authority' to clarify the equality or to expose the hypocrisy.

General Recommendation 16 of CEDAW requires unpaid work to be
valued and recognised and requires states parties to report on the
situation of unpaid women workers as well as to take steps to guarantee
payment, including benefits to unpaid workers in rural and urban
family enterprises. What we are talking about here, I think, is a farm or
a corner dairy. The household itself is not described as an enterprise.
But if a household is a school, and a school is an enterprise, why is the
home schooler not an unpaid worker in an enterprise? If the household
happens to be the residence of a doctor and the spouse has constantly to
answer the telephone, is she not an unpaid worker in the enterprise?

This margin is very blurred, yet it is the daily reality in the lives of millions of women.

If the woman is relieving an institution of the full-time responsibility of the care and attention of somebody, is she an enterprise or not? If she were not 'working', the service would have to be performed in an enterprise. There is no other place for it to be done. Isn't this work and service an important contribution to the livelihood, and the quality of life, of members of the household?

General Recommendation 17 of CEDAW states that the valuation of women's unpaid work is of major international importance. The committee requires the measurement and quantification of the domestic activities of women and the incorporation of the unremunerated domestic activities of women in national accounts.

So the CEDAW committee has no doubt that women's unpaid work is work and, in interpreting all the articles of ICESCR, 'due regard' (now overdue regard) is to be had to CEDAW.

THE 'SOFT' INPUT

Next we are directed by Article 38 of the Statute of the International Court of Justice to look beyond the covenants and conventions for evidence of customary international law, those resolutions, recommendations, gentlemen's agreements, etc. which in decades of soft law rise in status. At the UN World Conference for Women held in Nairobi in 1985, the final document stated, 'Governments should take concrete steps to measure the economic value of women's unpaid work with a view to taking it into account in national policy by 1995.' Furthermore, 'Governments and other appropriate bodies should by 1995 establish social support measures with the aim of facilitating the combination of parental and other caring responsibilities and paid employment, including policies for the provision of services and measures to increase the sharing of such responsibilities by men and women and to deal with specific problems of female-headed households that include dependants.'

At the UN Conference on Environment and Development, known as the Earth Summit, New Zealand endorsed 'programmes to promote the reduction of the heavy workload of women and girl children at home . . . and the sharing of household tasks by men and women on an equal basis . . . Countries should develop gender sensitive databases, information systems and participatory action oriented research and policy analyses . . . on the integration of the value of unpaid work, including work that is currently designated "domestic", in resource accounting mechanisms in order to better represent the true value of the contribution of women to the economy.'

The Vienna Declaration following the UN Human Rights Conference stressed that all human rights contained in the international instruments applied fully to women. Equal enjoyment of those rights should be closely monitored by each treaty body within the competence of its mandate, and a common strategy should be developed by the treaty bodies in that regard.

At its meeting in 1995, the UN Commission on Human Rights reaffirmed that discrimination on the basis of sex is contrary to the Charter of the United Nations, and noted that some human rights violations are specific to, or primarily directed against, women. The identification and reporting of such violations demanded specific awareness and sensitivity.

Other committees, definitely comprising 'experts of international standing', have contributed to a 'soft law' input. The Commonwealth Human Rights Initiative, an advisory group chaired by former Canadian External Affairs Minister Flora MacDonald, reported in 1991. In its recommendations it stated: 'Commonwealth programmes and reports should, as a matter of routine, be required to assess the impact of their activities and recommendations upon women. Cultural bias should be recognized where it exists. Economic measurements should include estimates of the value of women's labour and, where they fail to do so (for example in conventional recording of gross national product), this should be acknowledged.'[82]

The UN World Conference on Women held in Beijing in 1995 continued the resolutions and recommendations of previous conferences. The Platform for Action of the Fourth World Conference on Women commits governments to 'seek[ing] to develop a more comprehensive knowledge of work and employment through, *inter alia*, efforts to measure and better understand the type, extent and distribution of unremunerated work, particularly work in caring for dependants and unremunerated work done for family farms or businesses, and encourage the sharing and dissemination of information on studies and experience in this field, including the development of methods for assessing its value in quantitative terms, for possible reflection in accounts that may be produced separately from, but consistent with, core national accounts'.

The Platform for Action further *requires* government agencies and statistical services

> to develop a more comprehensive knowledge of all forms of work and employment by:
> (i) Improving data collection on the unremunerated work which is already included in the UNSNA, such as agriculture, particularly subsistence agriculture, and other types of non-market production activities;
> . . . and (iii) Developing methods, in the appropriate forums, for assessing the value, in quantitative terms, of unremunerated work that is outside national accounts, such as caring for dependants and preparing food, for possible reflection in satellite and other official accounts that may be produced separately from but are consistent with core accounts, with a view to recognising the economic contribution of women and making visible the unequal distribution of remunerated and unremunerated work between women and men.[83]

Beyond the international sources which provide evidence of customary consent, we are invited to look at judicial decisions which can assist us in our argument. *Andrews* v. *Law Society of British Columbia* is again paramount. In violation of human rights guarantees, women's unpaid work has historically been systematically and cumulatively exploited in a socially created environment to the universal advantage of men, and the disadvantage of women.

The Canadian Human Rights Commission has found that: 'Systemic discrimination . . . recognizes that long-standing social and cultural mores carry within them value assumptions that contribute to discrimination in ways that are substantially or entirely hidden and unconscious. Thus, the historical experience which has tended to undervalue the work of women may be perpetuated through assumptions that certain types of work historically performed by women are inherently less valuable than certain types of work historically performed by men.'[84]

You may remember my drawing attention to the words 'or other status' in Article 2 of ICESCR. In our work with WAM, it seemed important to demonstrate that, for example, to be a mother might well be grounds for human rights violations beyond those encompassed by sex. There seemed to be some support for this in *Brooks* v. *Canada*

Safeway Ltd, another judgement from the Supreme Court of Canada. Pregnant women workers had received unfavourable treatment in comparison with males and non-pregnant women in benefit provisions. The court did not find it necessary to locate a male equivalent of the condition of pregnancy. It specifically held that the disadvantage the pregnant women suffer comes about because of their condition – because of their difference. The Chief Justice placed the pregnant women in their own reality. Once this step was taken it was impossible not to find that differential treatment on the basis of pregnancy was anything but discrimination on the basis of sex.

The court stated: 'Combining work with motherhood and accommodating the childbearing needs of working women are ever-increasing imperatives. That those who bear children and benefit society as a whole thereby should not be economically or socially disadvantaged, seems to bespeak the obvious. It is only women who bear children; no man can become pregnant. As I argued earlier, it is unfair to impose all the costs of pregnancy upon one half of the population. It is difficult to conceive that distinctions or discriminations based on pregnancy could ever be regarded as other than discrimination based on sex, or that restrictive statutory conditions applicable only to pregnant women did not discriminate against them as women.' [85]

The court made it clear that the purpose of anti-discrimination legislation is the removal of unfair disadvantages which have been imposed on individuals or groups in society. Such an unfair disadvantage may result when the costs of an activity from which all of society benefits are placed on a single group of people. The reproduction of human beings is certainly such an activity, as is breast-feeding.

BIOLOGY – AND THE DESTINY OF SERVITUDE

Our intimate and gender-specific association with breast-feeding provides a universal case study of the sexist bias in economic value, production, reproduction and the human rights of workers.

Women work all by themselves to produce a milk product that cannot be qualitatively duplicated. Breast milk offers much more than ideal nutrition for the first six months of an infant's life, and thereafter the potential to contribute significantly to the nutrition and health of infants and young children. Breast milk is a living substance of great biological complexity that is both actively protective and immunomodulatory. Any breast-milk substitute, even the most sophisticated and nutritionally balanced formula prepared in accordance with Codex Alimentarius standards, cannot begin to offer the numerous and unique advantages that breast milk provides a child, or to approximate the significance of the act of breast-feeding for children and mothers alike.

Breast milk is frequently – and erroneously – described as 'free'. This is incorrect, if only from the stand-point of the energy cost to mothers and the value of their time during breast-feeding. There is also a nutritional cost. Maternal depletion is a common outcome of breast-feeding. Human milk has not usually been considered or classified as a food by planners or agronomists, as it is not grown agriculturally or purchased in a processed container. It is not conceptually difficult to measure the shadow price of breast milk. One could ascertain the 'opportunity costs' in terms of both the time a woman takes for breast-feeding and the additional food required for the mother. That assumes, of course, a value on the mother's time. One could investigate the availability of alternative forms of milk for a child, its price and the distance to the outlet to obtain that alternative form. But this, as a value measurement, does not emphasise the fact that breast milk is better for an infant.

Mounting evidence shows that breast-feeding provides for significant protection when practised for a minimum of thirteen weeks. The operative health policy conclusion is that maternity leave should never be less than three months after delivery.

The World Health Organisation (WHO) recognises at least three other points of particular interest in the economics of breast-feeding: 1. the health policy considerations of maternity protection measures for those employed outside the home; 2. the impact of breast-feeding on child spacing and the related costs or savings to society due to variable breast-feeding rates; 3. the potential savings in maternity wards and hospitals that are reorganised on WHO/UNICEF guidelines for protecting, promoting and supporting breast-feeding which help to make the health-care environment mother- and baby-friendly.[86] To this list can be added the huge energy costs in the daily sterilising of water and equipment for feeding breast-milk substitutes.

Breast-milk is the best food a new human being can have. It is a 'product' that does not enter the market, that must be 'served' to the consumer by a woman who is most certainly 'occupied' while performing this 'labour'. This 'subsistence worker' most certainly 'stores and carries out some basic processing of their produce'. Article 11 of

ICESCR states in part that 'parties to the present Covenant recognise the right of everyone to an adequate standard of living for himself and his [*sic*] family, including adequate food'.

A 1987 special report to the Economic and Social Council of the United Nations on the right to food expanded on this right. 'Everyone requires food which is (a) sufficient, balanced and safe to satisfy nutritional requirements (b) culturally acceptable and (c) accessible in a manner which does not destroy one's dignity as a human being. As well, food which is adequate, qualitatively, quantitatively and culturally, should be accessible in a sustained way'. This implies that 'the physical and institutional environment in which food is procured must be optimumly utilised and protected from erosion or distortion'. For our present purposes this involves three levels of state responsibility: 1. the obligation to respect the right to food; 2. the obligation to protect the right to food; 3. the obligation to fulfil the right to food.[87]

In the context of the work done during lactation, a further 'hard law' authority becomes relevant, the 1989 Convention on the Rights of the Child. Article 24(2) focuses on the child's right to the 'highest attainable standard of health' which states are required to assist through facilitating the 'right to enjoy adequate nutritious food'. The state is required to take measures to reduce infant and child mortality, which include appropriate pre- and post-natal health care for mothers. In addition, state parties are required to inform parents of the benefits of breast-feeding and to ensure adequate nutrition for mothers. Article 27 recognises that the child has a right to 'a standard of living adequate for their physical, mental, spiritual, moral and social development'.[88]

Statements by the WHO and the United Nations Children's Fund (UNICEF), while not legally binding, carry the moral and political weight of soft law. New Zealand as a member of the UN is a party to these resolutions. For instance, in 1978 the 31st World Health Assembly (WHA) prioritised breast-feeding as the preferred method of infant feeding. The Preamble to the WHA International Code of Marketing of Breast Milk Substitutes emphasises the right of every child and pregnant and lactating woman to be well nourished, and Article 4 requires governments to educate their populations on the best available infant-feeding method.

In 1989 WHO/UNICEF stated that 'breastfeeding is an unequalled way of providing ideal food for the health, growth and development of infants and has a unique biological and emotional influence on the health of both mother and child'. The statement required competent authorities in all countries to 'implement health and social measures' that will 'protect, promote and support breastfeeding'.[89]

INCOMPARABLE INEQUALITY

How is it, given the weight of all this evidence, that lactating mothers are not considered as producers, economically active subsistence workers, supplying an important basis of livelihood to the household? How is it that a human rights guarantee of equality supposes that any such worker can be compared with a man, who is utterly incapable of such work?

The Australian Senate Standing Committee on Legal and Consti-tutional Affairs has described gender bias as 'stereotyped views about the proper social role, capacity, ability and behaviour of women and men which ignore the realities of their lives and result in laws and practices which disadvantage women'.[90] All the work associated with reproduction makes this a stark reality. But women do much more work than that which is unique to their biology.

The 1995 Human Development Report tells us that, while women are the primary nurturers of families, they also spend more time than men at work. If their labour were paid or given a proper market value women would emerge as the major breadwinners in most societies. 'Many household tasks are unrelenting, meals must be prepared 3 times a day, childcare cannot be delayed until there is free time, this becomes clear on weekends. During weekdays men and women may have rela-tively equal total workloads but data from 18 industrial countries show that on Saturday women work almost 2 more hours than men and on Sunday one hour and three quarters more, a difference that widens if the family has young children.'

After describing of the undervaluation of the work women do and the lack of recognition of the contribution they make, the report states: 'the monetisation of the non-market work of women is more than a question of justice. It concerns the economic status of women in society. If more human activities were seen as market transactions the prevailing wages would yield gigantically large monetary values'.[91]

The legal, economic, social and policy changes required to redress the universal inequalities experienced by women because their work is not recognised are enormous. But the international legal instru-ments *require* the changes. Article 4(1) of CEDAW states: 'Adoption

by States Parties of temporary special measures aimed at accelerating
de facto equality between men and women shall not be considered
discrimination'.

Prof. Eliane Vogel-Polsky has commented: 'This is the first ever clear
statement in an international and universally applicable legal instru-
ment to the effect that positive action neither constitutes discrimination
nor derogates from the principle of equality (provided the measures
are temporary and aim to correct inequality where it is actually experienced). . . . It is an internationally accepted interpretation of a general
principle of law, the principle of equality between men and women.'

Article 4(1), according to Prof. Vogel-Polsky, 'is a principle of interpretation that has entered directly into the domestic legal order of
every state ratifying the Convention . . . Once the principle has entered
into a state's domestic legal order, it applies to all the laws, collective
agreements or statutory provisions in which equality of opportunity
and treatment is guaranteed to women and men.' The principle of
interpretation 'is not static; in essence it is dynamic since it enters into
every field where the issue of sexual equality arises and lends a new
dimension to legal standards adopted in the country's constitution, its
general or specific legislation, or the clauses of any collective agreement. Positive action measures must be adopted whenever and
wherever they are seen to be necessary for the achievement of equality
in this sense.'[92]

Early in 1996 WAM submitted its case to the New Zealand Human
Rights Commission, with all the covenants, soft law sources, judicial
precedents and expert statements gathered in specific subject areas
by my students. By the time of submission, students were already
applying what they had learnt to other political issues in their lives:
the immigration status of adopted refugee children, discrimination in
employment on the ground of sexual orientation, and tenancy disputes.

CONCLUSION

Internationally, there have been isolated instances of movement. The
Canadian government has finally approved questions which will recognise and count home management in the 1996 census. Question 30
will ask Canadians how many hours were spent (a) doing unpaid
housework, yard work or home maintenance, (b) looking after children,
and (c) providing unpaid care to seniors.

A key activist in securing this change, the Canadian Alliance for Home Managers, reported:

> We would not want to downplay our delight in simply being there, but we do have some concerns. We feel it is not proper to ask that the work day of home managers be broken down into separate tasks. This is not required of any other occupation, and, in any event, the census is not the proper statistical tool for detailed time use analysis. Question 31 records labour market activity by simply asking, 'Last week, how many hours did this person spend working for pay or in self-employment?' The same approach should have been used for unpaid work. Interpretation of data on household activities will be complicated by the fact that respondents are advised, where activities overlap, to report the same hours in more than one part of the questions. This will also make it impossible to compare hours of paid and unpaid work. We note that, whereas there is only one question on household activity, there are sixteen questions on labour market activity. We trust that a better balance between these two categories of work will emerge in future, and that volunteer community work will be added to more accurately reflect the work of all Canadians.[93]

Italy's 800,000 strong National Housewives Federation, formed thirteen years ago to press for housewives' rights to pensions and benefits, recently voted to turn itself from a pressure group into a union. It took that step after Italy's Constitutional Court ruled earlier in 1995 that housework had as much economic value as work done outside the home. The federation's founder, Frederica Rossi Gasparrini, hopes that union status will give her greater power to campaign for Italy's nine million full-time housewives and the six million who combine work in the home with outside employment.[94]

On 25 April 1995 a private member's bill entitled the Counting Unremunerated Work Bill was debated in the Senate of Trinidad and Tobago. It required the Central Statistical Office and other public bodies to include, in the production of statistics relating to GDP and other accounts, a calculation of unremunerated work performed in Trinidad and Tobago, and to include this calculation in the GDP. The bill was unanimously supported on its second reading and referred to a special select committee. On 9 May, the committee recommended a major amendment, that the value of unremunerated work be included in a set of 'satellite' accounts which do not form part of the official national statistics. Some government members feared negative consequences from publishing national income statistics computed differently from those of other countries. [95]

At the Beijing women's conference in 1995 Helga Conrad, Federal Minister for Women's Affairs in Austria, stated: 'The unequal distribution of power is implicitly based on the unequal distribution of paid and unpaid work, and the resulting power differential is the main obstacle to the equality of women in all parts of the world. The lengthy process of redistributing paid and unpaid work must be speeded up. For this purpose the obligation to share household child rearing and caring tasks in a spirit of partnership shall become part of the marriage and family law in Austria and non-compliance will be a matrimonial offence.'[96]

The UN does not need re-drafts or new covenants to improve the situation of women. The law is there and so are the mechanisms. What is missing is the political will. With the petition to the New Zealand Parliament on parliamentary representation, and the submission to the New Zealand Human Rights Commission, we are using the law to test political will. We are exhausting our domestic legal remedies. And, if the outcomes are negative, we will use the communication process to test the resolution of the UNHRC to hear these complaints of universal inequality.

I situate women in their own reality. We are, universally, half of humankind. We are guaranteed equal rights to participate in political and civil life. Nowhere do we experience this equality in reality.

I situate women in their own reality. Everywhere we work longer hours than men. We may not be paid, but no comparator is necessary. We may not be in servitude, we may even enjoy the time taken in all the production and services we furnish, but our reality is that this is work.

To refuse our participation with men on equal terms in political representation, and to refuse to recognise our economic production and reproduction as work, is a fundamental and universal breach of human rights.

Our lives are testimony.

International Covenant on Economic, Social and Cultural Rights

PREAMBLE
The States Parties to the present Covenant,
Considering that, in accordance with the principles proclaimed in the Charter of the United Nations, recognition of the inherent dignity and of the equal and inalienable rights of all members of the human family is the foundation of freedom, justice and peace in the world,
Recognizing that these rights derive from the inherent dignity of the human person,
Recognizing that, in accordance with the Universal Declaration of Human Rights, the ideal of free human beings enjoying freedom from fear and want can only be achieved if conditions are created whereby everyone may enjoy his economic, social and cultural rights, as well as his civil and political rights,
Considering the obligation of States under the Charter of the United Nations to promote universal respect for, and observance of, human rights and freedoms,
Realizing that the individual, having duties to other individuals and to the community to which he belongs, is under a responsibility to strive for the promotion and observance of the rights recognised in the present Covenant,
Agree upon the following articles:

Part I

ARTICLE 1
1. All peoples have the right of self-determination. By virtue of that right they freely determine their political status and freely pursue their economic, social and cultural development.
2. All peoples may, for their own ends, freely dispose of their natural wealth and resources without prejudice to any obligations arising out of international economic co-operation, based upon the principle of mutual benefit, and international law. In no case may a people be deprived of its own means of subsistence.
3. The States Parties to the present Covenant, including those having responsibility for the administration of Non Self-Governing and Trust Territories, shall promote the realization of the right of self-determination, and shall respect that right in conformity with the provisions of the Charter of the United Nations.

Part II

ARTICLE 2
1. Each State Party to the present Covenant undertakes to take steps, individ-

ually and through international assistance and co-operation, especially economic and technical, to the maximum of its available resources, with a view to
achieving progressively the full realization of the rights recognised in the
present Covenant by all appropriate means, including particularly the adoption
of legislative measures.

2.   The States Parties to the present Covenant undertake to guarantee that
the rights enunciated in the present Covenant will be exercised without discrimination of any kind as to race, colour, sex, language, religion, political or
other opinion, national or social origin, property, birth or other status.

3.   Developing countries, with due regard to human rights and their national
economy, may determine to what extent they would guarantee the economic
rights recognised in the present Covenant to non-nationals.

ARTICLE 3

The States Parties to the present Covenant undertake to ensure the equal rights
of men and women to the enjoyment of all economic, social and cultural rights
set forth in the present Covenant.

ARTICLE 4

The States Parties to the present Covenant recognize that, in the enjoyment of
those rights provided by the State in conformity with the present Covenant, the
State may subject such rights only to such limitations as are determined by law
only in so far as this may be compatible with the nature of these rights and
solely for the purpose of promoting the general welfare in a democratic society.

ARTICLE 5

1.   Nothing in the present Covenant may be interpreted as implying for any
State, group or person any right to engage in any activity or to perform any act
aimed at the destruction of any of the rights or freedoms recognized herein,
or at their limitation to a greater extent than is provided for in the present
Covenant.

2.   No restriction upon or derogation from any of the fundamental human
rights recognized or existing in any country in virtue of law, conventions, regulations or custom shall be admitted on the pretext that the present Covenant
does not recognise such rights or that it recognizes them to a lesser extent.

ARTICLE 6

1.   The States Parties to the present Covenant recognize the right to work,
which includes the right of everyone to the opportunity to gain his living by
work which he freely chooses or accepts, and will take appropriate steps to
safeguard this right.

2.   The steps to be taken by a State Party to the present Covenant to achieve
the full realization of this right shall include technical and vocational guidance
and training programmes, policies and techniques to achieve steady economic,
social and cultural development and full and productive employment under
conditions safeguarding fundamental political and economic freedoms to the
individual.

ARTICLE 7

The States Parties to the present Covenant recognize the right of everyone to the enjoyment of just and favourable conditions of work which ensure, in particular:

- (a) Remuneration which provides all workers, as a minimum, with:
    - (i) Fair wages and equal remuneration for work of equal value without distinction of any kind, in particular women being guaranteed conditions of work not inferior to those enjoyed by men, with equal pay for equal work;
    - (ii) A decent living for themselves and their families in accordance with the provisions of the present Covenant;
- (b) Safe and healthy working conditions:
- (c) Equal opportunity for everyone to be promoted in his employment to an appropriate higher level, subject to no considerations other than those of seniority and competence;
- (d) Rest, leisure and reasonable limitation of working hours and periodic holidays with pay, as well as remuneration for public holidays.

ARTICLE 8

1. The States Parties to the present Covenant undertake to ensure:
- (a) The right of everyone to form trade unions and join the trade union of his choice, subject only to the rules of the organisation concerned, for the promotion and protection of his economic and social interests. No restrictions may be placed on the exercise of this right other than those prescribed by law and which are necessary in a democratic society in the interests of national security or public order or for the protection of the rights and freedoms of others;
- (b) The right of trade unions to establish national federations or confederations and the right of the latter to form or join international trade-union organizations;
- (c) The right of trade unions to function freely subject to no limitations other than those prescribed by law and which are necessary in a democratic society in the interests of national security or public order or for the protection of the rights and freedoms of others;
- (d) The right to strike, provided that it is exercised in conformity with the laws of the particular country.

2. This article shall not prevent the imposition of lawful restrictions on the exercise of these rights by members of the armed forces or of the police or of the administration of the State.

3. Nothing in this article shall authorize States Parties to the International Labour Organisation convention of 1948 concerning Freedom of Association and Protection of the Right to Organise to take legislative measures which would prejudice, or apply the law in such a manner as would prejudice, the guarantees provided for in that Convention.

ARTICLE 9

The States Parties to the present Covenant recognize the right of everyone to social security, including social insurance.

ARTICLE 10

The States Parties to the present Covenant recognize that:

1. The widest possible protection and assistance should be accorded to the family, which is the natural and fundamental group unit of society, particularly for its establishment and while it is responsible for the care and education of dependent children. Marriage must be entered into with the free consent of the intending spouses.

2. Special protection should be accorded to mothers during a reasonable period before and after childbirth. During such period working mothers should be accorded paid leave or leave with adequate social security benefits.

3. Special measures of protection and assistance should be taken on behalf of all children and young persons without any discrimination for reasons of parentage or other conditions. Children and young persons should be protected from economic and social exploitation. Their employment in work harmful to their morals or health or dangerous to life or likely to hamper their normal development should be punishable by law. States should also set age limits below which the paid employment of child labour should be prohibited and punishable by law.

ARTICLE 11

1. The States Parties to the present Covenant recognize the right of everyone to an adequate standard of living for himself and his family, including adequate food, clothing and housing, and to the continuous improvement of living conditions. The States Parties will take appropriate steps to ensure the realization of this right, recognizing to this effect the essential importance of international co-operation based on free consent.

2. The States Parties to the present Covenant, recognizing the fundamental right of everyone to be free from hunger, shall take, individually and through international co-operation, the measures, including specific programmes, which are needed:

   (a) To improve methods of production, conservation and distribution of food by making full use of technical and scientific knowledge, by disseminating knowledge of the principles of nutrition and by developing or reforming agrarian systems in such a way as to achieve the most efficient development and utilization of natural resources;

   (b) Taking into account the problems of both food-importing and food-exporting countries, to ensure an equitable distribution of world food supplies in relation to need.

ARTICLE 12

1. The States Parties to the present Covenant recognize the right of everyone to the enjoyment of the highest attainable standard of physical and mental health.

2. The steps to be take by the States Parties to the present Covenant to achieve the full realization of this right shall include those necessary for:

(a) The provision for the reduction of the stillbirth-rate and of infant mortality and for the healthy development of the child;

(b) The improvement of all aspects of environmental and industrial hygiene;

(c) The prevention, treatment and control of epidemic, endemic, occupational and other diseases;

(d) The creation of conditions which would assure to all medical service and medical attention in the event of sickness.

ARTICLE 13

1. The States Parties to the present Covenant recognize the right of everyone to education. They agree that education shall be directed to the full development of the human personality and the sense of its dignity, and shall strengthen the respect for human rights and fundamental freedoms. They further agree that education shall enable all persons to participate effectively in a free society, promote understanding, tolerance and friendship among all nations and all racial, ethnic and religious groups, and further the activities of the United Nations for the maintenance of peace.

2. The States Parties to the present Covenant recognize that, with a view to achieving the full realization of this right:

(a) Primary education shall be compulsory and available free to all:

(b) Secondary education in its different forms, including technical and vocational secondary education, shall be made generally available and accessible to all by every appropriate means, and in particular by the progressive introduction of free education;

(c) Higher education shall be made equally accessible to all, on the basis of capacity, by every appropriate means, and in particular by the progressive introduction of free education;

(d) Fundamental education shall be encouraged or intensified as far as possible for those persons who have not received or completed the whole period of their primary education;

(e) The development of a system of schools at all levels shall be actively pursued, an adequate fellowship system shall be established, and the material conditions of teaching staff shall be continuously improved.

3. The States Parties to the present Covenant undertake to have respect for the liberty of parents and, when applicable, legal guardians to choose for their children schools, other than those established by the public authorities, which conform to such minimum educational standards as may be laid down or approved by the State and to ensure the religious and moral education of their children in conformity with their own convictions.

4. No part of this article shall be construed so as to interfere with the liberty of individuals and bodies to establish and direct educational institutions, subject

always to the observance of the principles set forth in paragraph 1 of this article and to the requirement that the education given in such institutions shall conform to such minimum standards as may be laid down by the State.

ARTICLE 14

Each State Party to the present Covenant which, at the time of becoming a Party, has not been able to secure in its metropolitan territory or other territories under its jurisdiction compulsory primary education, free of charge, undertakes, within two years, to work out and adopt a detailed plan of action for the progressive implementation, within a reasonable number of years, to be fixed in the plan, of the principle of compulsory education free of charge for all.

ARTICLE 15

1.   The States Parties to the present Covenant recognize the right of everyone:

(a) To take part in cultural life;

(b) To enjoy the benefits of scientific progress and its applications;

(c) To benefit from the protection of the moral and material interests resulting from any scientific, literary or artistic production of which he is the author.

2.   The steps to be taken by the States Parties to the present Covenant to achieve the full realization of this right shall include those necessary for the conservation, the development and the diffusion of science and culture.

3.   The States Parties to the present Covenant undertake to respect the freedom indispensable for scientific research and creative activity.

4.   The States Parties to the present Covenant recognize the benefits to be derived from the encouragement and development of international contacts and co-operation in the scientific and cultural fields.

International Covenant on Civil and Political Rights

PREAMBLE

The States Parties to the present Covenant,

Considering that, in accordance with the principles proclaimed in the Charter of the United Nations, recognition of the inherent dignity and of the equal and inalienable rights of all members of the human family is the foundation of freedom, justice and peace in the world,

Recognizing that these rights derive from the inherent dignity of the human person,

Recognizing that, in accordance with the Universal Declaration of Human rights, the ideal of free human beings enjoying civil and political freedom and freedom from fear and want can only be achieved if conditions are created whereby everyone may enjoy his civil and political rights, as well as his economic, social and cultural rights,

Considering the obligation of States under the Charter of the United Nations to promote universal respect for, and observance of, human rights and freedoms,

Realizing that the individual, having duties to other individuals and to the community to which he belongs, is under a responsibility to strive for the promotion and observance of the rights recognised in the present Covenant,

Agree upon the following articles:

Part I

ARTICLE 1

1.   All peoples have the right of self-determination. By virtue of that right they freely determine their political status and freely pursue their economic, social and cultural development.

2.   All peoples may, for their own ends, freely dispose of their natural wealth and resources without prejudice to any obligations arising out of international economic co-operation, based upon the principle of mutual benefit, and international law. In no case may a people be deprived of its own means of subsistence.

3.   The States Parties to the present Covenant, including those having responsibility for the administration of Non-Self-Governing and Trust Territories, shall promote the realization of the right of self-determination, and shall respect that right in conformity with the provisions of the Charter of the United Nations.

Part II

ARTICLE 2

1.   Each State Party to the present Covenant undertakes to respect and to ensure to all individuals within its territory and subject to its jurisdiction the rights recognized in the present Covenant, without distinction of any kind, such as race, colour, sex, language, religion, political or other opinion, national or social origin, property, birth or other status.

2.   Where not already provided for by existing legislative or other measures, each State Party to the present Covenant undertakes to take the necessary steps, in accordance with its constitutional processes and with the provisions of the present Covenant, to adopt such legislative or other measures as may be necessary to give effect to the rights recognized in the present Covenant.

3.   Each State Party to the present Covenant undertakes:

   (a) To ensure that any person whose rights or freedoms as herein recognized are violated shall have an effective remedy, notwithstanding that the violation has been committed by persons acting in an official capacity;

   (b) To ensure that any person claiming such a remedy shall have his right thereto determined by competent judicial, administrative or legislative authorities, or by any other competent authority provided for by the legal system of the State, and to develop the possibilities of judicial remedy;

   (c) To ensure that the competent authorities shall enforce such remedies when granted.

ARTICLE 3

The States Parties to the present Covenant undertake to ensure the equal right of men and women to the enjoyment of all civil and political rights set forth in the present Covenant. . . .

Part III

ARTICLE 7

No one shall be subjected to torture or to cruel, inhuman or degrading treatment or punishment. In particular, no one shall be subjected without his free consent to medical or scientific experimentation.

ARTICLE 8

1.   No one shall be held in slavery; slavery and the slave-trade in all their forms shall be prohibited.

2.   No one shall be held in servitude.

3.   (a) No one shall be required to perform forced or compulsory labour;

   (b) Paragraph 3(a) shall not be held to preclude, in countries where imprisonment with hard labour may be imposed as a punishment for a crime, the performance of hard labour in pursuance of a sentence to such punishment by a competent court;

(c) For the purpose of this paragraph the term 'forced or compulsory labour' shall not include:

    (i) Any work or service, not referred to in subparagraph (b), normally required of a person who is under detention in consequence of a lawful order of a court, or of a person during conditional release from such detention;

    (ii) Any service of a military character and, in countries where conscientious objection is recognized, any national service required by law of conscientious objectors;

    (iii) Any service exacted in cases of emergency or calamity threatening the life or well-being of the community;

    (iv) Any work or service which forms part of normal civil obligations. . . .

ARTICLE 23

1.   The family is the natural and fundamental group unit of society and is entitled to protection by society and the State.

2.   The right of men and women of marriageable age to marry and to found a family shall be recognized.

3.   No marriage shall be entered into without the free and full consent of the intending spouses.

4.   State Parties to the present Covenant shall take appropriate steps to ensure equality of rights and responsibilities of spouses as to marriage, during marriage and at its dissolution. In the case of dissolution, provision shall be made for the necessary protection of any children. . . .

ARTICLE 25

Every citizen shall have the right and the opportunity, without any of the distinctions mentioned in article 2 and without unreasonable restrictions:

    (a) To take part in the conduct of public affairs, directly or through freely chosen representatives

    (b) To vote and to be elected at genuine periodic elections which shall be by universal and equal suffrage and shall be held by secret ballot, guaranteeing the free expression of the will of the electors;

    (c) To have access, on general terms of equality, to public service in his country.

ARTICLE 26

All persons are equal before the law and are entitled without any discrimination to the equal protection of the law. In this respect, the law shall prohibit any discrimination and guarantee to all persons equal and effective protection against discrimination on any ground such as race, colour, sex, language, religion, political or other opinion, national or social origin, property, birth or other status.

ARTICLE 27

In those States in which ethnic, religious or linguistic minorities exist, persons belonging to such minorities shall not be denied the right, in community with the other members of their group, to enjoy their own culture, to profess and practise their own religion, or to use their own language.

Convention on the Elimination of All Forms of Discrimination Against Women

The States Parties to the present Convention,

Noting that the Charter of the United Nations reaffirms faith in fundamental human rights, in the dignity and worth of the human person and in the equal rights of men and women,

Noting that the Universal Declaration of Human Rights affirms the principle of the inadmissibility of discrimination and proclaims that all human beings are born free and equal in dignity and rights and that everyone is entitled to all the rights and freedoms set forth therein, without distinction of any kind, including distinction based on sex,

Noting that the States Parties to the International Covenants on Human Rights have the obligation to ensure the equal right of men and women to enjoy all economic, social, cultural, civil and political rights,

Considering the international conventions concluded under the auspices of the United Nations and the specialized agencies promoting equality of rights of men and women,

Noting also the resolutions, declarations and recommendations adopted by the United Nations and the specialised agencies promoting equality of rights of men and women,

Concerned, however, that despite these various instruments extensive discrimination against women continues to exist,

Recalling that discrimination against women violates the principals of equality of rights and respect for human dignity, is an obstacle to the participation of women, on equal terms with men, in the political, social, economic and cultural life of their countries, hampers the growth of the prosperity of society and the family and makes more difficult the full development of the potentialities of women in the service of their countries and of humanity,

Concerned that in situations of poverty women have the least access to food, health, education, training and opportunities for employment and other needs,

Convinced that the establishment of the new international economic order based on equity and justice will contribute significantly towards the promotion of equality between men and women,

Emphasizing that the eradication of apartheid, of all forms of racism, racial discrimination, colonialism, neo-colonialism, aggression, foreign occupation and domination and interference in the internal affairs of States is essential to the full enjoyment of the rights of men and women,

Affirming that the strengthening of international peace and security, the relaxation of international tension, mutual co-operation among all States irrespective of their social and economic systems, general and complete disarmament, and in particular nuclear disarmament under strict and effective international control, the affirmation of the principles of justice, equality and mutual benefit in relations among countries and the realization of the right of peoples under alien and colonial domination and foreign occupation to self-determination and independence, as well as respect for national sovereignty and territorial integrity, will promote social progress and development and as a consequence will contribute to the attainment of full equality between men and women,

Convinced that the full and complete development of a country, the welfare of the world and the cause of peace require the maximum participation of women on equal terms with men in all fields,

Bearing in mind the great contribution of women to the welfare of the family and to the development of society, so far not fully recognized the social significance of maternity and the role of both parents in the family and in the upbringing of children, and aware that the role of women in procreation should not be a basis for discrimination but that the upbringing of children requires a sharing of responsibility between men and women and society as a whole,

Aware that a change in the traditional role of men as well as the role women in society and in the family is needed to achieve full equality between men and women,

Determined to implement the principles set forth in the Declaration on the Elimination of Discrimination against Women and, for that purpose, to adopt the measures required for the elimination of such discrimination in all its forms and manifestations,

Have agreed on the following:

Part I

ARTICLE 1

For the purpose of the present Convention, the term "discrimination against women" shall mean any distinction, exclusion or restriction made on the basis of sex which has the effect or purpose of impairing or nullifying the recognition, enjoyment or exercise by women, irrespective of their marital status, on a basis of equality of men and women, of human rights and fundamental freedoms in the political, economic, social, cultural, civil or any other field.

ARTICLE 2

States Parties condemn discrimination again women in all its forms, agree to pursue by all appropriate means and without delay a policy of eliminating discrimination against women and, to this end, undertake:

(a) To embody the principle of the equality of men and women in their national constitutions or other appropriate legislation if not yet incorporated therein and to ensure, through law and other appropriate means, the practical realization of this principle;

(b) To adopt appropriate legislative and other measures, including sanctions where appropriate, prohibiting all discrimination against women;

(c) To establish legal protection of the rights of women on an equal basis with men and to ensure through competent national tribunals and other public institutions the effective protection of women against any act of discrimination;

(d) To refrain from engaging in any act or practice of discrimination against women and to ensure that public authorities and institutions shall act in conformity with this obligation;

(e) To take all appropriate measures to eliminate discrimination against women by any person, organization or enterprise;

(f) To take all appropriate measures, including legislation, to modify or abolish existing laws, regulations, customs and practices which constitute discrimination against women;

(g) To repeal all national penal provisions which constitute discrimination again women.

ARTICLE 3

States Parties shall take in all fields, in particular in the political, social, economic and cultural fields, all appropriate measures, including legislation, to ensure the full development and advancement of women, for the purpose of guaranteeing them the exercise and enjoyment of human rights and fundamental freedoms on a basis of equality with men.

ARTICLE 4

1.   Adoption by States Parties of temporary special measures aimed at accelerating *de facto* equality between men and women shall not be considered discrimination as defined in the present convention, but shall in no way entail as a consequence the maintenance of unequal or separate standards; these measures shall be discontinued when the objectives of equality of opportunity and treatment have been achieved.

2.   Adoption by States Parties of special measures, including those measures contained in the present Convention, aimed at protecting maternity shall not be considered discriminatory.

ARTICLE 5

States Parties shall take all appropriate measures:

(a) To modify the social and cultural patterns of conduct of men and women, with a view to achieving the elimination of prejudices and customary and all other practices which are based on the idea of the inferiority or the superiority of either of the sexes or on stereotyped roles for men and women;

(b) To ensure that family education includes a proper understanding of maternity as a social function and the recognition of the common responsibility of men and women in the upbringing and development of their children, it being understood that the interest of the children is the primordial consideration in all cases.

ARTICLE 6

States Parties shall take all appropriate measures, including legislation, to suppress all forms of traffic in women and exploitation of prostitution of women.

Part II

ARTICLE 7

States Parties shall take all appropriate measures to eliminate discrimination against women in the political and public life of the country and, in particular, shall ensure to women, on equal terms with men, the right:

(a) to vote in all elections and public referenda and to be eligible for election to all publicly elected bodies;

(b) To participate in the formulation of government policy and the implementation thereof and to hold public office and perform all public functions at all levels of government;

(c) To participate in non-governmental organizations and associations concerned with the public and political life of the country.

ARTICLE 8

States Parties shall take all appropriate measures to ensure to women, on equal terms with men and without any discrimination, the opportunity to represent their Governments at the international level and to participate in the work of international organizations.

ARTICLE 9

1.   States Parties shall grant women equal rights with men to acquire, change or retain their nationality. They shall ensure in particular that neither marriage to an alien nor change of nationality by the husband during marriage shall automatically change the nationality of the wife, render her stateless or force upon her the nationality of the husband.

2.   States Parties shall grant women equal rights with men with respect to the nationality of their children.

Part III

ARTICLE 10

States Parties shall take all appropriate measures to eliminate discrimination against women in order to ensure to them equal rights with men in the field of education and in particular to ensure, on a basis of equality of men and women:

(a) The same conditions for career and vocational guidance, for access to studies and for the achievement of diplomas in educational establishments of all categories in rural as well as in urban areas; this equality shall be ensured in pre-school, general, technical, professional and higher technical education, as well as in all types of vocational training;

(b) Access to the same curricula, the same examinations, teaching staff with qualifications of the same standard and school premises and equipment of the same quality;

(c) The elimination of any stereotyped concept of the roles of men and women at all levels and in all forms of education by encouraging coeducation and other types of education which will help to achieve this aim and, in particular, by the revision of textbooks and school programmes and the adaptation of teaching methods;

(d) The same opportunities to benefit from scholarships and other study grants;

(e) The same opportunities for access to programmes of continuing education, including adult and functional literacy programmes, particularly those aimed at reducing, at the earliest possible time, any gap in education existing between men and women;

(f) The reduction of female student drop-out rates and the organization of programmes for girls and women who have left school prematurely;

(g) The same opportunities to participate actively in sports and physical education;

(h) Access to specific educational information to help to ensure the health and well-being of families, including information and advice on family planning.

ARTICLE 11

1.   States Parties shall take all appropriate measures to eliminate discrimination against women in the field of employment in order to ensure, on a basis of equality of men and women, the same rights, in particular:

(a) The right to work as an inalienable right of all human beings;

(b) The right to the same employment opportunities, including the application of the same criteria for selection in matters of employment;

(c) The right to free choice of profession and employment, the right to promotion, job security and all benefits and conditions of service and the right to receive vocational training and retraining, including apprenticeships, advanced vocational training and recurrent training;

(d) The right to equal remuneration, including benefits, and to equal treatment in respect of work of equal value, as well as equality of treatment in the evaluation of the quality of work;

(e) The right to social security, particularly in cases of retirement, unemployment, sickness, invalidity and old age and other incapacity to work, as well as the right to paid leave;

(f) The right to protection of health and to safety in working conditions, including the safeguarding of the function of reproduction.

2.   In order to prevent discrimination against women on the grounds of marriage or maternity and to ensure their effective right to work, States Parties shall take appropriate measures:

(a) To prohibit, subject to the imposition of sanctions, dismissal on the grounds of pregnancy or of maternity leave and discrimination in dismissals on the basis of marital status;

(b) To introduce maternity leave with pay or with comparable social benefits without loss of former employment, seniority or social allowances;

(c) To encourage the provision of the necessary supporting social services to enable parents to combine family obligations with work responsibilities and participation in public life, in particular through promoting the establishment and development of a network of child-care facilities;

(d) To provide special protection to women during pregnancy in types of work proved to be harmful to them.

3. Protective legislation relating to matters covered in this article shall be reviewed periodically in the light of scientific and technological knowledge and shall be revised, repealed or extended as necessary.

ARTICLE 12

1. States Parties shall take all appropriate measures to eliminate discrimination against women in the field of health care in order to ensure, on the basis of equality of men and women, access to health care services, including those related to family planning.

2. Notwithstanding the provisions of paragraph 1 of this article, States Parties shall ensure to women appropriate services in connexion with pregnancy, confinement and the post-natal period, granting free services where necessary, as well as adequate nutrition during pregnancy and lactation.

ARTICLE 13

State Parties shall take all appropriate measures to eliminate discrimination against women in other areas of economic and social life in order to ensure, on a basis of equality of men and women, the same rights, in particular:

(a) The right to family benefits;

(b) The right to bank loans, mortgages and other forms of financial credit;

(c) The right to participate in recreational activities, sports and all aspects of cultural life.

ARTICLE 14

1. States Parties shall take into account the particular problems faced by rural women and the significant roles which rural women play in the economic survival of their families, including their work in the non-monetized sectors of the economy, and shall take all appropriate measures to ensure the application of the provisions of this Convention to women in rural areas.

2. States Parties shall take all appropriate measures to eliminate discrimination against women in rural areas in order to ensure, on a basis of equality of men and women, that they participate in and benefit from rural development and, in particular, shall ensure to such women the right:

(a) To participate in the elaboration and implementation of development planning at all levels;

(b) To have access to adequate health care facilities, including information, counselling and services in family planning;

(c) To benefit directly from social security programmes;

(d) To obtain all types of training and education, formal and non-formal, including that relating to functional literacy, as well as, *inter alia*, the benefit of all community and extension services, in order to increase their technical proficiency;

(e) To organize self-help groups and co-operatives in order to obtain equal access to economic opportunities through employment or self-employment;

(f) To participate in all community activities;

(g) To have access to agricultural credit and loans, marketing facilities, appropriate technology and equal treatment in land and agrarian reform as well as in land resettlement schemes;

(h) To enjoy adequate living conditions, particularly in relation to housing, sanitation, electricity and water supply, transport and communications.

Part IV

ARTICLE 15

1.   States Parties shall accord to women equality with men before the law.

2.   States Parties shall accord to women, in civil matters, a legal capacity identical to that of men and the same opportunities to exercise that capacity. In particular, they shall give women equal rights to conclude contracts and to administer property and shall treat them equally in all stages of procedure in courts and tribunals.

3.   States Parties agree that all contracts and all other private instruments of any kind with a legal effect which is directed at restricting the legal capacity of women shall be deemed null and void.

4.   States Parties shall accord to men and women the same rights with regard to the law relating to the movement of persons and the freedom to choose their residence and domicile.

ARTICLE 16

1.   States Parties shall take all appropriate measures to eliminate discrimination against women in all matters relating to marriage and family relations and in particular shall ensure, on a basis of equality of men and women:

(a) The same right to enter into marriage;

(b) The same right freely to choose a spouse and to enter into marriage only with their free and full consent;

(c) The same rights and responsibilities during marriage and at its dissolution;

(d) the same rights and responsibilities as parents, irrespective of their marital status, in matters relating to their children; in all cases the interests of the children shall be paramount;

(e) The same rights to decide freely and responsibly on the number and spacing of their children and to have access to the information, education and means to enable them to exercise these rights;

(f) The same rights and responsibilities with regard to guardianship, wardship, trusteeship and adoption of children, or similar institutions where these concepts exist in national legislation; in all cases the interests of the children shall be paramount;

(g) The same personal rights as husband and wife, including the right to choose a family name, a profession and an occupation;

(h) The same rights for both spouses in respect of the ownership, acquisition, management, administration, enjoyment and disposition of property, whether free of charge or for a valuable consideration.

2. The betrothal and the marriage of a child shall have no legal effect, and all necessary action, including legislation, shall be taken to specify a minimum age for marriage and to make the registration of marriages in an official registry compulsory.

Structure of the United Nations

GENERAL ASSEMBLY AND SUBSIDIARY BODIES

Under Article 13 of the United Nations Charter, one of the functions of the General Assembly is to initiate studies and make recommendations for the purpose of 'promoting international cooperation in the economic, social, cultural, educational and health fields, and assisting in the realization of human rights and fundamental freedoms for all without distinction as to race, sex, language or religion.' Most items relating to human rights are referred by the General Assembly to its Third Committee, which deals with social, humanitarian and cultural matters. Some, however, are considered by the assembly without reference to a main committee. Items which have a bearing on political, international security and disarmament issues are normally referred to the First Committee or to the Special Political Committee. Those of an essentially economic character are referred to the Second Committee, those relating to decolonisation to the Fourth Committee, and those of a legal nature to the Sixth Committee. The Fifth Committee deals with administrative and budgetary questions, including those arising from the consideration of human rights items.

ECONOMIC AND SOCIAL COUNCIL AND SUBSIDIARY BODIES

Under Article 62 of the United Nations Charter, the Economic and Social Council may 'make recommendations for the purpose of promoting respect for, and observance of, human rights and fundamental freedoms for all'. It may also prepare draft conventions for submission to the General Assembly and call international conferences on human rights matters. Under Article 68, the council 'shall set up commissions in economic and social fields and for the protection of human rights'.

To assist it in dealing with items relating to human rights, the council has established the Commission on Human Rights and the Commission on the Status of Women. The Commission on Human Rights, in turn, has established the Sub-Commission on Prevention of Discrimination and Protection of Minorities.

COMMISSION ON HUMAN RIGHTS

The Commission on Human Rights makes studies, prepares recommendations and drafts international instruments relating to human rights. It also undertakes special tasks assigned to it by the General Assembly or the Economic and Social Council, including the investigation of allegations concerning violations of human rights and the handling of communications relating to such violations. It co-operates closely with all other United Nations bodies having competence in the field of human rights. In addition, it assists the Economic and Social Council in the co-ordination of activities concerning human rights in the United Nations system.

HUMAN RIGHTS COMMITTEE

The Human Rights Committee, established in 1977 in accordance with article 28 of the International Covenant on Civil and Political Rights, consists of eighteen members of high moral character and recognised competence in the field of human rights, elected by states parties to the covenant from among their nationals. Members are elected for a four-year term by secret ballot at a meeting of the states parties, and serve in their personal capacity.

The tasks of the committee as set out in articles 40–45 of the covenant are: to study reports on the measures states parties have adopted to give effect to the rights recognised in the covenant, and on the progress made in the enjoyment of those rights; to transmit its reports, and such general comments as it may consider appropriate, to the states parties; to perform certain functions with a view to settling disputes among states parties concerning the application of the covenant, provided that those parties have recognised the competence of the committee to that effect; and when necessary to establish an *ad hoc* conciliation commission to make available its good offices to states parties involved in a dispute concerning the application of the covenant, with a view to a friendly solution of the matter on the basis of respect for the covenant. Such a commission must submit a report to the committee chairman, not later than twelve months after having been seized of the matter, for communication to the states parties concerned.

Under the Optional Protocol to the International Covenant on Civil and Political Rights, individuals who claim that any of their rights enumerated in the covenant have been violated and who have exhausted all available domestic remedies may submit written communications to the Human Rights Committee for consideration. No communication can be received by the committee if it concerns a state party to the covenant which is not also a party to the Optional Protocol. The committee considers communications in the light of all written information made available to it by the individual and by the state party concerned, and forwards its views to the state party concerned and to the individual.

The committee normally holds three sessions each year, and reports annually to the General Assembly, through the Economic and Social Council.

COMMITTEE ON ECONOMIC, SOCIAL AND CULTURAL RIGHTS

The Committee on Economic, Social and Cultural Rights, established in 1985 by the Economic and Social Council, is composed of eighteen experts with recognised competence in the field of human rights serving in their personal capacity. Its members are elected for a term of four years by the council by secret ballot from a list of persons nominated by states parties to the International Covenant on Economic, Social and Cultural Rights.

The committee carries out functions relating to the implementation of

the covenant. It examines reports submitted to it by states parties on the measures they have adopted and the progress made in achieving the observance of
the rights recognised in the covenant, and assists the Economic and Social
Council to fulfil its supervisory functions relating to the covenant by making
suggestions and recommendations of a general nature based on its consideration of reports submitted by states parties and the specialised agencies
concerned.

COMMITTEE ON THE ELIMINATION OF DISCRIMINATION AGAINST WOMEN

The Committee on the Elimination of Discrimination Against Women, established in 1982 in accordance with article 17 of the Convention on the Elimination of all Forms of Discrimination again Women, consists of 23 experts of
high moral standing and competence in the field covered by the convention.
Members are elected by secret ballot from a list of persons nominated by States
parties, and serve a term of four years. The Committee on the Elimination of
Discrimination Against Women meets once a year for two weeks in Vienna (or
New York).

The basic task of the Committee, as set out in article 17 of the convention, is
to consider the progress made in the implementation of the convention.

COMMITTEE AGAINST TORTURE

The Committee Against Torture, established in 1987 in accordance with article
17 of the Convention Against Torture and Other Cruel, Inhuman or Degrading
Treatment or Punishment, consists of ten experts of high moral standing and
recognised competence in the field of human rights, elected by states parties to
the convention from among their nations. Members are elected for a four-year
term by secret ballot at a meeting of states parties, and serve in their personal
capacity.

The tasks of the committee, as set out in articles 19 to 24 of the convention,
are: to study reports on the measures taken by states parties to give effect to
their undertakings under the convention; to make confidential inquiries, if it
decides that this is warranted, concerning well-founded indications that torture
is being systematically practised in the territory of a state party; to perform
certain functions with a view to settling disputes among states parties concerning the application of the convention, provided that those states parties have
recognised the competence of the Committee Against Torture to undertake
such functions; to establish when necessary ad hoc conciliation commissions to
make available its good offices to the states parties concerned with a view to a
friendly solution of inter-state disputes; to consider communications from or
on behalf of individuals subject to the jurisdiction of states parties concerned
who claim to be victims of a violation of the provisions of the convention,
provided that those States parties have recognised the competence of the
committee to that effect; and to submit annual reports on its activities to the
States parties and to the General Assembly of the United Nations.

UNITED NATIONS SECRETARIAT CENTRE FOR HUMAN RIGHTS

The Centre for Human Rights, located at the United Nations Office at Geneva, is the Secretariat Unit of the United Nations mostly concerned with human rights questions. The Centre, headed by the Under-Secretary-General for Human Rights, who is also Director-General of the United Nations Office at Geneva, is made up of the office of the Under-Secretary-General and six main sections. The centre maintains an office in New York at United Nations Headquarters.

Bibliography

Abdela, Lesley. *Women with X Appeal*. London, Optima, 1989.

Alexander, K.C. *Man in India: Patterns of Utilization of Time in Rural Households in Areas with Different Levels of Economic Development*. New Delhi, 1991.

Ankar, Richard, M. E. Kahn and R. B. Gupta. *Women's Participation in the Labour Force: a Methods Test in India for Improving Its Measurement* (Women, Work and Development 16). Geneva, International Labour Office, 1988.

Anthony, Susan B. and Ida Husted Harper (eds). *History of Woman Suffrage v.4 1883–1900*. New York, Arno & the New York Times, 1969, pp.444–45 (1st published, 1902).

Arendt, Hannah. *Crises of the Republic*. New York, Harcourt Brace Jovanovich, 1972.

Australian Bureau of Statistics. *Measuring Unpaid Household Work: Issues and Experimental Estimates*. Canberra, 1990.

Bernard, Jessie. *The Female World*. New York, The Free Press, 1981.

Brill, Alida (ed.). *A Rising Public Voice: Women in Politics Worldwide*. New York, Feminist Press, New York City University, 1995.

Brownmiller, Susan. *Against Our Will*. New York, Simon & Schuster, 1975.

Chisholm, Shirley. *Unbought and Unbossed*. Boston, Houghton Mifflin, 1970.

Clark, Margaret (ed.). *Beyond Expectations: Fourteen Women Write about Their Lives*. Wellington, Allen & Unwin/Port Nicholson Press, 1986.

Cook, Rebecca J. (ed.). *Human Rights of Women: National and International Perspectives*. Philadelphia, University of Pennsylvania Press, 1994.

Cook, Rebecca J. 'State Accountability Under the Convention on the Elimination of All Forms of Discrimination Against Women', in Rebecca J. Cook (ed.), *Human Rights of Women: National and International Perspectives*. Philadelphia, University of Pennsylvania Press, 1994.

Coomaraswamy, Radhika. 'Women, Ethnicity and the Discourse of Rights', in Rebecca J. Cook (ed.), *Human Rights of Women: National and International Perspectives*. Philadelphia, University of Pennsylvania Press, 1994.

Devereaux, Mary Sue. 'Time Use of Canadians in 1992', *Canadian Social Trends*, Autumn 1992. Ottawa, Statistics Canada.

Devlin, Bernadette. *The Price of My Soul*. London, Pan Books, 1969.

Fast, Janet E. and Brenda Munroe. 'Towards Eliminating Gender Bias in Personal Injury Awards: Contributions from Family Economics', *Alberta Law Review*, 32, 1, 1994.

Freedman, Marcia. *Exile in the Promised Land: a Memoir*. New York, Firebrand Books, 1990.

Gilman, Charlotte Perkins. *Women and Economics*. New York, Harper & Row, 1966.

Greig, Don. 'Reflections on the Role of Consent', in *Australian Year Book of International Law*, v.12. Canberra, Australian National University Faculty of Law, 1992.

Haines, Janine. *Suffrage to Sufferance*. Sydney, Allen & Unwin, 1992.

Handbook of Household Surveys, Studies in Methods F31. New York, United Nations Department of International and Social Affairs Statistical Office, 1984.

Hawrylyshyn, Oli. *Estimating the Value of Household Work in Canada*. Ottawa, Statistics Canada, 1978.

Henkin, L., R. Pugh, O. Schachter and H. Smit (eds). *International Law: Cases and Materials*. St Paul, Minnesota, West Publishing, 1980.

Hogshire, Jim. *Sell Yourself to Science: the Complete Guide to Selling Your Organs, Body Fluids, Bodily Functions and Being a Human Guinea Pig*. Washington DC, Loonipanics Unlimited, 1992.

Hussey, Gemma. *At the Cutting Edge: Cabinet Diaries 1982–87*. Dublin, Gill & Macmillan, 1990.

Improving Gender Disaggregated Data on Human Resources Through Agricultural Censuses. Rome, Statistical Development Service, Food and Agriculture Organisation, 1992.

International Rice Research Institute. *Gender Analysis in Rice Farming Systems Research: Does It Make a Difference?* Report of 1990 Workshop, Bogor, Indonesia. Manila, 1990.

Ironmonger, Duncan S. 'Modelling the Household Economy', in M. Dutta (ed.), *Economics, Econometrics and the LINK: Essays in Honour of Lawrence R. Klein*. North Holland, Elsevier Science Publishers, 1995.

Kennedy, Helena. *Eve Was Framed*. London, Chatto & Windus, 1992.

Kunin, Madeleine. *Living a Political Life*. New York, Knopf, 1994.

Lloyd, Denis. *Introduction to Jurisprudence with Selected Texts*. London, Stevens, 1959.

Lorde, Audre. *Sister Outsider: Essays and Speeches*. Freedom, California, Crossing Press, 1984.

McCallum, Janet. *Women in the House*. Picton, Cape Catley, 1993.

Myers, Virginia. *Head and Shoulders*. Auckland, Penguin Books, 1986.

Opfell, Olga S. *Women Prime Ministers and Presidents*. North Carolina, McFarland & Co., 1993.

Rich, Adrienne. *On Lies, Secrets and Silence: Selected Prose 1966–78*. London, Virago, 1980.

Rich Adrienne. *What Is Found There: Notebooks on Poetry and Politics*. New York, Norton, 1993.

Sarojini, T. K. *Women in India: a Review of the Implementation of the Nairobi Forward Looking Strategies 1985–92*. New Delhi, ESCAP, 1993.

Schachter, Óscar. 'The Charter and the Constitution: the Human Rights Provisions in American Law', in *4 Vanderbilt Law Review*, 1951, pp.399-659.

Statistics Canada. Canada Yearbook. Ottawa, 1990 and 1992.

A System of National Accounts and Supporting Tables, Studies in Methods 2. New York, United Nations Department of Economic Affairs Statistical Office, 1953.

A System of National Accounts. New York, United Nations Department of Economic Affairs Statistical Office, 1993.

Toffler, Alvin. *The Third Wave*. New York, Morrow, 1980.

Waring, Marilyn, *Women, Politics and Power*. Wellington, Allen & Unwin/Port Nicholson Press, 1985.

Waring, Marilyn, *Counting for Nothing: What Men Value and What Women are Worth*. Allen & Unwin/Port Nicholson Press, 1988.

The World's Women 1995: trends and statistics, 2 ed. New York, United Nations Statistical Commission, 1995.

Notes

Note: *All personal communications are indicated as such in the text, and are not referenced below.*

CHAPTER ONE: EQUALITY

1 Hannah Arendt, *Crises of the Republic*. New York, Harcourt Brace Jovanovich, 1972, p.4.
2 Adrienne Rich, *On Lies, Secrets and Silence: Selected Prose 1966–1978*. London, Virago, 1980, p.186.
3 Rabab Hadi, 'The Feminist Behind the Spokesman – a Candid Talk with Hanan Ashrawi', in *A Rising Public Voice: Women in Politics Worldwide*, ed. Alida Brill. New York, Feminist Press, New York City University, 1995, p.85.
4 In the 1996 Parliament, the Speaker, Peter Tapsell, is a member of the Arawa tribe. It is obvious that another Maori woman, the deputy leader of the Alliance party, Sandra Lee, finds it extremely difficult to get the call to speak. And even to write of this, and to criticise the Speaker, is a breach of parliamentary privilege, so that there is no place to raise the issue of the effective silencing of this woman MP.
5 Janet McCallum, *Women in the House*. Picton, Cape Catley, 1993, p.50.
6 Ibid., pp.84–85.
7 Ibid., p.110.
8 Olga S. Opfell, *Women Prime Ministers and Presidents*. North Carolina, McFarland & Co., 1993.
9 Jessie Bernard, *The Female World*. New York, The Free Press, 1981.
10 Radio New Zealand, 15 October 1994.
11 *New York Times*, 6 January 1987.
12 *Ms*, January 1988, p.75.
13 Joan Kirner, 'The Politics of Learning', paper delivered at the Women, Politics and Power Conference, Adelaide, October 1994.
14 Opfell, *Women Prime Ministers*, p.209.
15 Emiko Kaya, 'Mitsui Mariko – an Avowed Feminist Assemblywoman', in Brill (ed.), *A Rising Public Voice*, p.119.
16 *Eleftherotypia*, Athens, 29 January 1978.
17 Thenjiwe Mtintso, 'From Prison Cell to Parliament', in Brill (ed.), *A Rising Public Voice*, pp.113–16.
18 Ibid.
19 Gemma Hussey, *At the Cutting Edge: Cabinet Diaries 1982–1987*. Dublin, Gill & Macmillan, 1990, p.5.
20 Katherine Mansfield, *The Journal of Katherine Mansfield*, ed. John Middleton

Murray, London, Constable, 1962, p.333. T. S. Eliot, 'The Dry Salvages', in *Four Quartets*, London. Faber & Faber, 1944.

21 Quoted by Amanda Muir in her address to the Women, Politics and Power Conference, Adelaide, October 1994.

22 Diane Abbott, 'A Political Triple Whammy', in Brill (ed.), *A Rising Public Voice*, pp.170–73.

23 Mtintso, in Brill (ed.), p.113.

24 Lesley Abdela, *Women with X Appeal*. London, Optima, 1989, p.14.

25 McCallum, *Women in the House*, pp.122–23.

26 Abdela, *Women with X Appeal*, p.103.

27 Tom Hyde, 'Sandra Lee. A Year in the Bearpit', *Metro*, November 1994, p.60.

28 Marcia Freedman, *Exile in the Promised Land: a Memoir*. New York, Firebrand Books, 1990, p.96.

29 Susan B. Anthony and Ida Husted Harper (eds), *History of Woman Suffrage 1883–1900*, v.4. New York, Arno & the New York Times, 1969, pp.444–45. (1st published, 1902)

30 Shirley Chisholm, *Unbought and Unbossed*. Boston, Houghton Mifflin, 1970.

31 Great Britain. House of Commons, 'Parliamentary Debates 1989–90', v.171; 229–34.

32 Forty-eight in Congress and seven in the Senate.

33 *Ms*, January–February 1995, pp.84–90.

34 Ibid.

35 Ibid.

36 *The Nation*, Bangkok, 10 September 1992.

37 Doris Lessing, interview on the *Coming Out Show*, Australian Broadcasting Corporation, 1982.

38 Kirner, 'The Politics of Learning'.

39 Abdela, *Women with X Appeal*, p.14.

40 Virginia Myers, *Head and Shoulders*. Auckland, Penguin Books, 1986, p.167.

41 Freedman, *Exile in the Promised Land*, p.101.

42 Joan Eveline, 'The Politics of Advantage'. Unpublished D.Phil thesis, Murdoch University, Western Australia, 1994.

43 Rich, 'Women and Honour: Some Notes on Lying', in *On Lies, Secrets and Silence*, p.186.

44 McCallum, *Women in the House*, pp.122–23.

45 Ibid.

46 Gemma Hussey, 'Time for Change – Strategies for the Future', Women, Politics and Power Conference, Adelaide, October 1994.

47 Brill (ed.), *A Rising Public Voice*, p.17.

48 Hussey, *At the Cutting Edge*.

49 *Dominion*, 26 May 1989. Margaret Shields was elected to the New Zealand Parliament in 1981 and was a Cabinet minister from 1984 to 1990, when she lost her seat in the general election.

50 Katherine O'Regan, 'The Thread is Politics', in Margaret Clark (ed.), *Beyond Expectations: Fourteen Women Write about Their Lives*. Wellington, Allen & Unwin/Port Nicholson Press, 1986, p.153. Katherine O'Regan succeeded me

after I retired in 1984. In 1990 she was appointed a minister outside Cabinet, and at the time of writing in 1996 she still holds this position.

51 *Broadsheet*, September 1984. Judy Keall was elected in 1984 and defeated in 1990, and re-elected in 1993.

52 Madeleine Kunin, *Living a Political Life*. New York, Knopf, 1994, p.5.

53 Hyde, 'Sandra Lee'.

54 Myers, *Head and Shoulders*, p.171.

55 Kunin, *Living a Political Life*, p.29.

56 Bernadette Devlin, *The Price of My Soul*. London, Pan, 1969.

57 Kunin, *Living a Political Life*, p.5.

58 Hussey, At the Cutting Edge, p.128.

59 Ibid., p.32.

60 Marilyn Waring, *Women, Politics and Power*. Wellington, Allen & Unwin/Port Nicholson Press, 1985, p.12.

61 Freedman, *Exile in the Promised Land*, p.87.

62 Myers, *Head and Shoulders*, pp.158–59.

63 Waring, *Women, Politics and Power*, p.13.

64 Hussey, *At the Cutting Edge*.

65 Abdela, *Women with X Appeal*, p.26.

66 Kunin, *Living a Political Life*, p.189.

67 Opfell, *Women Prime Ministers*, pp.99–100.

68 Ibid., p.185.

69 Hussey, *At the Cutting Edge*, p.142.

70 Audre Lorde, *Sister Outsider: Essays and Speeches*. California, Crossing Press, 1984, pp.107–8.

71 Adrienne Rich, *What Is Found There: Notebooks on Poetry and Politics*. New York, Norton, 1993, p.17.

72 Waring, *Women, Politics and Power*, p.48.

73 Helena Kennedy, *Eve Was Framed*. London, Chatto & Windus, 1992.

74 Abdela, *Women with X Appeal*, p.164.

75 Myers, *Head and Shoulders*, pp.13, 164.

76 Abdela, *Women with X Appeal*, p.93.

77 Kunin, *Living a Political Life*, pp.4, 119, 29.

78 McCallum, *Women in the House*, p.145.

79 Janine Haines, *Suffrage to Sufferance*. Sydney, Allen & Unwin, 1992, p.4.

80 Kunin, *Living a Political Life*, p.30.

81 Virginia Woolf, *Three Guineas*. London, Hogarth Press, 1986, p.83. (1st published, Hogarth Press, 1938)

82 *NZ Herald*, 11 November 1994. It should be noted that, on 6 May 1995, Anderton reversed these decisions and resumed leadership of the party, and accepted the invitation to stand again for parliament.

83 Maria de Lourdes Pintasilgo, speaking at the Council of Europe's symposium on 'Equality Between Men and Women', Strasbourg, 1989.

84 Quoted in Brian Easton, 'A Modest Politician'. *NZ Listener*, 1 April 1995, p.56.

85 Brill (ed.), *A Rising Public Voice*, p.115.

86 Jo Fitzpatrick, speech delivered at NZ Women's Studies Association Conference, 1994.
87 Hyde, 'Sandra Lee'.
88 Denis Welch, 'Fletcher's Challenge', *NZ Listener*, 8 April 1995, p.26.
89 Kunin, *Living a Political Life*, p.13.

CHAPTER TWO: WORK

1   *Nepal: Poverty and Incomes: a World Bank Country Study*. World Bank, 1990.
2   See Marilyn Waring, *Counting for Nothing*, Wellington, Allen & Unwin/Port Nicholson Press, 1988, or *If Women Counted: a New Feminist Economics*. San Fransisco, Harper & Row, 1988, esp. Chs 2 and 3.
3   For further discussion of these, see Waring, *Counting for Nothing*, esp. Ch. 6.
4   *The World's Women 1995: trends and statistics*, 2 edn. New York, United Nations Statistical Commission, 1995.
5   Charlotte Perkins Gilman, *Women and Economics*. New York, Harper & Row, 1966.
6   Report of the World Conference to Review and Appraise the Achievements of the United Nations Decade for Women: Equality, Development and Peace. New York, United Nations, 1986. (A/CONF/116/28/Rev 1)
7   United Nations, Department of Economic Affairs Statistical Office. *A System of National Accounts*. New York, 1993.
8   To be pedantic, a subsistence household or unit is one that does not carry out economic transactions with other units but exists completely on what it produces. To be realistic, exchange activities with the rest of the economy do occur, but they are infrequent and do not represent the basic elements of the unit's or person's economic life. In practice, where most production is intended for own use, the term used to describe this is subsistence.
9   Oli Hawrylyshyn, *Estimating the Value of Household Work in Canada*, 1971. Ottawa, Statistics Canada, 1978.
10 Duncan S. Ironmonger, 'Modelling the Household Economy', in *Economics, Econometrics and the LINK: Essays in Honour of Lawrence R. Klein*, ed. M. Dutta. North Holland, Elsevier Science Publishers, 1995, pp.397–98.
11 Thirteenth International Conference of Labour Statisticians. Report II, Labour force, employment, unemployment and underemployment. Geneva, ILO, 1982.
12 Fifteenth International Conference of Labour Statisticians. Report IV, Revision of the international classification of status in employment. Geneva, ILO, 1993.
13 International Standard Classification of Occupations (ISCO-88). Geneva, ILO, 1988, p.171.
14 *A System of National Accounts*. New York, United Nations, 1993.
15 *The 1993 System of National Accounts* (6.14-16) suggests that in satellite accounts an extended (general) production boundary include estimates for household production of services for own use.
16 Women's Informal Sector Activities, para 57.
17 *Improving Gender Disaggregated Data on Human Resources Through Agricultural Censuses*. Rome, Statistical Development Service, FAO, 1992.

18 *Handbook of Household Surveys*, Studies in Methods series F, no. 31 (ST/ESA/
    STAT/SER.F/31). Statistical Office, Department of International and Social
    Affairs, United Nations, 1984, para. 13.15.

19 World Conference on Agrarian Reform and Rural Development. 'Declaration
    and Programme of Action'. Rome, FAO, 1979.

20 Convention on the Elimination of All Forms of Discrimination Against Women
    (1979). Prefatory text.

21 Implementation of the Nairobi Forward Looking Strategies 1985–92, New
    Delhi, ESCAP, 1993.

22 International Research and Training Institute for the Advancement of Women
    workshop, Women, Development Planning and Statistics, November 1986.

23 'Report to the Economic and Social Council' (E/CN.3/1993/18), para. 23.

24 'Report of the Seminar on the Use of Multi-round Surveys for Estimating Vital
    Statistics' (ESCAP.STAT/SUMS/Rep.14), June 1991.

25 Ibid.

26 Ibid.

27 De Graft Johnson, *Review of the National Household Capability Programme
    1979–1992*. New York, UN Statistical Division, December 1992.

28 Shamin Hamid, *Non-Market Work and National Income: the Case of Bangladesh*.
    Bangladesh Institute of Development Studies, April 1993.

29 T. K. Sarojini, *Women in India: a Review of the Implementation of the Nairobi
    Forward Looking Strategies, 1985–92*. New Delhi, ESCAP, 1993.

30 Ibid., see Table 12, p.43.

31 Richard Ankar, M. E. Kahn and R. B. Gupta, *Women's Participation in the Labour
    Force: a Methods Test in India for Improving Its Measurement* (Women, Work and
    Development 16). Geneva, ILO, 1988.

32 Farida Shaheed and Khawar Mumtaz, *Women's Economic Participation in Paki-
    stan: a Status Report*. Pakistan, UNICEF.

33 *Multi-purpose Household Budget Survey: a Study of Income Distribution, Employment
    and Consumption Patterns in Nepal*. Nepal Rastra Bank, 1989, p.9.

34 For Nepal, ibid., p.141; for India, K. C. Alexander, *Patterns of Utilization of Time
    in Rural Households in Areas with Different Levels of Economic Development*. Man
    In India, 1991, pp.305–29.

35 See e.g. Alexander, *Patterns of Utilization of Time in Rural Households*; see also
    studies in *Gender Analysis in Rice Farming Systems Research: Does It make a
    Difference?* Report of 1990 Workshop, Bogor, Indonesia. Manila, International
    Rice Research Institute, 1990.

36 International Standard Classification of Occupations (ISCO-88) Sub-major
    Group 62, 'Subsistence Agricultural and Fishery Workers', p.170.

37 See Sarojini, *Women in India*.

38 It should not be assumed that all aspects of this cycle occur in subsistence
    households. In *Women in Rural Australia*, Melissa Gibbs reported that, as the
    rural crisis continued and women had to take on more and more administrative
    and outside work, young girls had to take on their mothers' household tasks of
    caring for young siblings, cooking and cleaning.

39 Women in Australia, Australian Bureau of Statistics, Canberra, 1993, p.127.

40 Personal communication, Alexander Stephens, Regional Sociologist, FAO, Bangkok.

41 Shinawatra, Tongsiri and Pitackwong, *Differential Roles of Men and Women in the Farming Systems of Amphoe Phroa, Changwat Chiang Mai, Thailand*. Agricultural Economics Research Report No.18, Chiang Mai University, 1987.

42 *In Sirch*. Korea Institute for Social Information and Research, 1993, p.E.17.

43 *Women in Development: Nepal*. Asian Development Bank, July 1987.

44 Constitution of the Kingdom of Nepal, Part 3, para. 11.

45 *Women in Development: Nepal*.

46 *Nepal: Poverty and Incomes: a World Bank Country Study*. World Bank, 1990.

47 Simone de Beauvoir, *The Second Sex* (translated H. M. Parsley) London, Jonathan Cape, 1953.

48 *Gender Analysis in Rice Farming Systems Research*.

49 New Zealand Royal Commission to Inquire into and Report upon Workers' Compensation. 'Compensation for Personal Injury in New Zealand; report.' Wellington, Government Printing Office, 1967.

50 Deirdre Shaw, 'The Work of Farming Women'. Unpublished MA thesis, University of Waikato, Hamilton, 1993.

51 While war disrupts markets, the 'economic activity' it provides is of enormous value. War adds to growth. For a sustained analysis of this, see Waring, *Counting for Nothing*, Ch. 7.

52 For an excellent exposition on this, see Joni Seager, *Earth Follies*. New York, Routledge, 1993.

53 Personal communication, Petter Jakob Bjere.

54 For the history of the development of the UNSNA, and Stone's role in this, see Waring, *Counting for Nothing*, Ch. 2.

55 *Measuring Unpaid Household Work: Issues and Experimental Estimates*. Canberra, Bureau of Statistics, 1990.

56 *Sydney Morning Herald*, 7 March 1990, p.19.

57 Janet E. Fast and Brenda Munroe, 'Towards Eliminating Gender Bias in Personal Injury Awards: Contributions from Family Economics', *Alberta Law Review*, 32, 1, 1994.

58 *Toronto Star*, 9 May 1993.

59 Figures from Eric P. Nash, 'What's a Life Worth?', *New York Times* magazine, 14 August 1994, pp.34–35.

60 Jim Hogshire, *Sell Yourself to Science: the Complete Guide to Selling Your Organs, Body Fluids, Bodily Functions and Being a Human Guinea Pig*. Washington, Loonipanics Unlimited, 1992.

61 Conference of European Statisticians, *A Statistical System on Household Production and Consumption*, working paper 12. Geneva, 6-8 March, 1995.

62 Ibid., *Measuring Unpaid Work in the Harmonised European Time–Use Survey*, working paper 16.

63 For further details, see WINAP Newsletter, 10, June 1992. Bangkok, ECOSOC, ISSN 1011-3908.

64 By non-participant observation we meant placing trained enumerators in the respondent's household and recording all activities in a time–use diary for 24 hours.

65 Because the FAO funded the surveys, we were told this could not be done. All information collected under its regular programme funding is accessible to all member states and cannot be exclusive by imposing copyright over it. From an ethical standpoint, in respect of any research method and the principles of intellectual property, I would argue that results belonged to the respondents.

66 FAO Pilot Time–Use Studies, 1991, conducted in India, Thailand, Pakistan, Malaysia (unpublished), and replicated in New Zealand by Deirdre Shaw, 'The Work of Farming Women'.

67 Personal communication from Maurice Williamson, Minister of Statistics, 23 February 1993.

68 Letter from the Minister of Statistics to the Associate Minister of Women's Affairs, 22 July 1993.

69 I am grateful to Robin Fleming, New Zealand Ministry of Women's Affairs, who attended the conference and made available to me copies of papers, her report, and time for discussion.

70 *Canada Year Book 1992*. Statistics Canada, p.66.

71 *Canada Year Book 1990*. Statistics Canada, p.2–1.

72 See Chris Jackson, 'The Value of Household Work in Canada, 1986', *Canadian Economic Observer*, June 1992. Statistics Canada, Cat. no. 11-010, p.3.10.

73 Mary Sue Devereaux, 'Time Use of Canadians in 1992', *Canadian Social Trends*, Autumn 1992, Statistics Canada, Cat. no. 11-008E, p.14.

74 *Globe and Mail*, Toronto, 7 April 1994.

75 Conference of European Statisticians, *A Statistical System on Household Production and Consumption*.

76 Conference of European Statisticians, *Value of Household Production in Germany in 1992*, working paper 21. Geneva, 6–8 March, 1995.

77 Ibid., *Measuring Unpaid Work in the Harmonised European Time–Use Survey*.

78 Ironmonger, 'Modelling the Household Economy'.

79 Duncan Ironmonger, 'Why Measure and Value Unpaid Work?' *Conference Proceedings on the Measurement and Valuation of Unpaid Work*. Ottawa, Statistics Canada, 28–30 April 1993.

80 Ibid.

81 Alvin Toffler, *The Third Wave*. New York, Morrow, 1980.

82 Ironmonger, 'Modelling the Household Economy'.

83 Ironmonger, 'Why Measure and Value Unpaid Work?'.

84 Business Outlook, National Bank of New Zealand, December 1995.

85 Ironmonger, 'Modelling the Household Economy'.

CHAPTER THREE: HUMAN RIGHTS

1 'Refugee Status on Grounds of Sex', *Sydney Morning Herald*, 3 February 1993.

2 'Canada Gives Somali Mother Refugee Status', *New York Times*, 21 July 1994.

3 Susan Brownmiller, *Against Our Will*. New York, Simon & Schuster, 1975.

4 Geneva Convention (1949), article 27(2).

5 Information about the case of Amanita Diop was provided by Linda Weil Curiel.

6   Convention Relating to the Status of Refugees (1951), article 1A(2); Convention Against Torture and Other Cruel, Inhuman and Degrading Treatment (1984), article 16.

7   In November 1992, among those 28 states that had just signed the Convention Against Torture were Serbia and Montenegro.

8   The Geneva Convention relative to the Protection of Civilian Persons in Time of War, adopted 12 Aug. 1949

9   Convention Relating to the Status of Refugees (1951), article 33(1).

10   *New York Times*, 21 July 1994.

11   See Antonio Cassese, *Human Rights in a Changing World*. Oxford, Polity Press, 1990.

12   Oscar Schachter, 'The Charter and the Constitution: Human Rights Provisions in American Law', *4 Vanderbilt Law Review* 1951, pp.399–659.

13   Proclamation of Teheran, para. 2. *In A Compilation of International Instruments*, v.1, New York, United Nations, 1993.

14   *Human Rights Quarterly*. Baltimore, Maryland, Johns Hopkins University Press, 1987, pp.122–35.

15   E.g. the African Charter on Human and People's Rights, and the European Convention for the Protection of Human Rights and Fundamental Freedoms.

16   I am grateful to Christine Chinkin for her detailed explanation of these issues in 'Using the Optional Protocol: the Practical Issues', in *Internationalising Human Rights: Australia's Accession to the Optional Protocol*. Parkville, Victoria, Centre for Comparative Constitutional Studies, 1992, pp.6–15.

17   Ibid., p.7.

18   Ibid., p.9.

19   Ibid., p.10.

20   ICCPR, Article 23: '(1) The family is the natural and fundamental group unit of society and is entitled to protection by society and the state . . . (4) State Parties to the present Covenant shall take appropriate steps to ensure equality of rights and responsibilities of spouses as to marriage, during marriage and at its dissolution.'

21   No.35/1978, *Aumeeruddy Cziffra et al* v. *Mauritius*.

22   Communication No. 172/1984, 42 UN GAOR Supp. (No. 40) at 139, UN Doc. A/42/40 (1987).

23   Rebecca J. Cook, 'State Accountability Under the Convention on the Elimination of All Forms of Discrimination Against Women', in Rebecca J. Cook (ed.), *Human Rights of Women, National and International Perspectives*. Philadelphia, University of Pennsylvania Press, 1994, p.229.

24   L. Henkin, R. Pugh, O. Schachter and H. Smit (eds), *International Law: Cases and Materials*. St Paul, Minnesota, West Publishing, 1980, p.91.

25   Radhika Coomaraswamy, 'Women, Ethnicity and the Discourse of Rights', in Cook (ed.) *Human Rights of Women*, p.40.

26   *R*: v. *Morgentaler* (1988) 1 Canada: Supreme Court Reports 30, 171–72.

27   'Human Rights in the 21st Century', proceedings of Ninth Commonwealth Law Conference, Auckland, New Zealand, 1990.

28   Marilyn Waring, 'Gender and International Law: Women and the Right to

Development', *Australian Year Book of International Law*, v.12, Canberra, ANU, 1992, pp.177–89.

29 Denis Lloyd, *Introduction to Jurisprudence with Selected Texts*. London, Stevens, 1959.

30 'Alienating Oscar? A Feminist Analysis of International Law', in Dorinda Dallmeyer (ed.), *Reconceiving Reality: Women and International Law*. Washington DC, American Society of International Law, 1993.

31 Andrew Byrnes, 'A Feminist Analysis of International Human Rights Law', *Australian Year Book of International Law*. v.12, p.205.

32 International Court of Justice: Statute (1945), article 38.

33 Oscar Schacter, 'Recent Trends in International Law Making', *Australian Year Book of International Law*, v.12, pp.1, 11–12.

34 'The Identity of International Law', in Bin Cheng (ed.), *International Law – Teaching and Practice*. London, Stevens, 1982, p.32. Rosalyn Higgins, now Her Excellency Judge Higgins, was the first woman permanently appointed to the International Court of Justice.

35 Alain Pellet in 'The Normative Dilemma', *Australian Year Book of International Law*, v.12, p.26.

36 Cook (ed.), *Human Rights of Women*, p.362.

37 'Report of the World Conference to Review and Appraise the Achievements of the United Nations Decade for Women: Equality, Development and Peace, Nairobi, 15–26 July, 1985', E.85.IV.10.

38 'Monitoring the Implementation of the Nairobi Forward Looking Strategies for the Advancement of Women', Report of the Secretary General, 1 February 1995, E/CN.6/1995/3/Add.6.

39 Ibid., para 5 and 19.

40 Report of the United Nations Conference on Environment and Development, Rio de Janeiro, 1992. Proceedings of the Conference. New York, United Nations, 1993. Para 24.2(b), 24.3(a).

41 'Report of the World Conference on Human Rights, Vienna, 1993. New York, United Nations, 1993. A/CONF/157/24 (Part I), para 18.

42 *NZ Herald*, 14 November 1995.

43 Andrew Browne, Reuters report, Beijing, 7 Sept. 1995.

44 At the International Parliamentary Meeting on Gender, Population and Development, Tokyo, 31 Aug.–1 Sept. 1995.

45 Charlene Fu, Associated Press report, Beijing, 10 Sept 1995.

46 *Equality Before the Law: Justice for Women*, Law Reform Commission Report No. 69, Part 1. Canberra, Commonwealth of Australia, 1994, para 2.25.

47 'Isn't it Time for a Change?', Beijing, 6 Sept. 1995.

48 The Human Development Report, 1995. New York, Oxford University Press/UNDP, 1995, pp.7, 29, 41, 99.

49 The New Zealand public voted to change from the first-past-the-post system (e.g. in the House of Commons in Britain) to the mixed-member proportional system (e.g. in Germany and Israel).

50 The team, who commanded no fees, were Margaret Bedggood, former Chief Human Rights Commissioner of New Zealand and now Dean of the Faculty of

Law at the University of Waikato in Hamilton; Paul Hunt, formerly researcher at the UN Human Rights Centre in Vienna and now senior lecturer in international law at the University of Waikato; barrister and solicitor Prue Crossan; lobbyist and lawyer Anne Holden.

51 Submission on behalf of the petitioners to New Zealand Parliamentary Select Committee on Electoral Reform, November 1994.

52 Rebecca Cook, 'Women's International Human Rights Law: the Way Forward', *Human Rights Quarterly*, v.15, 1993, pp.230–61.

53 'What are "Women's International Rights"?', in Cook, *Human Rights of Women*, p.64.

54 'Report of the Human Rights Committee', UN Doc. A/45/40, 1990, v.1, Annex VI, pp.173–75.

55 Speaking at Ninth Commonwealth Law Conference, Auckland, 1990.

56 'Report of the Human Rights Committee', 1990, paras 10, 36, 38, 39, 3.29.

57 Ibid.

58 Discussion Paper 54, 'Equality Before the Law'. Sydney, ALRC DP 54, 1993, para 3.41.

59 Report No. 69, *Equality Before the Law: Women's Equality*. Law Reform Commission, Commonwealth of Australia, 1994, Part II, para 3.5.

60 Cindy A. Cohn, 'The Early Harvest: Domestic Legal Changes Related to the Human Rights Committee and the Covenant on Civil and Political Rights', *Human Rights Quarterly*, v.13, 1991, pp.316–17.

61 *Ashby* v. *Minister of Immigration* (1981), 1 NZLR 222 (CA).

62 *D.* v. *Minister of Immigration* (1990), 2 NZLR 673.

63 1994, 2 NZLR 257.

64 1989, Canada: Supreme Court Reports, 143.

65 Ibid.

66 Seventh session, 1988, UN Doc. A/43/38 (1988), 109.

67 Report to Council of Europe's symposium on 'Equality between Women and Men', Strasbourg, 1989.

68 See Waring, *Counting for Nothing*.

69 Andrew Clapham, *Human Rights in the Private Sphere*. Oxford, Clarendon Press, 1993, p.97.

70 ICCPR, Article 8(3)(c).

71 Richard Lillich, 'Civil Rights', in *Human Rights and International Law: Legal and Policy Issues*. Theodor Meron (ed.), Oxford, Clarendon Press, 1984, pp.125–26.

72 Updating of the Report on Slavery Submitted to the Sub-Commission in 1966, Report by Benjamin Whitaker, Special Rapporteur. UN Commission on Human Rights, E/CN.4/Sib.2/1982/20/Add.1/7 July 1982, paras 31, 72, 33, 41.

73 M. Bossuyt, *Guide to Preparatories of the ICCPR*. Boston, Kluwer Academic Publishers, 1987, p.486.

74 *Human Rights Quarterly*, 9 (1987), pp.122–35, para 45.

75 Ibid., para 71.

76 Ibid., para 72.

77 Constitution of the International Labour Organisation and Standing Orders

of the International Labour Conference. Geneva, International Labour Office, May 1989.

78 Karen Knop, 'Rethinking the Sovereign State', in Cook (ed.) *Human Rights of Women*, p.157.

79 Mary Chinery-Hesse, Deputy Director General of International Labour Office, Bejiing, 6 September 1995.

80 'Progress Achieved in the Implementation of the CEDAW', Report by CEDAW, Beijing, A/CONF/177/7, 21 June 1995, para. 18, 2.

81 'What Are "Women's International Human Rights?" ', in Cook (ed.), *Human Rights of Women*, p.59.

82 Flora MacDonald/Commonwealth Human Rights Initiative, *Put Our World to Rights*. London, Commonwealth Human Rights Initiative, 1991.

83 'Report of the Fourth World Conference on Women', A/CONF/177/20, 17 Oct. 1995, para 165(g), 206.

84 *Public Service Alliance of Canada and Canadian Human Rights Commission* v. *Canada (Treasury Board)* 1991, 14(5). Canadian Human Rights Reporter, D/341, D/349.

85 1 Canada: Supreme Court Reports, 1219 (1992).

86 Personal communication.

87 Robert Robertson, 'The Right to Food in International Law', in K. Mahoney and P. Mahoney (eds), *Human Rights in the Twenty-First Century: a Global Challenge*. Dardrecht, Martinus Nijhoff, 1993.

88 See Geraldine Van Bueren, *The International Law on the Rights of the Child*. Dardrecht, Martinus Nijhoff, 1995.

89 'Protecting, Promoting and Supporting Breast-feeding: the Special Role of Maternity Services', A Joint WHO/UNICEF statement, 1989. Geneva/New York, WHO/UNICEF, 1989.

90 'Gender Bias and the Judiciary', Canberra, Senate Printing Unit, 1994.

91 'The Human Development Report', 1995. New York, UN Economic & Social Council, 1995, pp.6, 90.

92 Report to Council of Europe's symposium on 'Equality Between Women and Men', Strasbourg, 1989.

93 *FALL*, 6, 1995.

94 *Medicine Hat News*, Calgary.

95 Newsletter, Caribbean Association for Feminist Research and Action, Tunapuna, Trinidad and Tobago.

96 Mike Osbourne, AAP, Beijing, 10 Sept. 1995.

Index